WORKING
THROUGH AGEING

Rethinking Work, Ageing and Retirement

Series Editors: **David Lain**, Newcastle University,
Sarah Vickerstaff, University of Kent and
Mariska van der Horst, Vrije Universiteit Amsterdam

This is multidisciplinary series brings together researchers
from a range of fields including management and organizational studies,
gerontology, sociology, psychology and social policy, to explore the
impact of extended working lives on older people and organizations.

Also available in the series:

Rethinking Financial Behaviour
by **Ariane Agunsoye**

Menopause Transitions and the Workplace
edited by **Vanessa Beck** and **Jo Brewis**

Older Workers in Transition
edited by **David Lain**, **Sarah Vickerstaff**
and **Mariska van der Horst**

Find out more at:
bristoluniversitypress.co.uk/
rethinking-work-ageing-and-retirement

WORKING THROUGH AGEING

Experiencing Growing Up and Older at Work

Kathleen Riach

BRISTOL
UNIVERSITY
PRESS

First published in Great Britain in 2025 by

Bristol University Press
University of Bristol
1–9 Old Park Hill
Bristol
BS2 8BB
UK
t: +44 (0)117 374 6645
e: bup-info@bristol.ac.uk

Details of international sales and distribution partners are available at bristoluniversitypress.co.uk

https://doi.org/10.51952/9781529245837

British Library Cataloguing in Publication Data
A catalogue record for this book is available from the British Library

ISBN 978-1-5292-4580-6 hardcover
ISBN 978-1-5292-4581-3 paperback
ISBN 978-1-5292-4582-0 ePub
ISBN 978-1-5292-4583-7 ePdf

Cover design: Andrew Corbett
Front cover image: Unsplash/David Hoefler

For Martin, Keelan and Alba, who embody
the messiness, paradoxes, possibilities and
joys of ageing in the best possible way

Contents

Series Editors' Preface

David Lain, Sarah Vickerstaff and Mariska van der Horst

A new book by Kathleen Riach is a major event and a gift for those of us with interests in ageing and work. When we started the Rethinking Work, Ageing and Society series, we wanted to publish books that shine a critical light on the issues that affect people as they age. Significant changes in the landscape include extended working lives and rising state pension ages, changes to job transitions in later life, an increasing recognition of health transitions in the workplace, and shifts towards individual responsibility and risk in private pensions saving. Volumes in the series have successfully explored some of these issues through critical, theoretically informed social science research. However, there is an important broader issue to be explored about how people experience ageing today and how we can make sense of this. This is not about focusing on a particular life stage, on older workers per se, or working in 'later life', although this remains important; rather, it relates to ageing as a *process* that proceeds and is experienced over the life course.

In this context, we are delighted to welcome Kathleen Riach's excellent new book, *Working through Ageing*. Throughout her distinguished career, Professor Riach's research has encouraged us to think more deeply, and differently, about ageing and work. This ambitious new project presents the theory of 'working through ageing', which seeks to avoid the common imbalance of focusing exclusively on ageing as something imposed upon individuals within organizational contexts or as something that is purely the locus of the individual. The book develops a phenomenological approach influenced by the work of Simone de Beauvoir, a writer Riach convincingly argues deserves contemporary reassessment for her work on ageing. This phenomenological approach is used to analyse data on individuals (previously) working together in a UK hedge fund, who are tracked, and interviewed qualitatively, over a ten-year period. This major methodological undertaking allows Riach to explore and theorise the rich dynamics of ageing in the context of financial capitalism. The individuals interviewed are therefore able to reflect on their own ageing over time and how this has been influenced by their positionality. The book is full of insights that are revealed through the presentation of fascinating interview data, a wide critical reading of the literature, reflections on the personal experiences of the author, and engagement with the ideas of Simone de Beauvoir. *Working through Ageing* makes an important contribution to the literature, plotting a new and exciting way forward; its influence will be felt for many years to come.

Preface:
Ageing, Ageing, All Around ...

This is a book about how people experience ageing in the context of organizational life. Specifically, it is about how we negotiate growing up and older in highly competitive professional contexts, while attending to the quality of ageing as an embodied and situated experience. It recognizes that ageing is not a process that is incidental to how, where and when we work, and who we work with, and nor is it separate from the way we come to know ourselves as ageing subjects more generally. Rather, ageing at work should be understood as simultaneously a making of the self through the constitution of dynamic organizational subjectivities – a 'being' of ageing – and a 'doing' of ageing through particular and specific embodied acts that are shaped by the occupational and work-based contexts of our lives. In other words, working through ageing is a practical accomplishment underpinned by a particular relational and experiential organizational ontology.

Such a concern rides on a wave of political and institutional attention to age and work. Much of this has been fuelled by dual socioeconomic concerns surrounding a fear of an increasingly 'top-heavy' demographic, and the need to maximize labour force participation across the life course. These trends are neither universal in their intensity nor in the way they pattern across different national landscapes. However, under the banner of ageing as a 'global challenge', multiple governments and international agencies have invested considerable time and resources to try and establish the most effective policy interventions that encourage and enable participation in the labour market across the life course. For the past 30 years, targets have been used to help set levels of participation for particular cohorts, multi-agency strategies have explored the economic viability of different demographic patterns, and national legislation has been introduced to combat discriminatory practices based on age. To support this, there has been a demand for research that explains and predicts behaviour based on chronological benchmarks, leading to studies that explore the differential effects of particular interventions and practices for certain age groups and their labour force participation.

My own understanding of ageing as a more phenomenological experience is a little different. When I began researching age identities at work during my doctorate around 20 years ago, studying the experience of ageing as a process constituted in the dynamics of organizational life was still embryonic. At the same time, the area of age and employment studies held much promise, given its evolution within a truly multidisciplinary landscape. Critical gerontology was informing a variety of frameworks to understand broader conditions of health-based age, although age-and-stage functionalist models remained influential more broadly More psychologically informed schools of thought focused on identifying age-related stereotypes based on, for example, ingroup and outgroup behaviour. Meanwhile sociological perspectives enabled the explanation of how biography and social structure coalesced across the working lives of people, while broader political economy perspectives considered patterns of structural disadvantage in the labour market at a national and international level and the practicalities of considering age as a protected characteristic in legislation.

Similarly, studies of discrimination and marginalization have dominated the recent landscape in age and employment studies, showing how age-based inequality emerges at various levels of organizational and institutional life. Here we see how age-based identities and ideas are shaped by, and in turn shape, certain organizational norms, and how the experience of age-based norms or assumptions intersect with other axis of power such as gender or ethnicity. As highlighted in Chapter 1, age-related discursive and ideological repertoires play out in the context of contemporary workplaces and impacts the way in which workers are indexed and subsequently positioned, enabling us to see the variegated ways in which organizational members are subject to being marginalized or misrecognized. Such an approach has been incredibly valuable in terms of showing how organizations produce a variety of unintended effects for the socially situated worker subject.

Most notably, intellectual attention to the life course has blossomed and created a language and means of understanding how trajectories are shaped though the confluence of various social, demographic, economic and physical elements that are inherently linked with other people. Taking a life course perspective highlights how our lives are 'intimately shaped by many social contexts both near to, and far from, individuals-including families, peer and friendship groups, schools, neighborhoods, work organizations, health care institutions, social programs and policies, historical events and periods of social change, and culture' (Settersten, 2003: 3). For Richard Settersten, Glen Elder (1994) and Laura Bernardi (Bernardi et al, 2019), among others, ageing lives are both linked in their sense of dependencies with others and situated in terms of where ageing and its meaning takes place. Given that this work has emphasized that institutions, organizations and policy may inform people's ageing experiences, how such social spaces and places more broadly inform the ontological processes of ageing is a question begging to be addressed by organizational theorists. These intersections must be the concern for any social scientist if we are to offer a richer understanding of how our own individual experience comes from a world where more of us than ever are growing older in contexts that are marked by constraining social expectations and culturally inculcated assumptions around ageing.

Collectively, these branches of literature have provided a rich heritage for age and employment studies to inspire ideas around how age informs work and vice versa. However, there has been an enduring tendency to take ways of perceiving, behaving and relating to age in general and simply apply them to ageing in and around organizational life. At worst, it is assumed that the workplace is nothing more than a replica or microcosm of broader society, ignoring the unique and historically entrenched dynamics of power, control and authority that govern the ways in which we come to recognize and evaluate ageing at work. At best, attention to the organizational context has been positioned as a handmaiden to broader political and economic patterns of ageing rather than a complex, particular and active context itself. Both undermine the potency of the organizational context where work not only shapes the ageing experience, but where work itself is also constituted by the ageing process. This is a dyadic relationship between the embodied, situated experiences of ageing in a particular context and the processes of organizing that are themselves constitutive of ageing. Ignoring the ways in which workplace dynamics are central to how we come to be and know ourselves and others as ageing subjects is not only a significant oversight but also limits the possibility of organizational accounts shedding theoretical light on the experience of ageing in contemporary society more broadly.

Yet something else is also missing. In our attempts to try and understand, there is something unsaid about why we as scholars might be drawn to certain classifications or solutions around age, and any sustained attention to the experience of *ageing* in a work context has remained tantalisingly elusive. This is not to say that ageing is a silent topic in the world of work; if anything, ageing is around us more than ever in popular culture. For example, celebrities and influencers provide weekly anecdotes about how they celebrate or resist ageing processes.Most recently we have seen this in the UK through the recent groundswell of menopause-related commentary that is often underpinned by ideas that the 'cure' to delaying ageing-related experiences resides within us and our bodies and hormones, as long as we make the right lifestyle and consumer choices or financial decisions. More generally, journalists share insights about the trials or pleasures of ageing, often universalizing the challenges faced as we grow older, while the $62 billion anti-ageing beauty market sells the promise of interventions to 'solve' the ageing process. Commentators provide evocative accounts of the emotions and experience of how to fight ageing, while other thought leaders advise us how to age, not age or age differently. Sayings around old dogs and new tricks, wrinkles as smiles and being as old as you feel are presented as truisms that fuse attributes or behaviours to the passing of time and slip out of our mouths without a second thought. The ubiquity of ageing often means we passively swallow age-related platitudes or ideas and push them into the world in our everyday talk and actions, only choking when someone pushes them back onto us in a way that jars with our sense of self. This might also happen when we catch our reflection, see photos of our younger self or have encounters that spark momentary reminders of ageing that we might not have been aware of, or want to be aware of.

Together, this all contributes to the continuing irony of ageing and its absent-presence. To borrow from the sentiment of Samuel Coleridge's poem 'The Rime of the Ancient Mariner' that refers to 'water, water everywhere, Nor any drop to drink', ageing is everywhere, but is often an ambiguous or inaccessible experience, and ways of talking and thinking about ageing at work are few and far between, and often beyond our access. We witness it and feel it through our bodies and with those around us, but ageing is an experience that itself is rather miasmic, with few opportunities in life to reflect upon its meaning to us or others beyond clichés or metaphors around its rejection, reversal or inevitability. We are still not sure how to make sense of the fullness of this experience, particularly in a workplace setting where everything we say and do carries the costs and consequences of being evaluated, judged or a threat to both our financial and ontological security.

The common response I receive when talking about ageing to other people has been 'of course I don't think about it' or 'it's too much a reminder of the end point', suggesting that the reason for ageing and its subsequent exclusion from social and organizational commentary is due to its close connection with an inevitable end point: death. Here ageing is situated as a journey towards an ultimate destination where points of reflection only emerge when we are prodded into recognizing our own existential inevitability. This is indeed a powerful framing, and the conflation of ageing as predominantly or even exclusively understood through death is in many ways historically and institutionally embedded in both medical legacies in the Global North and the overarching concern with death or finitude in a range of social, psychological and psychoanalytic theories. However, while ageing as 'resulting' in death may be a truism, it is not *only* what ageing means to and for us. It seems a rather sweeping diminution to suggest that one of the most important features of living can be best explained only in relation to its inevitable end. Surely there is more to ageing than that?

In beginning to take this question seriously in the context of work, I went in search of what an ontology of organizational ageing might look like. This was – and still is – a process of reflection and exploration rather than this book representing a final or declarative conclusion. I began this current study in 2010 by spending six months in a London-based hedge fund, which was the result of a chance conversation with a friend about the challenges of asking people about ageing. His invitation to come and 'hang out' at his firm formed the basis of a decade-long relationship with many of those who worked there. After returning for another period of observation in 2012, I continued to interview those I had originally spoken to every two years, and without them, this study would simply not exist. As such, in this book, I have tried to give priority to direct accounts of participants where I can, as well as provide details of the year we spoke, and if this was in year 0, 2, 4, 6, 8 or 10 of the project. While I have used pseudonyms, there are also a small number of times within Chapters 5, 6 and 7 when it felt better to anonymise their narratives completely. As I will discuss in Chapter 3, the numerous inverviews, observations and informal conversations I had during this time were vital in terms of how I began to understand the oscillating dynamics between the organization of ageing and ageing as constituting our organizational lives. They also enabled me to appreciate how individuals, even when relatively economically and socially privileged, were dependent on undertaking a process of reckoning around ageing in order to continue feeling recognized, valuable and meaningful as workers and humans more generally. When talking with them, everyday ageing encounters and moments were marked by relations of power, conflicts, normative career patterns and other organizational cultural values over time. I had the privilege of repeated conversations with space to reflect in between them, and in doing so, it became clear that ageing was indeed everywhere, often in implicit or hidden ways; within norms and systems that formed webs of meaning around how we are encouraged to think and feel about ageing. More significantly, it began to emerge that within these webs of meanings and relations, there appeared to be a particular *quality* to ageing that provided possibilities, perspectives and sometimes expansive ways to negotiate working life and 'do ageing' differently as a generative organizational project.

To account for these experiences, in this book I introduce a theory of 'working through ageing'. Working through ageing refers to both the theoretical articulation and everyday practices that are concerned with having to grasp our selves and the working world around us, while simultaneously contending with our dynamic embodied experience of growing older. The aim is to circumvent the imbalance of focusing on ageing at work as either exclusively imposed through organizational regimes and cultures or something that is purely the locus of the individual, by highlighting the oscillation between embodied experience and organizationally situated lives. Working through ageing is simultaneously a practical and ontological accomplishment of being an ageing worker and how this happens in the ongoing situated negotiations, everyday activities and politics, informal interactions and mundane practices in workplaces. To theoretically explore this idea, I draw on the work of Simone de Beauvoir, whose work *Old Age* (1985 [1970]), memoirs and fictional work concerned with ageing build out from her well-known treatise on gender, *The Second Sex* (2015 [1949]), and earlier works on ethical relations (2004 [1944]; 2018 [1947]; 2005 [1959]). In conversation with de Beauvoir, and her interlocutors who have since forged a path for critical and political phenomenology, I explore how working through ageing demands a commitment to recognizing ageing as an organizing principle that is inseparable from beingness, as constituted through people, experiences and encounters in and across multiple workplace settings over time. It is in working through ageing that we gain a sense of recognition, meaning, belonging and purpose as an organizational subject, but also feel moments of doubt, ambiguity and uncertainty as to who we are.

My own journey in developing these ideas over the past ten years has involved thinking with and against the seams of phenomenology and philosopher Simone de Beauvoir. In doing so, it feels important to emphasize upfront that this project is not one that offers either a philosophically exhaustive or a purist commitment to de Beauvoir's thesis. I take seriously the possible limitations of de Beauvoir's position on old age, which she once proclaimed a projectless realm, as well as her own self-identification of being in 'the land of shades' when aged 44 (1985 [1963]: 291). Her fictional work also shows an aversion to recognizing a plurality of older ageing subjectivities and in places her work carries a scorn for women who betray the normative accoutrements of acceptable ageing. While she may be ironically mirroring the dominant views of her time, at times her accounts of mid-life and older age feel restrictive and sometimes cruel. More broadly, I am also very aware that de Beauvoir's own biography and choices have been criticized as standing in contradiction to an ambition and aspiration for a more communal and generous ageing experience. Many commentaries have suggested that de Beauvoir was complicit in leveraging normative age-based power dynamics through her own questionable actions around students or other young women who crossed her path. Working with and against her ideas is not to become an apologist for her own life, but rather to recognize that she was both complicit and fallible to the manifold political and power bases that organize ageing relations and experiences.

Notwithstanding these critical points, her intellectual project provides a fertile backdrop for thinking about what a political phenomenology of ageing might entail and how different elementals around working life and working ageing bodies come together to produce a variety of ontological effects. I hope that the interplay between these strands will become clear in the later chapters, but to set up the backdrop for why a new theory of ageing and organization is needed, Chapter 1 begins by exploring how recent commentaries help us understand ageing as an organizational and organizing phenomenon. Chapter 2 starts to explore what a phenomenology of working through ageing might attend to, considering how contemporary critical and political phenomenological approaches might be extended in conversation with de Beauvoir. After introducing the empirical work informing this study in Chapter 3, Chapters 4, 5 and 6 empirically focus on working through ageing as a being and doing via three interrelated phenomenological figures. Specifically they explore the self-other-setting dynamics that constitute working through ageing; concepts that are simultaneously committed to an ontological concern with intersubjectivity and a refusal to distil or reduce the fecundity of embodied lived experience. Chapter 4 focuses on how ageing is disclosed in and and through relations with others. Chapter 5 then explores grasping as an ongoing tension in the being and doing of ageing as a subject-object that must contend with the simultaneity of being a self-for-others and their own dynamically situated embodiment as they age. Chapter 6 draws on the figure of anchoring to consider how working through ageing plays out through both the organizational aged conditions and parameters, and the inescapable situatedness of our own carnal temporality– an experience I refer to as chronochoreography. The final chapter reflects on these accounts to discuss how age surfaces through the being and doing of working life, and how this may point to a psychosocial depth that is particular to ageing. In doing so, I discuss how 'compostability' as a way of conceptualizing the onto-organic folds of time, power and organizing, suggests a more promiscuous mode of subjectivity, which in turn provides for the possibility of generative lines of recognition in the ageing experience.

Such an endeavour is of course carried out in and through my own ageing experience, and I remain indebted to a myriad of people who have been involved in my research and life during this time to help support this book coming to fruition. The fieldwork and thinking in this inevitably parallels my own experience of moving from my 30s into my 40s alongside multiple places, contexts and people. I migrated across the world from the UK to Australia and then back, changed jobs, lost and gained loved ones and had two children. While I'm very aware of the privilege, mobility and choice I have had in this decade of living, I have also been incredibly fortunate to have both generosity and commitment to the wonderful participants who were vital to the fieldwork on which this study is based. Over the course of a decade, the people I interviewed tolerated my incessant questioning and were so gracious with both their time and their openness. While they are anonymous in the book, I hope they can all see how indebted I continue to be to their time and trust.

The British Academy generously awarded me a Midcareer Fellowship that provided vital space and time to realize the ambitions of this project, and the drafts of the ideas in this book have benefited from feedback at a range of conferences and presentations, which has shaped my ideas and this project for the better. Ellen Pearce and Izzie Green from Bristol University Press went over and above in their support, and I am beyond grateful to Melissa Tyler, Kate Kenny and Nancy Harding, who formed an enviable clan of critical friends over a number of years, donating so much time they did not have to discussing and pushing this book into existence, chapter by chapter. Alongside them, my gratitude goes to Leanne Cutcher, Gavin Jack, Lesley-Anne Barnes MacFarlane and numerous friends and colleagues who have been such a source of intellectual inspiration, humour and general love and support over the years.

I have also been fortunate throughout this time to be in three academic departments that were characterized both by a fierce collegiality and a strong expertise in organization studies and where theoretical hybridity was encouraged. Colleagues from Essex, Monash and Glasgow Universities have been formative in the evolution of my thinking around how embedded structural and power dynamics, and the ways social and psychic processes of ageing are bound up in our desires or demands relating to economic and labour experiences. Collectives such as the CROS interest group provided multiple spaces for helping me craft and rehearse the practicalities of how to talk theoretically about ageing, which were also supported latterly by Eleanor Kirk, who was a dynamite force in organizing writing sessions that offered a permission field to write among a range of institutional pressures. The opportunity to do this study was also facilitated by two former heads of department, Julie Wolfram Cox and Veronique Ambrosini, who were masterful in proactively giving me space to return to research and writing after my periods of parental leave. Academic leadership and the associated bureaucracy of workload models in university are often unattractive, unrecognized and a significant act of sacrificial labour, but they both chose to make it an ethical and feminist praxis.

Finally, this book has brought to bear how much of our ageing subjectivities are beholden to significant others in our life. My mum has always been unconditional in her support and confidence to pursue what I was passionate about, while my dad continues to embody an openness and joy of learning that still inspires me. Anna, Chris and their families provided an engineer and scientist voice in my head telling me to be as clear as possible, and continue to be solid companions in the journey of life. I owe the completion of this book to Martin, who has not only supported me through taking the burden of the mundane aspects of family and domestic life that afforded precious hours to write, but also being there to gently remind me that the richest experiences are 'in the gaps of life' if you give them time on their own terms, which I am still learning to do. And, finally, thank you to Keelan and Alba, who have patiently (for the most part) lived with this study for the full duration of their lives.

These intertwining lives are fundamental to making this book, although all mistakes and theoretical hiccups are inevitably my own. I hope that it will show that ageing is of course fraught with negotiating paradoxical and often painful or negating experiences that rebound across interdependent individual and social worlds, but that it also provides the possibilities for uncovering, recovering or creating new ways to negotiate how, where and why we work and live in a meaningful way as we grow up and older. In this sense, the book's aim is rather a humble one: to render visible how people 'work through' – both practically as an everyday series of encounters, and phenomenologically as an ontological process of being – organizational ageing as an experience that is worthy of pausing and reflecting on in and of itself, and to explore all the contradictions, ambivalences, feelings and potential that it involves.

Kathleen Riach
September 2025

Constellations of Organizational Ageing: Controlled, Commodified, Conferred

You do not have to look far to see how ageing is built into the world of work, from images of the workforce in recruitment advertisements, industrial action on pensions eligibility, and reports of productivity diminishing as the population grows older. These are not only underpinned by ideas of the working life course, but also a compulsion to be able to view ageing as a source of possible control and mediator of value or meaning. Yet age as a workforce concern has become more complex during the historical present as we see the move towards more fluid patterns of entry and exit, more flux in the workforce, and global changes in terms of how economies are structured. Systems of workplace forecasting are central to people management policies and are still predicated on the idea of a 'hard stop' at a certain point in time, usually based on chronological age. In some professions, this has been supported through using occupational pension eligibility to symbolically 'mark' the end of work. Other mechanisms may seek to control pathways around work, such as transition to retirement programmes, often called 'phased', which are increasing in popularity across the public and private sectors.

Such challenges are often felt most acutely at a local level, as revealed in a conversation I had with one senior manager in the National Health Service (NHS) on workforce planning. At this point, post-COVID-19 job vacancies were at crisis point, not only due to Brexit but also to employees choosing to retire around 18 months earlier than had been forecast, and a fear that the NHS was not able to protect older bodies at work. At the scale of a national workforce, this had seismic consequences for the workforce overall, leading to several short-term, quick-fix and expensive solutions to backfill staff shortages, such as previously employed nurses now returning as per diem staff through agencies that were able to provide more flexibility than NHS work structures. Yet the striking point of this conversation was not the challenge per se, but how steadfastly the manager hung on to the idea that there was a possibility of being able to easily correct the situation. What she felt was needed were better systems of control, better systems to garner as much value out of older employees as possible, and a communications campaign emphasizing the value of the older healthcare workforce. This replicated many of my previous exchanges with managers where they recognized that ageing was a 'grand challenge', but there was an ongoing hesitancy to consider it central to how work itself was structured and organized.

To explore this further, this chapter embarks on exploring when and how age and ageing have entered the lexicon of institutional and organizational life through a prism of ageing as controlled, commodified and conferred. This helps to highlight how ageing is both an organized and organizing phenomenon. By this, I mean that ageing as a phenomenon is organized: made and shaped through normative organizational and institutional discourses and ideas that inform and colour how we perceive and experience ageing in ourselves and others. But simultaneously, the human experience of ageing also shapes and governs the organizational and institutional systems and practices that we often assume to be the 'neutral' apparatus of everyday careers and working lives. As I will suggest later on, recognizing the organized/organizing helix of ageing situates the experiential and situated dynamics of growing up and older in the context of financial capitalism, helping us to interrogate ' "the familiar" as a site of oppression' (Stanier et al, 2022: 4).

In many ways, what we recognize as contemporary modes of organizational life provide the conditions of possibility that lubricate the organizing processes surrounding ageing. Attending to such a context when theorizing ageing is even more important, given that contemporary organizations now have just as much power and influence over people's ageing experiences and lives more broadly as other actors, such as the state, community or family. Much of the Global North is now governed through a logic of financial capitalism as an extension of late capitalism – an overarching term used to speak to a global circulation of people, products and profit, governed by increasing abstract modes of labour and capital rather than industrialized labour. In recognizing its aspirations to be 'a purer stage of capitalism than any of the moments that preceded it' (Jameson, 1991: 55), late capitalism thrives on streamlining a desire for rational and often economically orientated ways of thinking. In financial capitalism, we see how this manifests itself through the way in which economies and national jurisdictions are dependent on financial institutions and the international flow of capital. Power becomes the dominion of corporations such as banks and organizational entities that undertake private equity and trading with financialized logics underpinning national strategies and intercountry economic – and subsequent political – relations. Financialized logics subsequently underpin national strategies and influence intercountry economic and political relations. The consequences (or, some might say, the intention) of such patterns and logics have been attributed to increasing wealth for an increasingly small proportion of people, while exacerbating inequalities both within and across countries.

Central to this is recognizing that a veneer of egalitarianism or meritocracy shrouds how systems and logics of working life operate in ways that benefit some groups or people and marginalize others. These organizing mechanisms fuel how organizing structures and norms enable and highlight particular ways of thinking about ageing at work, while precluding or silencing other experiences of ageing. In suggesting that ageing is a central charge through which organizations and institutions are experienced in financial capitalism, I focus on a prism of ageing as controlled, commodified and conferred. Ageing as controlled constitutes ageing as something that can be managed, identified and subsequently contained in ways that legitimize organizational power or defer responsibility, as well as shape systems of governance. Ageing as commodified pays attention to circuits of value that become a locus of commodification in external markets and internal organizational spaces, while ageing as conferred focuses on the way that we are pulled into desirable subject positions through age marked patterns of subjectification. Together, these three elements operate in symphony with each other, but are not necessarily experienced in synchronicity, and can undermine attempts to move towards more age inclusive and democratic practices. In other words, they create 'aged' systems of organizing, a term I use in this book to refer to processes that are constituted by, and in turn reproduce, normative expectations around chronology, bodies and biographies that generate uneven effects for people on the basis of their perceived position on the life course.

Ageing as controlled

Understanding ageing as controlled sets up ageing and its corollaries as something that can be managed, identified and contained. This logic shapes how ageing and its related lexicon (around age, generation and cohorts, *inter alia*) are discussed, manifest or absorb into everyday practices in ways that lead to a closing down of ways to acknowledge the full spectrum of the ageing experience. Ageing as controlled not only sets certain conditions surrounding organizational duties or responsibilities, but also governs the way in which some elements of ageing are prioritized or ordered in terms of their policy or socioeconomic importance. However, it also has a broader consequence for ageing: suggesting that age can be a focus of control not only paints a (partial) picture of ageing at work but also symbolically represents ageing as a phenomenon that *can* and *should* be controllable through institutional or organizational structures and processes. In other words, it enables ageing to become a 'target' for institutional, organizational and management control.

This desire to control ageing is imprinted into the historical and social imagination of the Global North. It underpins a master narrative of decline that has dominated ways of thinking about ageing as intrinsically a unidirectional and inevitable deterioration. The discourse of decline is rooted in biological and medical foundations that shaped early gerontology and has resulted in multiple legacies in health as well as society more broadly. For example, it is one reason why gerontology remains a 'Cinderella service' (compared to, say, paediatrics) and shadows the narratives around offsetting or 'freezing' time that characterizes the double standard of ageing for older women (Sontag, 1979). By comparison, ageing masculinities as constituted through a forever virile motif framed virility as proof of being able to master or triumph over ageing, most recently taken up by the pharmaceutical promotion of Viagra (Marshall, 2002). Yet this desire to control or ward off the decline associated with ageing can also be found in historical accounts. Most notable is endocrinologist Brown-Séquard (1889, p 106) self-injecting an elixir made of his own blood and the semen from various animal's crushed testicles as reported in *The Lancet* in 1889). As Brown-Séquard (1889) himself reported, it had a rejuvenating effect where he 'regained all the strength [he] possessed a good many years ago'. Such an endeavour draws startling parallels with the pursuit of the millionaires of Silicon Valley trying to 'trick' mortality through various body hacks that also involve various bodily fluids and transfusion processes (Walter, 2020). Here we see how attempts to control and master ageing are synonymous with broader projects to control and transcend nature as the final anthropocentric triumph.

There is a similar compulsion to control and understand ageing through ideas of classifying and categorizing age. Early accounts about ageing sought to understand ageing identities as shaped predominantly through the idea of stage-based dispositions predicated on chronological age that in turn connect to work-related behavioural or motivational factors. Such ideas are shaped through functionalist perspectives and a lifespan-based understanding of age similar to Shakespeare's 'seven ages of man', where expectations are bestowed upon different bounded groups on the basis of the meaning and activities that they are likely to engage with or have to negotiate. Approaches such as Erikson's (1994) rich account of the lifespan, written for the National Institute of Mental Health and underpinned by a psychosocial approach, counter these simplistic interpretations through considering how development alters over the course of one's life due to multiple social demands and expectations. Yet a selective reading of Erikson's work was used to further support a stage-based approach that served as the glue to underpin identification between chronological age and sets of behaviours or outlooks that could be expected. This assumes a sequential approach to ageing as the dominant mode of experience, and that chronological age could provide significant explanatory insight into the predictive intentions or motivations of workers; a position that latterly informed studies of age stereotypes around ingroup and outgroup identification (for example, Kleissner and Jahn, 2020).

Ageing as a controllable or predictable phenomenon is also part of a broader political landscape. Since the 1970s, a gradual shift from a welfare state model towards advocating for individualization and responsibility for the self (Cairns et al, 2020) has shaped the way in which ageing has been shorn up into areas of policy concern. This has led to cohort-based silos where younger and older groups in the workforce are often the concern of different government portfolios and distinct policy spaces, a pattern that was also replicated in academic disciplines, as seen in the fields of youth studies and social gerontology. For younger workers, often defined as those aged between 16 and 25, youth employment initiatives promoted transitioning into work and establishing a sustainable trajectory, embedded with a concern around 'employability' (McQuaid and Lindsay, 2005). Here, particular initiatives, such as apprenticeships, focus on skills acquisition rather than the structural or cultural discrimination individuals may face in the labour market. Central to these interventions has been the attempt to control and counter the uneven impact of economic shocks on the younger workforce, such as the Global Financial Crisis that had a disproportionate impact on youth unemployment (Choudhry et al, 2012). Yet controlling age through employability is also underpinned by the broader moral panic around controlling a disaffected and unengaged youth (Crisp and Powell, 2017); a paragon that has underpinned class-based perceptions of youthful masculinity (Pain, 2003).

Policy efforts to control older workers have followed a somewhat different path. Until the 1990s, several labour market policies and initiatives across the Global North had encouraged both the 'early activation' of retirement and the targeted redundancy of older workers. Yet the awareness of changing demographic patterns resulted in a significant U-turn whereby policies that previously legitimized exit strategies were reframed as ageist or economically unviable. Since then, political and policy commentaries have emphasized the need to offset the peril of demographic trends in many countries in the Global North, given that populations are 'ageing' due to more older people per capita vis-à-vis younger people. In response, a policy mandate of extending working lives has involved initiatives and targets for labour market returnees after the age of 50, as well as encouraging more flexible ways to combine work and pensions (DWP, 2017; Phillipson, 2019) or leaving paid employment more gradually (Vickerstaff and Loretto, 2017).

In the UK, the removal of retirement ages and the increase in the pension eligibility age have been justified by a reported need to control the economic consequences of a demographic swell, but these moves have been met with significant resistance from individuals as well as trade unions and employee representatives. Part of this is the difficulty of usurping the social imagination of retirement as a prolonged period that rewards a working life, breaking a social contract surrounding work and comfortable postwork lives (Crawford et al, 2020), even though statistically this is only the experience of a privileged minority (Fasang, 2012). Broader critiques of retirement cite a failure to create policies that support women and those whose careers are marked by more interrupted or precarious patterns of paid work. The success of policy interventions in transforming cultural ideas or social patterns surrounding working for longer while addressing potential political economic inequalities has also been questioned. For example, many face a persistent 'zone of insecurity' in their late 50s to early 70s, with declining incomes on the one hand and contracting job opportunities on the other (Philipson, 2019). Despite noble attempts to control ageing and its impact on the national landscape, ageing policy is still an ongoing work in progress in terms of trying to reconfigure the policy worlds of ageing that enable 'new social and sematic spaces, new sets of relations, new political subjects, and new webs of meaning' (Shore et al, 2011: 1).

Ageing as a phenomenon subject to control is central to organizational life, given that 'How long and how hard an individual works are influenced by national policy but determined locally' (Beck and Williams, 2015: 275). Policies flow into organizational life, but for the most part, organizations decide where and how resources are distributed and ordered in ways that shape how people think about relationships between labour and life over time. Increasingly, and as was suggested at the beginning of this chapter, age management is part of broader workforce systems that seek to predict and manage the flow of work. Succession workforce planning targets both 'young workers', and 'older workers', two groups regularly considered in age diversity initiatives. On the one hand, this organizing and representation of categories enables the production of evidence on shared trends across groups, reifying the legitimacy of classifying them in this way. But this can come at a cost through producing monolithic representations of those categories that shut down the possibility of looking at the more slippery and complex process of ageing that defies such easy classification.

Within the landscape of work and employment, there are certain areas where ageing is more or less explicitly referred to, and tackling discrimination in the labour market has been a major area where age as a workplace issue is located and discussed. EU legislation required Member States to introduce age discrimination legislation in the early 2000s, with default retirement ages ending in the UK in 2011, although employer-justified retirement ages are still possible. Older workers are evidenced as suffering from structural discrimination, as well as in interpersonal workplace relations shaped by enduring stereotypes around age-related categories. Here youth might be marked by energy and new ideas, but a flightiness or lack of resilience. By comparison, 'old' is correlated with an inability to change, slowness or unproductivity, and ill health, as well as potentially standing up for rights compared to younger workers (Maltby, 2007). Age inequality in a work setting also manifests through a mixture of relative measures and chronological benchmarking. For example, one study of performance appraisals noted that supervisors and employees would often draw on ideas of age groups (such as young and old workers) or number of years served as a shorthand to discuss workplace experiences (Previtali and Spedale, 2021). Although age-based prejudice remains under-researched in social psychology relative to gender and race (North and Fiske, 2015), it is recognized that the incidence, validity or experience in different cultural or occupational processes of age-based stereotyping is still a feature of the labour market (Fiske, 2017; Petery et al, 2020), as highlighted in attitudinal studies about perceptions of older people (Sharps et al, 1998; Chonody and Wang 2014). While these vary across countries, in general, workplace strategies echo broader social stereotypes regarding age.

Given the prevalence of these age-based stereotypes, it is unsurprising that the incidence of formal employment disputes continues to rise, particularly during the COVID-19 pandemic. While this provides one route for addressing injustices, controlling ageing inequality predominantly through legislation is unlikely to eradicate age-based bias more broadly. It also leaves out the fact that ageist perceptions and attitudes do not necessarily lead to age discriminatory practices, suggesting that ageing inequality is not quite as easy a creature to 'capture' as equality legislation suggests (Tornstam, 2006). Yet setting up ageing as predominantly a matter for discrimination or diversity policy in workplaces situates work-related ageing dynamics as fully possible to control. Through this lens, there is a targeted perpetrator who can be identified and possibly re-educated through inclusion or unconscious bias training and interventions, and a victim (the age-marked worker) who can be supported through human resource processes. It suggests the possibility of identifying specific places or hot spots where ageing is more likely to nestle into relevance within organizational practice and taint otherwise 'objective' practices such as recruitment, performance assessment and other ways of measuring and ordering the workforce. In doing so, ageing as a workforce issue can become contained as a personnel problem that has a set of tools to generate a solution that also contains its applicability to organizational life.

We can also see this desire to control ageing in broader discussions that frame ageism as the underbelly of organizational practice, suggesting that it both preys on the darker dynamics in human relationships and threatens to undermine the efficiency and productivity of ageing economies. For example, in launching a worldwide campaign to tackle ageism, the World

Health Organization and the United Nations jointly called for 'urgent action to combat ageism and better measurement and reporting to expose ageism for what it is – an insidious scourge on society' (WHO, 2021). In these policy narratives, the labour market is seen as a vital actor in purging age bias, allowing employment to provide economic security and psychological wellbeing. This conceptualizes ageism as a foreign and parasitic entity in an otherwise smooth economic efficiency that can be controlled, isolated and subsequently expelled from the workplace, which in turn makes it difficult to account for the many forms of age bias that occur in institutions.

At the same time, ageism itself is controlled as an organizational phenomenon through being ordered alongside other '-isms'. Anti-ageism initiatives may be seen as competing for similar resources (Riach, 2009), less recognized than other forms of discrimination (Jenkins and Poulston, 2014) or not viewed as important as tackling other forms of bias, given that 'ageist language did not seem to have the power to shock in the way that overtly racist or sexist language nowadays might' (van de Horst and Vickerstaff, 2021: 6). This desire to control ageing is also part of broader processes of organizing that seek to externalize, rationalize and subsequently measure value and manage aspects of organizational life. A number of organizational scholars have already demonstrated how imposing institutional structures seek to shape what employees do in ways that mark out certain bodies as more capable or suitable than others. As Dale (2005: 650) suggests, these manifest in ways of ordering in the workplace and also serve to regulate how work-based identities might be fostered – for example, ' "horizontal" forms of control are combined with and intrinsic to "deep" forms of control that seek to tap into ever more of individuals' sense of self and their experience of the world'.

Of course, behind organizational systems of control such as policy and organizational practices are lives and ageing experiences that do not neatly fit into patterns or dominant narratives about working lives. The enduring organizational expectations of a planned, defined and unidirectional process of stepping in and out of the labour marker contrast significantly with lived experience of labour force entry and exit as a fragmented, iterative and often improvised process. For those at the beginning of their working lives, the complex pathways into employment are rarely a clear, linear journey. Instead, there is more a yo-yoing between independence/dependence and insecurity/security than seen previously within the Global North (Biggart et al, 2001; Furlong and Cartmel, 2006). Similarly, the end of working life is increasingly marked by risk and uncertainty (Lain, 2018). Large numbers of individuals still find themselves de facto retired due to ill health or being unable to re-enter the labour market after retrenchment, redundancy or leaving a job (Blöndal and Scarpetta, 1999; Vickerstaff, 2006) – an experience that is exacerbated through gender where women are more likely to have more fragmented or 'frayed' careers over their working life course (Sabellis and Shilling, 2013).

This begs the following question: if controlling ageing is not possible, then why is it such a seductive trope for organizations? One reason may be that ageing as implanted into normative organizational mechanisms of control can help to maintain a veneer of rationality and objectivity, while disproportionately impacting certain groups of workers. Here, categorization through chronological markers or parameters is valorized through systems that attribute meaning and legitimacy. Chronology becomes a 'neat' way of explaining, presenting and organizing people. Even when age markers are not invoked, other organizing mechanisms may work in conjunction with age-based expectations. For example, Cutcher et al (2022) highlight how in one call centre, attributes ascribed to 'older workers' were not recognized within tightly controlled performance development spaces or regular evaluations. This reproduced an age-stratified and bureaucratically sanctioned valuation of the workforce that was reflected in performance management regimes and disproportionately impacted older workers.

What we see then is that underpinning this desire to control ageing lies a set of uneasy assumptions supported by a propensity to control workers and, by implication, to control ageing. The looming demographic crises, fear of the unemployed and moral panics around disaffected youth push us to contain ageing to discussions of discrimination and ageism. These are not simply facts valorized through statistical forecasting or predictions about the lack of capacity and skills needed for the workplaces of the future. They garner their momentum and emphasize a worldview that ageing *can* and *should* be controlled, simultaneously calling on a nomothetic logic and a felt crisis that relies on affective ways of emotionally reacting to and relating to ageing through containment in and through rationalistic logics and practices. Such an achievement results in 'capturing' something that can then be ascribed a value and put to use, as will be discussed next.

Ageing as commodity: devaluing/revaluing the ageing body

If controlling ageing is about bringing together different constellations of policy, people, practices and processes to manage, delineate, regulate and authorize ageing, this often requires assigning and organizing various qualities as more or less important or valuable. Just as ageing is controlled through a sanctioning of where it might be found and in what form, commodifying ageing ascribes particular modes of value to ageing and its various corollaries.

Since the emergence of industrialization, the ageing body at work has been associated with conversations on productivity. Early accounts surrounding the labouring body often mention age, from narratives of enslaved people and their ageing bodies correlated with price (Genovese, 2012) to Frederick Taylor's early writings on scientific management, which recorded the age of an employee next to information about their physical strength and capability (Bahnisch, 2000). In these instances, we see the early flickers of how ageing shaped by a master narrative of decline closely aligns with a broader economic logic where labour value is situated within a body that can have symbolic or differential worth. At the same time, how 'old' or young' bodies are is a relative rather than absolute measure, since classifications such as 'old' or 'young' are highly contextual and can depend on the organizational setting or sector (Bytheway, 1994; Featherstone and Wernick, 1995; Hockey and James, 2002). This means that the commodification of ageing is a complex terrain, but is also one worthy of pursuing, as success can lead to significant profit and power.

Aesthetic labour, where value is attributed to the set of visual or body-based characteristics deemed most appropriate to a particular sector or profession, has highlighted a congruence between age and value, particularly in service industries and customer experience roles where the worker as embodying a brand image or aspiration has been closely correlated. For example, Duffy et al (2017: 262) explore how Virgin Airline's 'Still Red Hot' 25th anniversary campaign plays with the postfeminist assumption of 'cultural sexualization, marked by a symbolic vocabulary of youthful, unselfconscious pleasure seeking'. A similar sentiment is found in earlier reference to the 'PanAm smile' within the airline industry and the adage of 'use them till their smiles wear out, then get a new bunch' (Neilsen, 1982: 81): a pattern that assumes an unending supply of 'fresh' bodies that can be extrapolated for labour as well as the loss of sexualized modes of capital as employees grow older. The absence of manual labour in post-industrial economies can also mean that the symbolic representation of the body is considered a material manifestation what are otherwise highly abstracted and invisible modes of labour. This is not only influenced by social attributions around ageing and fitness (Tulle, 2008), but is part of aspiring to embody what an 'ideal worker' may look like, where normative health, fitness and wellbeing ideals are conflated with workplace performance (OECD, 2006; Rudman, 2006; Waring and Waring, 2009). As is the case with gendered, racialized and sexualized forms of workplace commodification, ageing is attributed to ideas of what is seen as 'appropriate' or 'fitting' and thus more valuable in a particular occupational setting. The inscription of such value is often highly gendered. For example, Jyrkinen and McKie (2012) note that the gender coding operating around professional ageing bodies is particularly cruel to women in terms of conflating a diminishing cultural value with a diminishing organizational value, while men's authority may increase as they begin to look older. Similarly, Trethewey's (1999) study of women's occupational identities highlights how the gendered ageing body is not only a site of work in terms of labour, but also a site that should be voluntarily 'worked on', through cosmetic procedures, fitness or wellbeing pursuits. She shows how gendered tensions emerge between having a fit body as synonymous with professionalism and being in control, and the danger of distraction from professional credibility due to its sexualized inscription.

While less concerned with the right look, ageing as a site of valuation has also been central to the business case for age diversity. Promoted by the UK government in the early 2000s, the 'business case for older workers' was incredibly influential in determining how ageing-related economies of value were sanctioned and legitimized. This suggests that positive organizational outcomes could be gained from employing older workers through, for example, accessing a larger pool of talent, knowledge retention, or reflecting the broader population and thus potential market. The business case framing the value of older workers was also significant in the run-up to anti-age discrimination law. Unlike other legislation surrounding race and gender in Northern European countries which was driven by concerns relating to civil rights and equality, age discrimination legislation enacted in 2006 in the UK was strongly underpinned by a market-driven logic. To make a business case, examples of best practice older worker recruitment and management focused on entry-level customer service roles and were supported by evidence. This included emphasizing how elderly customers preferred salespeople that reflect their own age (Johnson-Hillery et al, 1997), a term Foster and Resnick (2013) refer to as 'matching and mirroring'. Similarly, customers may view retail employees who look younger or older as more or less useful depending on what they are buying, which may also be attributed to gendered-aged ascriptions about men or women's differential capacities to 'serve' in a more or less acceptable way (McDowell, 2009).

The fallacy of a business case approach was quickly recognized when Duncan (2003: 108) noted that 'fighting stereotypes with stereotypes' was unlikely to tackle more deep-seated modes of age inequality in the labour market. For example, attributing the value of older workforce to their flexibility can lead to framing older workers as a contingent army that can be demobilized during economic downturns (Kindelan, 1998). In other words, if age is legitimized as a means of valuation, then it can just as easily be justified as a means of devaluation – a currency that can be used to mark or cast out people with few negative ramifications.

Commodification also emerges from a consideration of age as a relational point of value where people 'fit together' in a way that provides benefits to the organization over and above the sum of their parts. Generations and intergenerational contact or cooperation are seen as a basis for increased productivity or competitive work advantage (Pitt-Catsouphes et al, 2013; Čič and Žižek, 2017), although organizations are also warned to be mindful of tension or conflict (North and Fiske, 2015). Pritchard and

Whiting (2014: 1622) suggest that the commodification of the generations concept serves to 'stabilize particular understandings of age while obscuring differences that might be more pertinent to issues of work entitlement, responsibility and their consequence'. This has a performative effect, as promoting age-based relations as a source of conflict may serve to decentre opportunities for 'the social reproduction of the collective worker' to resist the demand of work intensification more broadly (Roberts, 2006: 81). Yet age-based assumptions underpin a business case and shore up generations as a phenomenon that can be 'put to work' for the benefit of organizational outcomes. This aids the digestion of ageing in organizational practices and narratives as marked by difference, in that there is an 'essence' of age that can, under the right conditions, be bottled, marketed and leveraged to the benefit of businesses and shareholders.

In much of the Global North, economically driven attributions of workforce value and age currently rest upon a neoliberal political and economic logic that underpins 'active ageing' and 'successful ageing'. Active ageing emerged as a policy solution to assist in optimizing opportunities for health, participation and security that enhance quality of life as people age (Walker, 2002; WHO, 2002). In its early inception, it echoed early tenets of activity theory: a functionalist approach that promoted meaningful engagement throughout one's life (Havighurst and Albrecht, 1953). Active ageing often focused on health maximisation, although its translation into the context of work and the economy creates a moral economy built on assumptions relating to choice, self-responsibility and individualization of the ageing self as active and useful, and this useful body as an aspirational and achievable possibility for all. The focus on health has also shaped how expectations of professional embodiment are increasingly crafted through ideals of fitness and 'healthism'. As Calasanti and King (2005: 6) note, such underlying assumptions fail to consider how intersectional trajectories play out in our experience of growing older within different circumstances, contexts and conditions, given that: 'The dictate to age successfully by remaining active is both ageist and ignorant of the lives of the working classes. Spurred by the new anti-aging industry, the promotional images of the "active elder" are bound by gender, race, class, and sexuality.'

While ageing is suggested as something that can be unsuccessful or successful, its commodification cannot prevent the ageing body being finite in its capacities. Parts can become subject to excessive strain or even break under certain conditions. This is not to take a biologically deterministic view, but rather to recognize that work can lead to modes of extraction, such as exploitation and overwork that harm the body. Such harms are often displaced in narratives that focus on ageing as a source of value or become invisible as employees move across different employers who do not recognize previous excesses or the body toil of past labour. Moreover, they fail to acknowledge that an ability to recover from work-related excesses and harms may alter over the life course and be compounded or exacerbated by how the employee is perceived. Modes of commodification serve to simplify and occlude this aspect and, in doing so, they open up or close down spaces that seek to situate ageing as an asset or liability. The challenge becomes not just the fecundity of the ageing process being occluded, but may lead to suggestions that organizations should discharge certain bodies before they lose their normative value.

Just as organizations can commodify ageing as a source of value, workplaces can also be the site of aged decommodification and devaluing, as highlighted in accounts of workforce recruitment, development or engagement. Those aged over 50 in the labour market are less likely to receive training, although in part this is due to their higher representation in parts of the labour market where training is less widespread, such as self-employment or small businesses (Canduela, 2012; Vickerstaff et al, 2015). Elsewhere, Beck (2014) points to an assumption that older workers may undertake informal training, but that this form of learning is generally less valued. Yet, underresourcing training can also be due to employers' negative assumptions of older workers' value based on ideas around wage-productivity gaps and a perceived difficulty in guaranteeing a return on investment (Conen et al, 2012; Istenič et al, 2024; de Meulenaere et al, 2016). Some studies point to these elements as part of a larger age-devaluation thesis that stems from the dynamics of a political economy wherein skills and knowledge are assumed as going 'out of date', making older workers more vulnerable to structural inequalities (Bowman et al, 2017: 476). Others have suggested that older workers are positioned as less valuable due to the roles they are more likely to occupy. For example, Egdell et al's (2023) study of the later working lives of firefighters shows how 'valuable' work is delineated around age-marked bodies and how jobs where older firefighters are more often located beyond the 'front line' are the targets of cuts due to austerity measures. Reasons for this devaluation vary but we can see that a discourse of decline once again underpins diminishing opportunities and value in the labour market.

When points of valuation correlate with age indexing, there remains a problematic pattern of relying on more value than is being 'paid for'. This can be an underlying rationale in jobs that forefront the social benefits of employment for older workers and in doing so undermine the economic premium their labour potentially has (Riach, 2007). In contrast, those at the beginning of their working lives find that institutional and policy sanctioned models such as apprenticeships or internships, while being significantly underpaid (or not paid), are justified on the promise of future 'payback' (Grant-Smith and McDonald, 2018). Nickson and Baum also point out 'the reliance of younger workers in hospitality and retail is simply a structural one', given that the sector assumes that this cohort in the workforce will accept flexibility relating to working hours for low wages, while being more likely to have an 'outgoing middle-class sociability' that is beneficial in customer-facing work (Nickson and Baum, 2017: 545).

The organization of ageing suggests certain age-indexed knowledge as more valuable to organizations than others. Farrugia (2018: 513) suggests that youthfulness is about an 'accumulation of capitals that are possessed by young people and sold on the labour market in exchange for a wage', which is especially important in the context of the immaterial labour that characterizes contemporary work. Yet they also suggest that older worker disadvantage may emerge from how 'older managerial and professional workers are marginalized because they have *more* human capital than organizations want'. This points to a tension within current accounts of older worker diversity, whereby organizations suggest they want an accumulative mode of knowledge and yet fail to articulate how particular modes of knowledge have more or less currency in a given work context.

At its heart, ageing as commodified plays out through a paradox. On the one hand, the ideal body at work is one that is not subject to any marks of ageing; it is commodified through promoting the idea of being an unending source of value and labour, with an ability to renew and regenerate itself, given the right products and techniques. Organizational accounts also 'write out' the organic experience of the ageing body in subtle ways. Framing the body as a site of labour requires the ageing body to aspire to always be a site of 'successful ageing' and not damaged by the labour process itself. This effectively 'writes in' an assumed ability to endure, self-discipline and have a neverending capacity for labour on their bodies. Increasingly, the biodynamics of ageing are seen as running counter to other professional discourses. Even when the changing corporeality of the ageing body is acknowledged, there are assumptions that the aspiration should be for the body to maintain a constant generative capacity that can keep going or at least recover and mend itself back to its full, required functionality. Similar to the 'ideal worker' subject, such a reification of presumed, essentialized qualities is conflated with other axes of power that make this expectation a more distant ambition for certain groups or people. The consequence of such aspirations and often unachievable benchmarks is intimately felt by employees themselves, as we will explore next.

Ageing as conferred: the making of an ageing subject

Ageing as controlled and commodified is powerful not only because it complements and reinforces broader systems of organization, but because it informs and shapes an individual's desire to make sense of ageing. Ageing as conferred speaks to the way organizational ideals connect to lived experiences around what it means and how it feels to grow up and older in the context of work. In exploring this, we begin to see ageing at work as a practical project of the self that, creates desiring positions that align with certain organizational roles, positions and identities.

Since the 1970s, academic studies paying attention to the dynamics of labour and the economy began to recognize how the conferral of age-based identities emerges through economic or organizational projects, structural or economic modes of transformation, or social reproduction. For example, processes of modernization could render a worker 'too old' by making their skills appear out of date or irrelevant (Banks and Casanova, 2003), while those exploring the political economy of youth have suggested that economic inequality and a structural lack of opportunity is central to how people identify collectively as 'youths' (Rogers and Terriquez, 2016). Such concerns have been foundational in youth studies, highlighting how employment and transitions in and around work not only shape experience at a particular time of life, but also inform what it means to be a 'young' person in the economy more generally (Furlong, 2012). Youth identities are also intertwined with the stratification of class-based dispositions and expectations in terms of how work forms part of a trajectory into adulthood. Within these traditions, seminal work such as Paul Willis' *Learning to Labour* (1978: 146) highlights how 'manual labouring comes to take on, somehow, a significance and critical expression for its owner's social position and identity, which is no part of its own proper nature'. In other words, structural conditions coalesce with socially situated spaces in and around work in ways that simultaneously develop the self and shape the material conditions under which work is expected or experienced.

The specificity of context to this process is captured in Krekula's (2009: 8) notion of age coding: 'practices of distinction that are based on and preserve representations of actions, phenomena, and characteristics as associated with and applicable to demarcated ages'. Age coding can draw on particular economic identities and suture them with normative images of age, such as what 'enterprising' means (Ainsworth and Hardy, 2008: 290) where the 'enterprising self is not uniformly accessible but, rather, an inherently aged construction'. Likewise, age coding can position older women's 'talent' for being more flexible and adaptable, subsequently sidelining their status in policy(Ainsworth, 2002).

Such representations of ageing can also turn inwards and result in individuals producing self-marginalizing identities. Studies focusing on the phenomenon of 'internalized ageism' suggest a person sets self-limiting features on themselves in accordance with their age that often play out within an ageist environment (Köttl et al, 2021; Ayalon, 2022). Partly, this may be down to 'age stereotype threat', where it is the perception (rather than the outcome or actual incidence) of age-based stereotypes that impacts how workers feel about their age relative to their career or work opportunities (Lamont et al, 2015).

The turn towards poststructural approaches to identity within studies of work and organization has resulted in increasing focus on the way in which the 'aged subject' is discursively produced. Noting the 'inadequacy of the "victim–perpetrator" paradigm dominating mainstream scholarship' (Spedale, 2019: 41), studies have considered how biased or unequal ideological repertoires underpin the language used to create social worlds that define the 'older worker' subject position (Rudman and Molke, 2009; Spedale, 2019). Such subject positions are particularly potent as they are often in the realm of the 'universe of the undiscussed' (Bourdieu, 1977: 168): taken-for-granted or unspoken assumptions and beliefs that are central to the production of ageism and disavowal of individuals or groups who are 'attached' to a particular age norm. Increasingly, this manifests within 'new ageism' (McVittie et al, 2003), where bias emerges through latent, indirect or seemingly benign ideas rather than visible or explicit forms of discrimination. In the context of work, new ageism operates through a façade of neutrality, objectivity and meritocratic practices, making it difficult to call out, even though it may limit positive or generative subject positions for those recognized as 'older workers' (Biggs and Powell, 2001; Riach, 2007; Gendron, 2018) or who is viewed as 'young' or 'older' (Ainsworth and Hardy, 2008).

The dynamics of ageing as conferred do not impact everyone equally, but highlight that ageing is never 'just' about ageing. Echoing the work of Crenshaw (Cho et al, 2013), ageing scholars have shown the intersectional effects of various axes of power around age and other social categories. For example, studies of the life course have shown how women experience a 'double jeopardy' in relation to age and gender at multiple times over their life course (Arber et al, 2007). This emerges through problematic subject positions such as the cranky old women or the dolly bird at work (Itzen and Newman, 2003; Irni, 2009). It also underpins lines of recognition where certain forms of gendered-aged labour is highly demanding but undervalued. Similarly, women are more likely to be subject to ageist bias across the life course and viewed as 'never the right age' for work (Duncan and Loretto, 2004) due to assumptions around caring responsibilities or the 'threat' of a female body getting pregnant and disrupting the normative labour process (Jyrkinen and McKie, 2012; Berger, 2021). Cutcher's (2021: 1448) study of being an older manager and mothering discourses suggests an expectation to defers one one's own needs or ambitions, pointing to a 'precarious subjectivity as the older women perform work outside their formal role and focus on furthering the career of their younger, male manager, not themselves'. Elsewhere, younger women are more likely to undertake additional emotional labour within customer services interactions compared to their male counterparts (Riach and Wilson, 2014). And similar studies have explored the marginalizing effects surrounding ageing and disability (McLaughlin and Neumark, 2024) and how youth unemployment and older worker disadvantage highlights the way in which those in lower socioeconomic groups are more vulnerable to age-biased practices (Bratt et al, 2018; Ugargol and Parvathy, 2023). Just as disadvantage and advantage can accumulate (Willson et al, 2007) over the working life course, being subject to bias can also have a compounding impact, although the systems and organizing regimes around control and commodification often diffuse temporal and spatial boundaries that would enable us to better account for the cumulative impact of ageism.

The 'ideal worker' position is central to processes of ageing identification, where 'access to a single, univocal identity – such as that of successful older worker … is difficult and problematic' (Spedale, 2019: 48). The ideal worker operates as an unattainable aspiration. In other words, the combination of attributes ascribed through discourse is almost impossible for one individual to inhabit in practice. When broken down into its constituent parts, the 'ideal' ageing worker can be seen as a Frankenstein-like make-up of paradoxical trajectories and a compendium of aesthetic, bodily capacity and skills that would be impossible for one person to embody. For example, they should have significant experience while also being willing to work long hours and accept the salary and terms offered by the employer, they should be able to leverage a significant professional network but have flexibility and a willingness to move when and where the organization requires; and they should never be unwell or subject to health episodes, while always able to absorb the stress and encroachment of labour into life.

Such an unattainable aspiration may be theoretically easy to dismiss, but they are often part of the pigment of organizational life that we are reliant upon for a sense of self. To be caught up in such practices is not only to respond to an organizational demand but is entangled with an ontological demand. In other words, there is an inherent reliance on work and organizational settings, interactions and relations as a means of constituting who we are and this subsequently makes us vulnerable to lines or markers of aged conferral. Work is formative to a sense of self across the life course, from aspirations during 'emerging adulthood' (Arnett, 2000) right through to later life, as show in Gabriel et al's (2010) study of unemployed managers in their 50s. Ageing subjectivities are often deeply intertwined with organizational dynamics and markets, meaning that resistance not only undermines personal experiences of ageing, but is also perceived as an attack on a normative mode of organizing. Farrugia (2018: 512) highlights this in his study of immaterial labour, suggesting that 'youth and youthfulness is becoming deeply intertwined with the labouring subjectivities, practices and products of the new economy'. Of particular importance to the conferral of ageing at work is a chrononormative matrix: 'the use of time to organize individual bodies towards maximum productivity' (Freeman, 2010: 3). While the continuum of ageing rarely dissolves into dualisms that we might see play out in the case of gender, it does compel certain recitations, for example, through age-and-stage ideas, and when and what is recognizable as a legitimate older or younger worker. This is particular challenging against a backdrop of temporally biased cultural norms at work often predicated on a preference for newness (Riach and Kelly, 2015).

This ongoing project of the organizational self, often termed 'identity work' (Brown, 2015), place demands on different people by virtue of social and organizational positions in order to be recognized as professional. A desire for age-based identification can even ironically operate in ways that prevent people returning to work. In other words, the desire and demands for ontological security may result in economic insecurity and are part of a broader story of 'ontological precarity' (Lain et al, 2020: 93) where older worker marginalized identities emerge from 'both the "objective" conditions structuring older workers' lives and individuals' subjective interpretations of their situations'. For example, the shock of redundancy or the stigma of unemployment for those over 50 can mean that crafting a 'non/worker identity' is such a precarious task that it can prevent individuals from seeking job opportunities, for fear of breaking or shattering the sense of self they had tentatively built up while not in paid employment (Riach and Loretto, 2009). Such concerns around the uneven landscapes of recognition and intelligibility in the conferral of ageing highlight how the conditions of organizational subjectivity rest on an oscillation between the experiential and relational dynamics of ageing and the organizational context in which one grows older. Given that our own identity projects are not 'fixed', but rather constituted in ongoing modes of interaction, work operates as a powerful signifier that informs the meaning of ageing and how we make sense of our ageing self.

While discourse play a key role in the constitution of organizational ageing subjectivities, age identities are in many ways 'a body-based system of social categorization' (Ainsworth 2002: 581) and are subsequently entangled with a more embodied experience and reception. On the one hand, scholars are keen to avoid a biomedically determined approach that pathologizes ageing and older workers. On the other hand, the need to recognize the material, embodied experience of ageing is vital if the ageing experience of work is to be fully acknowledged. Studies concerned with normative modes of embodiment highlight the ways in which selfhood is constituted through the corporeal experience of enabling and constraining dynamics in organizational life as we grow up and older. For example, accounts of the menopausal transition highlight how women's ageing bodies can require women to have to negotiate the 'deficient, passive, frail or overdetermined bodies of dominant menopausal discourse or the disparaging representations of the older female body/worker' (Jack et al, 2019: 139). Such organizational subjectivities are imbued with aged conditions of intelligibility, in part due to terms such as 'older worker' or 'menopausal employee', which provide social scripts or ways of recognizing ourselves and others as an organizational subject, even when this may also be a marginalized or devalued position or identity. Similar accounts of maternal bodies at work have demonstrated how ageing is more subtly marked through becoming a body-for-others within the life course, and how this may become a site of organizational abjection. For women, the ageing body experienced as a biocultural site of fertility over time can also result in the need to negotiate being viewed as excessive and unable to be controlled within labour processes.

As such, how we experience the body as a gendered-aged phenomenon in an organizational context is always undertaken through day-to-day practices and protocols that seek to 'maintain "order" and perceived efficiency in organizations, effectively punishing ... for disturbing the embodied codes of practice which "govern" how workers are expected to present themselves' (Gatrell, 2019: 428–429). While women may seek to explore the 'multidimensional power of embarrassment' as they grow older (Butler, 2020: 697), ignoring age-based modes of organizational subjectivity can come at a cost. Rejecting aged normative lines of recognition have the consequence of people being rendered invisible or problematic, given that organizational ageing as conferred feeds off broader social norms. For example, narrow parameters of recognition reify readily available age-based archetypes, such as 'fluffy young girl', 'cranky old women' (Irni, 2009) or 'lecherous old man'.

Resisting these modes of age-orientated conferral may also require a more radical rejection of the broader norms around organizational life. Chrononormativity and its corollaries mean that organizational systems of conferral – even when not explicitly about age – have uneven effects for different organizational bodies. They may operate through a sheen of objectivity that is comforting and compelling for all, but are inscribed by certain lines of directionality about what is appropriate, legitimate and recognizable. They are difficult to argue against because employees are also contained 'within them', subject to their norms and parameters that enclose where, when and how they may explore ways of being an ageing worker. They may even give us a sense of comfort: even if they are not what we might choose them for ourselves, they provide a sense of feeling 'in time', as Wanka's study of work-retirement transitions suggest (2020: 497). Such processes do not happen in a vacuum, but are deeply intertwined with organizational life. At the heart of organizing, we can see a chronobiopolitics around the ageing working body through setting up a presumption that the working body should be a predictable and controllable entity through which organizations can guarantee a consistent and ever-efficient mode of labour. At the same time, the ageing process may be read as producing an instability that challenges the organizational demand for the static body where productivity must and should be predicted. Recognition, or legitimacy as an age-situated subject at work requires employees to become 'the subject [that] produces its coherence the cost of its own complexity' (Butler, 1993: 115), compelled to negotiate, silence, compromise or repress the fecundity of their ageing experience.

Discussion: the chronotopics of ageing at work

Recognizing our increasing reliance and dependency on organizations for both our economic security and ontological security demands a framework that is both sensitive to ageing and ageing in the context of work. Controlling, commodifying and conferring ageing at work help us understand why, despite legislative and policy intervention, culture change programmes, and the increasing incidence of age diverse workplaces, ageing at work is still marked by biases, exclusion and limited ways of recognizing the fullness of growing up and older. Ageism and various forms of age-based organizing are not simply *incidental* to the labour process, but are an *enduring feature* of the organizational and economic landscape in contemporary society. In other words, normative prescriptions of ageing are not simply a parasitic force that can be expunged from workplaces, but are intimately woven into how we think about and experience work.

The trinity of controlling, commodifying and conferring highlights how ageing at work is a process that is negotiated through material bodies, economic circumstances and organizational contexts coming together. In other words, the conferral of ageing at work operates as an embodied and socially situated experience within the context of aged organizing processes and workplace settings. This is by no means a passive, objective or universal process, but rather is always undertaken in and through the context of organizational, occupational and institutional norms and systems. Ageing is both ideologically inscribed and situated as part of a complex interplay between one's habituated experience of being a temporally dynamic body, and the experience of broader organizational systems of power and recognition. As a heuristic, control, commodification and conferral highlights possibilities and challenges in relation to how we begin to understand ideas, norms and assumptions around ageing as entangled in practices and individual working lives.

What I have attempted to show is that organizing ageing marks out different territories and spaces that are ordered as more or less important. Constellations of controlling, commodifying and conferring processes of organizational ageing operate as a chronotope, binding together different times of life with different spaces in the workplace or labour market. Just as Bakhtin (1981) suggests that chronotopes are never neutral, ageing chronotopes are incredibly powerful as they enable the diffusion and sanitation of different forms of organizational order and modes of organizing that are accorded more or less value by an organization or economy. They encourage us to think about what we should receive or expect at certain chronological benchmarks or times of our life. For example, viewing careers through the lens of ageing chronotopes provides a critical lens on positioning early careers as places where the exertion of labour is more about investment than immediate financial reward, or highlights why managers expect candidates for particular positions to be found within a chronological age range (Martin et al, 2014). Similarly, a chronotopic understanding of a 'later' career may orientate towards a duty to mentor, or to feel a responsibility to share accumulated knowledge. Such assumptions are not neutral, and are often for the benefit of organizations or those in power and serve to reproduce a normative, stable order, even at the cost of individual trajectories or preferred identities.

However, controlling, commodifying and conferring also expose the limitations of the organizational project to fully account for the ageing experience. It helps us understand why scholars themselves might be tempted to take a shortcut and stake a claim on ageing at work being either predominantly the outcome of broader ideas or discourses, or predominantly determined through our own individual embodiment at a particular moment in time. But this does not provide a clear way to understand what it means to grow up and older as a worker or how we might do this as we ourselves change over the life course. It is true that some experiences will mean we invariably prioritize the abstracted logics, agendas and norms shaped by ageing as controlled, commodified and conferred through organizational and institutional systems of governance. But at other times, it is likely that organizational stakeholders will focus on the intimate, quotidian and often private moments or flashes of awareness, where ageing feels like a dynamic but sedimented experience. If we are always situated in contexts that seek to implant modes of ageing upon us, while negotiating the inherent temporality of an embodied ageing experience, we must not only consider organizational subjects as situated, but also as constituted in, and constituting, the world-making activities that make up ageing in work and organizations. In other words, the dynamically situated person who grows up and older at work is not simply beholden to the organizational posturing of control, commodification and conferral, but is continually involved in constituting ageing at work. To consider this further, we need a theoretical intervention to think through the reciprocal processes through which the ageing embodied self and ageing world meet and mingle as we work through ageing.

2

Towards a Phenomenology of Working Through Ageing

In this chapter, I introduce what a theory of working through ageing might encompass. Specifically, I consider how a phenomenological approach can help to further conceptualize working through ageing as the amalgam of self-world encounters experienced in and over the life course. To inform this, I draw together recent critical phenomenological accounts with a revisiting of the work of Simone de Beauvoir, exploring the fertility of her theoretical conversations for understanding the practical and ontological experiences of growing up and older in work.

Phenomenology is an approach emerging from accounts in early 20th-century continental Europe and traditionally associated with the intellectual canon of Husserl, Heidegger and Merleau-Ponty. This initially sought to interrupt the backdrop of distance and objectivity associated with the scientific method through declaring a 'going back to the things themselves'. Here 'going back' is not simply about understanding an object or phenomenon in its context, but also grasping how perception is an active, situated, relational activity that is always doing something. Rather than think of judgement, acknowledgement or thought as a neutral filter that happens after an a priori or independent act of cognition, phenomenology considers the very act of perception as imbued with meaning or intentionality.

Such ideas have been subject to valuable critical interventions within feminist theory that show the experiential realm is neither neutral nor apolitical. Feminist theory has emphasized a contemporary phenomenological concern with being-in-the-world with others as an inherently and profoundly uneven and interdependent experience grounded in our corporeality. Corporeality here is neither singular in terms of an individual's definitive fleshy experience nor fully made through culture, but an amalgam of different elementals of historical, social and political features of the world that informs how different bodies come to experience power or subjection. This theoretical evolution serves to correct ideas that assume ethnocentric or phallocentric points of origin and has led to a rich legacy of critical phenomenological accounts of gender, as well as disability and ethnicity both in society and, to a lesser extent, within organizations. Such work is not abstract, but seeks to generate a political call to action.

However, amid this critical turn, ageing has remained curiously absent from the phenomenological playbook. In part, this echoes a broader hesitance to theorize ageing on its own terms in social theory and empirical philosophy. Instead, scholars have often relied on theorizing within cohort-bounded parameters, such as 'youth studies' or 'gerontology', or have viewed mortality as the guiding preoccupation in relation to ageing. Elsewhere, there has been a tendency to apply theoretical apparatuses from other disciplines, such as gender studies, situating ageing as a genus of other modes of subjectivity or inequality. Such approaches have reaped valuable insights, as discussed in the previous chapter, but invariably also do a disservice to the specific, dynamic qualities of the ageing experience. To begin considering this specificity, I will consider ageing as contingent on a phenomenological dis-ease that tends us towards displacing, sanitizing and externalizing the lived experience of ageing in a way that may render it partially coherent, but flattens the prolificity of the ageing experience in and around work. Yet this attention to dis-ease requires us to begin a phenomenological account that attends to the simultaneity of the practical and ontological project of growing up and older. What I suggest here is that the compulsion to shore up ageing through the limited parameters of control, commodification and conferral, as discussed in the previous chapter, might be dismantled, at least in part, through attention to the phenomenology of ageing as a critical intervention.

To further explore what a phenomenology of working through ageing might consider, the chapter turns to the work of Simone de Beauvoir, one of the few social theorists to produce a sustained philosophical treatise on age and who persistently revisited the dynamics of ageing across her literary and biographical accounts. Through a critically responsive conversation with her work, I suggest that her ideas spark new ways to think about working through ageing as simultaneously an ontological and practical undertaking, and one that is pursued within an organizational context through the One/Other dialectic as experienced through the dynamically situated body. Notwithstanding the limitations of some of her empirical accounts of growing older, de Beauvoir's theoretical oeuvre helps to map out what working through ageing as a phenomenological project might look like. This leads to a broader consideration of how organizational experiences of ageing are inherently bound up in ontoepistemological conditions that arise from being simultaneously interdependently situated in the world while required to assert our own sense of self.

A phenomenological invitation into organizational ageing

The classical phenomenological method aims to explore the process through which things come to us as a primary experience. Departing from a concern for either an objective scientific method or a subjective individual perspective, it invites us into the fold of understanding how identity is not simply a matter of the self, but always about the self-in-relations. This provides the basis for considering how we are *of* the world, in terms of how world making occurs in the way in which we come to be meaningful and recognizable among a constellation of different settings, relations and objects. It encourages us to denaturalize the taken-for-granted, overlooked ways in which we operate *in* the world as embodied subjects, while also recognizing the impossibility of transcending or escaping our own embodied inheritance *of* the world – in other words, phenomenology is committed to a sociality that is both situated and inherently intersubjective. Such a position highlights an inherent tension around the vulnerability of being interdependent on others, while striving for a level of integrity that allows us to be recognized as individual. On the one hand, we are never able to fully guarantee an ontologically stable self because we are beholden to relations between the self, others and settings. We cannot escape our dependency and reliance on the 'second person', who in turn must also rely on us for their own ontological pursuits. On the other hand, our desire for stability also makes us vulnerable to the illusion that our selves, others and various settings are 'already-made' and absolute.

Central to a person's indelible connection with the world is how actions, perceptions and representations are not part of an objective process, but always come from a situated directedness born from our embodied, lived experience. This directedness is central to the phenomenological precept of 'intentionality' that emphasizes the experience and process of how 'things' – objects, people and ourselves – are always orientated towards something, rather than there being a possibility of asserting neutral, objective or disinterested purview. Husserl's successors, notably those positing an more existentialist phenomenological commitment such as Merleau-Ponty (1964a: 118), emphasize how 'the corporeal relevance of every being' is fundamental to how we come to be in and of the world. Intentionality unfolds through situated, embodied ways of knowing and being, as if our lived experience operates as a centrifugal force of comprehension. It orientates us in particular ways towards a constellation of 'things' that is inseparable from our situated embodiment. These relations and reciprocities between ourselves and things inform something about us and the organizational world in which we come to be situated, rendering us both coherent and vulnerable.

Two main perspectives on intentionality exist. Traditional phenomenological methods imply that there is still an essential point of origin, even if it is impossible to access. This suggested the possibility of reduction, or a nomothetic aspiration of suspending, or 'bracketing' – in other words, that there is a theoretical possibility of removing the 'noise' that occludes the structure of 'the thing itself'. In contrast, more critically inflected phenemonologically informed accounts have critiqued this idea of a point of essence or structure that may somehow imply the possibility of a stable and fixed essence of structure of consciousness. This school of thought emphasizes how intentionality has no a priori state beyond the constellations of intentionality and directedness we live by and through. Importantly, these ontoepistemological constellations are not neutral, but are patterned through historical, cultural and institutional matrices that make up the world.

Such a perspective is valuable when considering how to 'explicitly thematize power relations, structural forces, and unequal distributions of privilege in their phenomenological analyses of lived experience' (Stanier et al, 2022: 3). It acknowledges that power is not simply corruption of an ex ante ontopoetic process of intentionality, but rather that consciousness itself is constituted through conditional access and uneven epistemic modes that shape how the human condition is disclosed. Notably, this focus has placed concerns of inequality and injustice at the heart of phenomenological inquiry, although mainly in relation to racialization and gender rather than ageing.

One of the earliest sustained phenomenological analyses of this uneven structuring of consciousness is found in Frantz Fanon's work on race. Working through a critique of his former teacher Merleau-Ponty, who was formative in emphasizing the centrality of the body to phenomenology, Fanon exposes the dangers of assuming that grand narratives (such as racialization and colonialism) are an empirical manifestations separate from the structuring of consciousness and intentionality. To do so, he demonstrates how anti-Blackness is not simply a dialectical history we passively read, but is textured over consciousness, time and bodies to produce a 'zone of non-being'. As such, he highlights how intentionality through being and access to the world is a conditional and corporeal accomplishment constituted through an inherently uneven reciprocity:

> I arrive slowly in the world; sudden emergences are no longer my habit. I crawl along. The white gaze, the only valid one, is already dissecting me. I am fixed. Once their microtomes are sharpened, the Whites objectively cut sections of my reality. I have been betrayed. (Fanon, 2008 [1952]: 95)

Understanding phenomenology as not only an embodied theory, but one that also provides a basis for exploring inequality and uneven recognition has revitalized, extended and transformed the critical phenomenological turn in recent years. Notably, it has helped to consider power as not simply an axis, but as central to the condition of lived experiences of gender, disability, race and ethnicity as corporeally, culturally and organizational constituted. Scholars such as Iris Marion Young, Sara Ahmed, Judith Butler, Gail Wiess, Kay Toombs and Lauren Berlant have all emphasized how lives are constituted through uneven relations and modes of attachment between bodies, objects and contexts that either afford or negate recognition. In doing so, they show our inevitable (but often uneven) dependence on others to constitute our self, often through considering plurality within reciprocity as an ontological imperative that provisions political and ethical modes of living and organizing.

Phenomenological lines of thinking have been formative to the study of organizations and institutions. Traditional phenomenological incursions have influenced ideas on how meaning is made in workplaces – for example, we can see an indebtedness to Husserl's concept of 'lifeworld' and 'bracketing' in Weick's (1995) widely cited sense-making approach. Elsewhere, Heidegger's concept of 'dwelling' has been applied to settings including strategy (Chia and Holt, 2006), while Tim Ingold's reworking of the dwelling concept as a theoretical intervention has been used to explore sensory experience within organizations (Brown et al, 2020). We also see the phenomenological focus on embodiment underpinning approaches to situating corporeal relations in organizational spaces, such as Taskin et al's (2023: 717) account of resisting organizational change through 'the embodiment of objects (using them as extensions of individual bodies) and their emplacement (putting them somewhere and letting them occupy the place)'. The language and vocabulary of phenomenology has also reached into contemporary policy. Notably, the term 'lived experience' can be found in national workforce guidelines or on building effective policy (Australian Government, 2025: 17; DWP, 2021), while charities and advocacy bodies regularly draw on the term to encourage a people-centred approach to policy and strategy (for example, MIND, 2023; National Survivor User Network, 2023). While not fully attending to the ontological concerns with the being and doing of subjectivity, it hopefully points to an increasing openness to recognizing how conditional relationality and reciprocity are central to an uneven experience of the world.

More recently, paying attention to a phenomenology of organizational recognition has been central to studying the contours of dependency and vulnerability that make the employee experience are subject to organizational and organizing effects. Butler's (1990; 1993) performative ontology of gender has enjoyed significant popularity, both inspiring queer or feminist organization studies and wider analyses of organizational subjectivities and recognition. As highlighted in the rich empirical work of Kate Kenny

(2019), Melissa Tyler (2019) and Nancy Harding (2013), among others, organizational subjectivities are reciprocally played out in the regimes of organizational life, often through mundane or quotidian acts that condition (but do not determine) us as embodied organizational subjects. Such a concern focuses on our ontological 'desire for recognition comes to be organized, and how recognition comes to be conferred or denied on the basis of organizing and organizational regimes that render some lives intelligible or other not, or less so' (Tyler, 2019: 19).

For me, the previous work undertaken by organizational scholars is vital in terms of highlighting how a phenomenology of 'making a living' is simultaneously a practical and ontological undertaking that is unevenly enacted in businesses, institutions, places of work and other sites of organizational power and control. Here we feel the compounding dynamics of a material necessity for work entangled with our desire and bodily demand for recognition as viable subjects. At the same time, both in studies of work and social sciences more broadly, attention to a phenomenology of organizational ageing has lagged behind. In part this is symptomatic of a more general philosophical hesitance to take a sustained look at ageing. Despite historical treatises often referring to ageing, notably Cicero's *Cati Maior de Senectute* (*On Old Age*) written in 44 BC (Cicero, 2016 [44 BC]), ageing has often been subsumed into philosophical attention to death and finitude. From Plato's *Phaedo* (2010 [360 BC]) to Heidegger's (1951) account of death as central to the experience of finitude in terms of being-towards-death, theoretical accounts of ageing are often driven by a concern relating to impending mortality. These of course inform the broader ageing-as-decline narrative discussed in the previous chapter and present it a truism that occludes more plural considerations of ageing. Elsewhere, contemporary philosophical thinking has also tended towards a focus on age as a point or position (often older age) from which knowledge about a 'good life' takes place, as we see in Nussbaum and Levmore (2017). Alternatively, age has suffered from being situated as an addendum to other modes of situated experience where 'some feminists mention age-based oppression but treat it as a given – an "et cetera" on a list of oppressions' (Calasanti and Slevin, 2006: 1).

That said, phenomenological thinking has impregnated theoretical accounts of ageing, predominantly through a concern with temporality. Phenomenology ideas have provided a means of exploring the qualitative experience of being *in* time, rather than as a spectator looking upon or capturing time through objective or externalized measurement. For example, Jaan Baars (2012: 165, emphasis added) draws on Husserl and Heidegger to 'deepen our understanding of what it may mean to live *in* time to correct and counterbalance the under-reflected overemphasis on chronometric time and age'. Yet, connected to this is the way in which temporality through our past and futures operate in consciousness. Here the ageing self is always charged by both mnemonic and transcendental demands. The past and future are associated with manifold retrospective or prospective capacities that are central to intentionality; our temporally situated self is required to grasp who we are through who we were and who we might be. This is extended in Lynne Segal's (2014) nuanced feminist account *Out of Time*. While she does not explicitly refer the phenomenological condition, Segal's account of growing older is imbued with a concern for ontological reciprocity and situated embodiment in the world as part of the ageing experience. For her, how we remain attached to the world is not simply something that we can do at the sidelines of life, but demands attention to an ethical imagination that is situated in the life course.

Most of these scholars note that Simone de Beauvoir's treatise *Old Age* is one of the few texts over the past hundred years to have a sustained attention to age. However, it is fair to suggest that none is effusive about its potential to provide us with generative insight. Baars consigns its reference to a fleeting discussion in the introduction to his main work. Segal (2014: 10) gives it its rightful intellectual place, although notes a double bind in de Beauvoir's own life whereby 'Beauvoir recognized her ageing self, and yet, simultaneously she repudiated it'. Nussbaum is less generous and suggests that de Beauvoir's account of old age is 'the most preposterous famous works of philosophy that I have ever encountered' (Nussbaum and Levmore, 2017: 18–19). This seems a surprising and rather sweeping dismissal, given the growing number of theoretically rich commentaries around Beauvoir, most notably the edited compendium led by Sylvia Stoller in 2014 inspired by de Beauvoir's work on age. Such contributions from Bonnie Mann, Sonia Kirks, Gail Weiss and other notable philosophers are complemented by Kristana Arp's (2016) work on de Beauvoir's existentialist account of older age. And the echoes of a Beauvoirian dialogical account of age-based identification are also reflected in Margaret Cruikshank's *Learning to Be Old* (2009: 180) where she claims: 'An older woman becomes old not by any words or gestures, necessarily, but simply by having projected onto her young women's culturally shaped notion of what old is.' While not concerned with work and organization, and often focussing on the realm of the old rather than ageing, these studies suggest that de Beauvoir's work, far from being preposterous, or even an 'act of collaboration with social stigma and injustice' (Nussbaum and Levmore, 2017: 20), may present us with exciting new vistas for articulating a phenomenology of ageing.

Ageing with and against Simone de Beauvoir

While critical phenomenology's debt to Simone de Beauvoir might be clear to many, it is often foreshadowed by her broader reputation as the founding mother of feminism, more often cited than read. Until recently, a relative lack of attention to the fullness of her intellectual project stands in contrast to the sustain attention her peers have enjoyed, such as her long-time partner Jean-Paul Sartre, and Maurice Merleau-Ponty, who was a close member of her intellectual circle and a co-founder of *Les Temps Modernes* with de Beauvoir and Sartre. However, recent commentaries (Tidd, 2004; Simons, 2006; Moi, 2008; Hengehold and Bauer, 2017) have sought to correct the previous discrepancy of not recognizing the full breadth and richness of her oeuvre. We can of course muse on the various reasons for de Beauvoir's relative lack of recognition as a philosopher, although the obvious reasons all seem to be distinctly gendered. There is a lingering patriarchal misapprehension that her work was somehow more a companion to her partner Sartre's work rather than groundbreaking in its own right. The fact that her focus and attention to gender has subsequently been foundational in feminist thought may also have inadvertently led to the broader theoretical potential of her work being displaced. Alternatively, it may be that the ambidexterity she displays in writing that spans across philosophy, autobiography and fiction has been unfairly viewed as detracting from the intellectual lines of inquiry she pursues in her project. This is despite the possibility that such work could be positioned as one point of origin for an early form of the feminist praxis of ecriture feminine and 'writing differently'.

Whatever the reason, de Beauvoir's work is one of the few in the existing phenomenological canon that explicitly and systematically attends to ageing. Given the aforementioned lack of attention to ageing by phenomenologists, this in itself is notable. Yet while she is best known for her treatise on gender, theoretical reflections on ageing run throughout the oeuvre of her work. The second section of *The Second Sex* is in part a book that speaks to different biographical scenes, with sections four and five written as a commentary on the situated experience of 'The Young Girl' and 'The Mother'. Her fictional work, notably *Misunderstanding in Moscow*, *The Inseparables* and *She Came to Stay*, draws on the dynamics of ageing and the troubling of age matrices as infused with modes of power through which relations and selfhood are disrupted. In these works, we witness the consequences of normatively implanted age indexes and their effects in her protagonists' lives. Even when we are unsympathetic to the characters, we feel the intimacy of their struggles to negotiate an integrity and coherence of the self within relations, contexts and themselves as they grow up and older. Alongside de Beauvoir's fictional work, her memoirs of course classify themselves through different periods of her life, reflecting on her changing expressions and encounters as she grows older, most stridently in *The Prime of Life*. Such accounts contain the constant murmur of an ontology of ageing which is finessed in *Old Age*.

A Beauvoirian account of ageing as a phenomenological encounter requires a recognition of her broader intellectual oeuvre that concerns the human condition as governed by an existential concern around the possibilities of freedom (transcendence) and constraint (immanence). However, although existentialism fuels the vocabulary of her intellectual programme, her ambitions for a good life are sedimented within phenomenological conditions of what we would now term reciprocity, recognition and an ongoing and embodied engagement with the world that is never entirely of our making. Within this, intentionality rests in the self as a *disclosing being* (de Beauvoir, 2018 [1947]: 53) who is situated in the particularities of their body and the context through which they come to experience the world.

From her earliest work, de Beauvoir lays out an ontology marked through a phenomenological paradox. On the one hand, we need to feel we are a creative and agential subjects in and of ourselves, a conviction that is marked through the possibility of an open future. At the same time, we are an object, both through the facticity of our past lives and experiences, and through being an 'object for others' (de Beauvoir, 2018 [1947]: 6). Working through this ambiguity is a situated project, relying on an interdependence with the world, with settings and with others:

> To will that there be being is also to will that there be men by and for whom the world is endowed with human significations. One can reveal the world only on a basis revealed by other men. No project can be defined except by its interference with other projects. To make being 'be' is to communicate with others by means of being. (de Beauvoir, 2018 [1947]: 50–51)

To 'cast oneself into the world' (de Beauvoir, 2018 [1947]: 31) is always done while carrying with us the risk that 'at every moment others are stealing the whole world away from [us]' (2018 [1947]: 51). In other words, by necessity we must engage with the world and others to become a viable and coherent subject, but doing so always carries with it the possibility of negation. The contingent project of striving to become an autonomous and fully agential subject in the world is therefore never complete or stable. Moreover, this disclosure is not something we choose, but are compelled to do, all the while constantly enmeshed in the entanglement of subject and object, world and self. Such a process is often both desired and disturbing, as metaphorically summed up in one of de Beauvoir's autobiographically experiences when she visited a clairvoyant. While she was not surprised of what she was told, 'I was astonished to find that I had shown myself from the outside as both the projector and the projected' (de Beauvoir, 1988 [1972]: 48). Such is an example of how our compulsion to know ourselves and the world means we are relationally held and disclosed at the same time in ways that we cannot completely control or even be fully aware of. However, it also highlights that while there is no alternative, in practice, the experience of being subject and object is often one of surprise, catching us off guard.

This contingency is more precarious for some than for others. In her earlier work, de Beauvoir suggests that it is predominantly 'up to him to justify the world and to make himself exist validly' (2018 [1947]: 611). This of course is not a universal 'him' and forms the basis for her most notable work, *The Second Sex*, in which she evolved her concept of 'en situation' that is introduced in earlier work. *En situation* is not a category, but rather the inexplicably intertwined striving for individual freedom and in a world that appears already made by others. In some ways, this is akin to Merleau-Ponty's ideas of 'attitude' and 'bodily schema', or even aspects of Bourdieu's later concept of 'habitus'. It also speaks to Sartre's own concept of situation, where Being is marked by an ambiguity of knowing that muddies any possibility of experiencing a purely subjective or objective realm. However, importantly, de Beauvoir's writing suggests that *en situation* is not about equal pursuits of projects of freedom, but rather an unequal structuring of consciousness that is never possible to extract from the corporeal experience of being a women; a point that has been central to subsequent commentaries within the critical phenomenology traditions discussed earlier.

From here, we see her contribution to one of the most formative motifs of the 20th century: the 'Other'. In accounting for the ways in which gendered subjectivity is constituted through women becoming Othered and alienated from their body (while inescapably and always 'a' body), de Beauvoir explicitly considers how historical plots serve as irrefutable ontological obstacles that differentially impact certain bodies and people. Here, intersubjectivity unfolds through a world that is marked by unequal access to epistemic and ontological integrity. It is layered into political, social and historical conditions that may receive individuals as inessential, or 'Other', providing terms through which to be acknowledged only through 'secondary' modes of recognition. However, this Other is of course constituted reciprocally, though unevenly. The 'One', and the dialectic of One (or self) and 'Other' is central to de Beauvoir's consciousness and 'the human condition as defined in relation with the Other' (2015 [1949]: 284). She continues that 'through the Other I accede to the Whole, but it separates me from the Whole; it is the door to infinity and the measure of my finitude' (2015 [1949]: 284). This idea is developed through Hegel's master-slave dialectic (1988 [1807]) in order to recognizes that intersubjectivity is imbued within reciprocal relations and a co-dependency between One and Other relation which is required to constitute the self. However, de Beauvoir suggests that while this is the case for everyone in terms of an ontological demand, men are accorded the privilege of the myth of sovereignty given 'The representation of the world as the world itself is the work of men: they describe it from a point of view that is their own and that they confound with the absolute truth' (2015 [1949]: 282). By comparison, women can only 'strive' towards what is a male norm of an anatomized, rational and independent subject, which their embodied situatedness precludes them from being accorded recognition on their own terms. At the same time, they are percieved in the Other as a subject of terror and subsequently the target of possession, repression or oppression.

This notion of 'one' and 'other' is also central to de Beauvoir's empirical attention to age in together an existential concern regarding freedom and constraint with a postdualist phenomenological notion of the making of the aged self. Importantly, this occurs *in* time. De Beauvoir's key work on ageing, *Old Age* (also published in the US as *The Coming of Age*), is predominantly about old age, yet is underpinned by a broader concern with how we come *into* old age through a gradual process of social and ontological denigration. Its focus is a concern with exploring how an immanent facticity emerges through a historical and cultural 'plot' skewed into rendering old age as a project-less realm. While death is important to this process, de Beauvoir does not fall into the trap of other thinkers through previously showing us in earlier work that death is not the definitive condition through which all projects are orientated in that: 'The human being exists in the form of projects that are not projects toward death ... but projects toward singular ends' (de Beauvoir, 2004 [1944]: 115). Rather, she emphasizes the significance of the social negation of old age and how it unevenly patterns across our intersubjective dependence on others, noting how those who are old are both viewed and positioned as objects; oppressed and systematically deprived of humanity.

Noting that old age is simultaneously 'a biological but also a cultural fact' (de Beauvoir, 1986 [1970]: 13), many of the examples in the first part of *Old Age*, 'Old age seen from without', are underpinned by a flavour of dialectical materialism, focusing on the conditions which produce negation and a dehumanizing of people as they age. This draws on accounts of systemic marginalization where we see how ageing is socially, political and historically aligned with a biology of inevitability and is presented not so much as a fact, but a justification for oppression, given that de Beauvoir has earlier explored how 'one of the ruses of oppression is to camouflage itself behind a natural situation since, after all, one cannot revolt against nature' (2018 [1947]: 89).

While particularly novel at the time that de Beauvoir was writing, this also sets the stage for a deeper theoretical incision in the second part of her treatise, 'The being-in-the-world' through considering how the boundaries between organic tenacity and recognition become sedimented as absolute, denying any possibilities for a richer consciousness of old age. This involves a recognition of *en situation* as an embodied temporal project where, as Debra Bergoffen (1997) notes, de Beauvoir's conception of the body is not simply one determined through biology or society, but lived a particular way over and across time and space. Thus, when we do something and relate to something, we do so not from a position of absolute autonomy or an atemporal deterministic prism, but through actions endowed with lines of historically impregnated directionality that accord possibilities or consequences depending on the dynamically situated body. For de Beauvoir, these are the lines that lead to the inessential aged Other.

However, they also carry the potential to be undermined or challenged through our situated and dynamic inhabitation, most explicitly found in de Beauvoir's autobiographical canon. Her own personal account of ageing appears to contradict her explicit claims in *Old Age*, but is certainly in line with her broader ideas across her intellectual oevre; that there is no reason why ageing precludes being as 'not a thing but a project of self towards the other' (2004: 93) over the complete life course. Throughout her autobiographies, notably *Memoirs of a Dutiful Daughter* (1976 [1958]), *The Prime of Life* (1960) and the two-volume *Force of Circumstance* (1985 [1963]), we can see the dynamically situated self-in-situation at play. Here, de Beauvoir orientates herself in the text, temporally situating her ideas at an embodied nexus of past, present and future. For example, at the end of *The Prime of Life*, de Beauvoir suggests that it is the dynamic, situated nature of life that means we always have the potential for recognition and an integrity of self: future is not bound by a 'quantity' of time left, but an intentional quality. This suggests the ontological project as developmental and encased within the situated experiences of ageing. However, I would also suggest it provides the opportunity to suggest that ageing bodies may carry a particular corruptive quality due to being organic, dynamic entities that move us across and over ageing planes and contexts.

Old Age also delves beyond an account of Othering that simply mirrors *The Second Sex* through paying more attention to the paradoxical tension between the 'Other' and 'the One' as it plays out in the conferral of the ageing subject. Here ageing is a process of conferral that involves understanding how ageing subjects may become 'old'. Suggesting that Othering is propagated by any group seeking to maintain status and authority, de Beauvoir stresses in *The Second Sex* that alterity is a 'fundamental category of thought' (2015[1949]: 43) that impacts not simply on how we identify, but also how we come to experience ourselves and others as ordered, marginalized or as somehow 'lesser'. At first, this emphasis when approaching ageing (as Other) might seem contradictory – surely 'every' person is 'an age'? However, while everyone is or 'has' an age, not all are identified as (too) old or (too) young. As de Beauvoir suggests, the privileged subject (the 'One', in her words) can always become a subject of aged othering. We see an Othering akin to gender where the 'too-old' (or, indeed, the 'too-young') subject, is necessary in society given 'the subject posits itself only in opposition: it asserts itself as the essential and sets up the other as inessential, as the object' (2015

[1949]: 44]. In other words, the 'aged' Other – be that of the denigrated position of an older worker, the 'green' younger worker, the too-fertile professional, the distracted working mother and so on – are positions aged organizing provides to valorise 'the One'. Such aged archetypes are both inessential *and yet* depended upon to reify the importance or value of other groups. The idea that people are 'made' secondary in this way rather than a de facto chronological or biological-based inferiority provides a valuable way of reorientating the conversation about ageing and work as not about increasing or decreasing capability or skill, but about how capacity is inscribed into the aged totems we use to understand and organize ageing. It also opens up a conversation about the inessential 'Otherness' of the aged worker as essential to the 'One' found in contemporary accounts of the ideal worker subject. De Beauvoir's accounts of the unsteadiness of the One-Other dialectic as intersecting with gender or other modes of privilege strike me as suggesting ageing consciousness presents us with a more complex ontological task that hitherto considered. This surrounds the sociality of ageing as dynamically situated in a body that changes, grows older and moves across realms of the One and the Other over the life course. In other words, the hows and whys around the One becoming the Other are not simply part of *en situation*, but are temporally based and operate through an intertwined embodiment; the ageing self as simultaneously a past, present and future body.

Tidd (1999: 92) has already pointed to this temporal concern as a comfortable extension to de Beauvoir's ontological commitments, given what we can see in 'Beauvoir's notion of subjectivity is that choices are made "en situation", and here her choice is made according to temporal and physical constraints produced by the ageing process'. On the one hand, this is not about the 'facts' of the past, present or future, but about 'coherence, which functions as a detailed testimony of experience' (1999: 92) and an embodied dynamic process where we are always a body-that-changes. Attending to what we might call an onto-organic bodily component is central to ageing, in that our world changes through the intentionality or directedness involved in taking up the world and dwelling within it. It becomes central to how we come to cohere our ageing selves in the nexus of self, others and settings, while being a changing body where certain contexts, spaces, mechanisms, roles, relations or sets of behaviours are made to feel more natural, familiar, welcoming or habitable than others.

This dynamically situated ageing body thus corrupts any mirage of a division between the self and the Other that we or the organizations in which we are situated may seek to assume. However, while we might recognise this theoretically, in practice, de Beauvoir suggests that such potential to dispell this mirage is thwarted by the 'unrealizability' of age. Here she suggests that ageing carries an ambiguous quality that makes the dynamics of subjectivity even more opaque; where 'even if the body does send us signals, they are ambiguous' (de Beauvoir, 1986 [1970]: 316). This denial or unawareness of age is not simply down to a case of denial or bad faith, but comes from the 'unrealizable' condition of being old as something irrecoverable in origin. We might extend this further through suggesting there is a significant challenge in recognizing being 'with age' – what we might be called age-ful – as an intelligible and multifaceted mode of subjectivity, especially since we are bombarded with aged systems that percolate the parameters of social recognition and 'tell' us about our age. For de Beauvoir, this is unsurprising given that an inherent age bias against 'older' is patterned into society, meaning that the older self is dispossessed of holding any agential potential by a 'project' through which to enact viable forms of recognition. As such, it is unsurprising that old age is 'something beyond my life, outside it – something of which I cannot have any full inward experience' (1985 [1970]: 324).

Such a position has its limitations in providing a theoretically fertile entry to explore ageing more generally and I would share the same concerns as Cole (2016: 210), who has suggested that de Beauvoir somewhat undermines her existentialist commitment through assuming that growing older is a passive experience. However, I would temper this through recognizing de Beauvoir's empirical concern is with old age. By comparison, I would suggest her broader theoretical oeuvre does allow us to move towards understanding the phenomenological experience of the dynamically situated ageing self. To do so, I reverse and pause on my earlier reading of the hesitance for phenomenology to engage more explicitly with the ageing experience. I interpret this as not simply down a distinct unease or uncomfortableness regarding growing old that de Beauvoir suggests, but that ageing presents a condition of a deeper ontoepistemological dis-ease: an 'apartness' from ageing that I suggest may be formative in structuring ageing consciousness and modes of intentionality.

The dis-ease of the dynamically situated condition of the ageing subject

When I first began researching workforce ageism and older worker identity during my masters degree over 20 years ago, my choice of academic field was often met with surprise. 'But you are so young!' was the common remark, followed closely by 'but that's so depressing!' I rarely get such exclamation-filled responses anymore, in part due to an increased awareness of age being a 'grand challenge' and invariably down to the changing cask of my own body. However, what does persist is an awkwardness when talking about ageing or growing older at work: a feeling that there are not enough words to describe it, or a quelling of discussion for fear of saying the wrong thing, either dismissed through humour or part of a rigid, stilted and uncomfortable conversation – synonymous with profound unease, or what we might call dis-ease. Ageing as dis-ease in this context speaks not simply to the occlusions or deferrals when talking about ageing, even though the uncomfortable experience of talking about age is often felt as an embodied experience; rather, it is about ageing being ontoepistemologically implanted into consciousness in ways that manifest through modes of uneasiness, awkwardness and hesitance.

Dis-ease as a phenomenological condition of the dynamically situated ageing subject simmers beneath the ideas discussed in the previous chapter that point to where and how ageing differentiation and distribution is enacted in interpersonal relations, organizational processes and instituting structures. In practical terms, dis-ease traps us into misrecognizing the experience of ageing at work itself where there is a simultaneous desire to explore the meaning of ageing in and around work, but also a compulsion close down ageing and its potential to rupture 'business as usual'. At the same time dis-ease is a phenomenological experience of apart-ness: a more complex and incomplete directionality that ebbs away from us, making it easy for fallible and imperfect proxies such as the unequivocal and fixed directedness found controlling, commofidying and conferring ageing to take precedence.

In some ways, this may manifest in a way described by Leder (1990) as bodily dys-appearance when our bodies are mainly remembered or made visible in problematic or dysfunctional ways. However, I would argue that dis-ease in terms of the ageing body is also saturated with a unique tension that originates from the ageing body being a dynamically situated entity that invariably changes. Due to our reciprocal and dependent relationship with the world for our sense of self, bodily changes shape how we perceive the world and how we are also perceived by the world. This means disruption and moments of reckoning are inevitable. The experience of apart-ness as a corollary of the dis-ease of ageing becomes ever more complicated through the clashes between our desires to try and be in symphony with the world and remain recognized as a legitimate subject, while being aware of unpredictable breaches that may emerge from our dynamically situated embodiment. In other words, the dis-ease of ageing has the potential to unstitch our selves, the ontological imperative that fuels the world-self experience, and the processes of organizing that build up, maintain and manicure the dis-ease of ageing.

Ignoring, overlooking or forgetting about this dis-ease in the ageing experience might promise to deliver a feeling of ontological comfort; a delicious feeling of synchronicity and attunement with the world that we may have experienced in our working lives previously, although we are only aware of it in retrospect. Such a feeling reflects Ahmed's (2007: 158) suggestion that 'to be comfortable is to be so at ease with one's environment that it is hard to distinguish where one's body ends and the world begins'.

However, in doing so we sidestep addressing the inconvenient or inconceivable boundaries, biases and contradictions that organize ageing, immune and untouched within the deep structures of meaning that make up the workplace. Ageing is left to be absorbed and neutralized through the lustre of processes and practices in workplaces that make us feel comfortable, but also make us vulnerable to their effects.

By comparison, working through ageing as a phenomenological project must fully embrace this dis-ease as a condition of apart-ness, recognising that it has profound theoretical possibilities for exploring ageing as both a practical and ontological endeavour in and around work. Just as various modalities shape the received wisdoms and ways in which we come to know about ageing more broadly (Hagestad and Settersten, 2015), organizations and institutional processes might also provide us with modalities through which we come to know ageing that can both partially appease and rupture the experiential apart-ness of ageing. For example, it may provide insights into how ageing's apart-ness is complicit in working with or against instituted modes of work intensification and exploitation, or encouraging compliance. Alternatively, apart-ness as a condition of ageing may help us better understand what binds together subjects, objects and settings in particular ways that index age with particular roles, jobs or positions in the hierarchy. In both cases, dis-ease, in symphony with the One/Other dialectics of a dynamically situated self, help to move us towards a more particular theory of working through ageing.

Discussion: working through ageing

I began this chapter by considering how we might wriggle out of the prohibitive regimes of organizational ageing as controlled, commodified and conferred, doing so by developing a phenomenology of ageing. Here ageing is considered through our embodied subjectivity being inescapably entwined in the trinity of self-other-setting relations that make up organizational lives. Articulating this through a critical phenomenological lens that focuses on the uneven structuring conditions of consciousness, we can see how ageing demands us to pay attention to the particular ontological negotiations that constitute ageing through the One/Other dialectic as experienced in the dynamics situatedness of growing older. Thinking with and beyond de Beauvoir's work through attention to the dis-ease of ageing experienced as a phenomenology of apart-ness further attends to the relational, situated and embodied dynamics of ageing as compelled by a consciousness that is reciprocal but not necessarily equally experienced by everyone.

De Beauvoir's accounts of uneven outcomes, situations or ways of experiencing the world provides fertile ground for beginning to consider ageing in work: a context imbued with power and a systematic desire for organizing, ordering, preferring and excluding. While work was never the main focus of any of her publications, de Beauvoir shows at least an empirical appreciation for the particularities of institutions and organizations, and how they shape the parameters and restraints on human subjectivity. Her historical assessment of women's position in society highlights economic participation, along with social roles, as central to women's freedom where 'woman wins concrete autonomy because she has an economic and social role' (de Beauvoir, 2015 [1949]: 203). In *The Prime of Life* (1965 [1960]: 57), she discusses how visiting a factory making light bulbs 'was my first encounter with industry and made a violent impression on me'. Labour also feels central to forging a politics of subjectivity that appears more explicit in parallel works, where she states that:

> The standard of living that the worker demands is not required by his immediate needs, nor is it called forth by dreams of compensation. It is the actualization, the expression of the idea that the worker has of himself, in the same sense that our body is the expression of our existence. It is the objective form that a transcendence takes on. (de Beauvoir, 2005 [1945]: 183)

Elsewhere, she positions work or economic participation as a 'hold upon the world' (de Beauvoir, 1986 [1970]: 602], where hold is similar to Merleau-Ponty's (2002 [1945]: 470) concept of a grip through which the self can gain a sense of recognition and situatedness, albeit within sanctioned parameters. A concern with the economic context also appears in *Old Age*, where she discusses how 'society turns away from the aged worker as though he belongs to another species' (1986 [1970]: 603), suggesting that once men retire, their experience of being economically 'projectless' translates into an ontological negation and that this process is all the more intensely experienced given that they move between occupying the status of the One or Other, and 'the movement from one group to the next may amount to a promotion or to a fall' (1986 [1970]: 101). And her insistence on the role of instituting structures in how the subject comes to be recognized and othered as 'old' makes it clear she was aware of the weight of power, authority, control and resistance that organizations held.

Calling out de Beauvoir's attention to organization and labour is important, not least because it suggests that a Beauvoirian ageing is a process where work provides an important and active location in which a relationally situated and experienced self is disclosed. It allows us to see that for her, claims of subjectivity are always both an ontological and a practical situated project: an undertaking or 'working through' of ontological demands in everyday relations, encounters and contexts. In other words, de Beauvoir guides us to an organizational ontology of ageing where organizational lives operate at the intersection of 'the concrete and particular thickness of this world and the individual reality of our projects and ourselves' (2018 [1947]: 75). Through this thickness, the intensive inhabitation and attunement of organizing absorbs and shapes particular practices, relations and bodies into becoming more essential than others, and, in doing so, it essentializes and subsequently marginalizes along aged lines of recognition. All of this is achieved as an organizational project that disappears and naturalizes a particular totem of ageing, reified through a selective reliance on certain ways of culturally, socially and bodily experiencing ageing that culminate in orientating what particular bodies can, might or want to do in the everyday act of working.

What I have sought to introduce above is how the elements of the One/Other, dynamic situatedness, and dis-ease are central to a phenomenology of ageing. Working through ageing as a modus operandi for understanding the organizational experience of growing up and older requires us to be and to know the porosity of how our dynamic and changing bodies are made in the rebounding of the receptions and perceptions of other people in situ. Such onto-organic processes are not just about a biological or material conditions but also holds an intentionality that emerges through an aged point of orientation. This may generate a disruption to the way we are in the world, requiring a recalibration or creating an unsteadiness that demands attention and recohering. But doing so may also provide opportunities for more creative and experiential practices showing that there are different ways of being webbed into relations and contexts. Moreover, it provides a basis for highlighting the ambidexterity of the experiential self, and relating over the life course as holding the potential for different modes of organizational subjectivity.

Working through ageing as a phenomenological project of the dynamically situated self requires continual maintenance in the way in which ageing organizes work, and work organizes ageing. On the one hand, working through ageing is the stitchwork that draws together particular groups by virtue of their life course, such as older or younger workers, middle (career) managers, graduate cohorts or pre-retirees, providing a sense of belonging and community but also sanctioning age-correlated experiences, such as occupational entry or exits, how much we are paid, when we are eligible to receive a pension and, in some countries such as the US, when we are protected by law from age discrimination. Such practices work alongside more subtle 'felt economies' that valorize difference and thwart the potential to build solidarity across the workforce and quell spaces for potential community building beyond age-based categories.

However, within the context of organizations, this onto-organic process constituted through negotiating the One/Other, dynamically situated experiences, and dis-ease is neither absolute nor complete. Working through aging is invariably enmeshed in relations and reciprocal bonds that are never fully of our making but still allow the potential for ageing to be an active and dynamic project in which we come to be and know the world in situ. It shows us how ageing is not the sum and substance of what normative organizational discourse or teleological scripts demand, but rather an experience that we are continually living through that is revealed throughout our lives in different, albeit uneven, ways, often in the cracks, contradictions and possibilities beyond what was previously presented as organizational modes of age-related practice. From this arises a new impetus to reckon with ageing, and with it comes different disruptions and new possibilities for living and working.

I am not suggesting that working through ageing leads to one best way to grow up and older in an organization and I am certainly not implying that the workplace is the sole or even the most important context in which we create or harvest an ageing consciousness. However, work does provide the opportunity to empirically explore how the ageing experience comes together and is rendered coherent in a setting where people are subject to various power dynamics, systems and institutions that invariably constitute lived experience. To explore working through ageing as central to these experiences, in the next chapter, I will introduce how the theoretical ideas introduced above inform the empirical study of a group of workers and their experience of growing up and older at work. Supporting this, I develop Jennifer McWeeny's account of 'phenomenological figures' as an aperture to build a mode of analysis that takes critical phenomenological commitments into the field and onto the page. I then present three chapters that further extend an analytical vocabulary of working through ageing through empirical accounts of negotiating self, other and setting in the context of working lives.

3

Figuring-in Conversations About Working Through Ageing

This chapter shares an empirical account of what became a longitudinal phenomenological study of working through ageing. However, it would be disingenuous to suggest that it began as either longitudinal or wedded to a critical phenomenological way of viewing the world. Rather, the research started in 2010 in a North London pub talking to a group of friends about ageing. At the time, we were all in our mid to late 20s, living in London but working in very different sectors, and I was using their personal anecdotes about office politics to test drive some thoughts. At that point, my idea was to sequentially look at different occupations in order to compare how people talk about their experience of ageing at work, spending a few months in three different organizations. There was never any intention to start a decade-long endeavour: rather, I was keen to focus on the way in which ageing 'gathered ground' through reference to different relations, objects and bodies at a particular point in time. One of our group casually mentioned that 'I work at a hedge fund. Why don't you come and talk to us, our boss would like this kind of thing'. I quickly Googled 'hedge fund' and his company, which I will refer to here using the pseudonym HFUK, wrote up a one-page research overview which was emailed to the firm via my friend and waited. What followed was speaking to group of 25 people, plus a wider constellation of people associated with the firm over the course of the next ten years.

My encounters over this decade emphasize how the experiential quality of ageing must always be considered methodologically rather than simply as an 'object' of research. It means taking seriously the reciprocal dynamics within the research and analytical process itself as researchers work with respondents. We need to acknowledge how the me, you, they and us involved in research share – or not – in what 'we' mean when we talk about ageing in and over time, and how this can be both a source of antagonism and a glimpse into understanding the dynamics of organizational lived experience more broadly.

At the same time, any researcher concerned with ageing must avoid being methodologically seduced by a 'Petrificus Totalus' spell, where the desire for a stable or generalizable methodological and analytical process produces 'frozen' subjects that become the object of research. While respondents as frozen objects might be easier to analytically account for, such accounts undermine a phenomenological commitment to ageing. It was this fear of petrifying the experience of ageing that was at the forefront of my mind as I began this project, and reckoning with temporal ambiguity marks both the research process and ageing, meaning that we need to consider working through ageing as not simply an ontological and organizational project, but a mode of analysis.

In response to this challenge, I present the research process here as a practice of 'figuring-in': a methodological commitment and analytical approach that provides one way of practically engaging with a phenomenological ethos in fieldwork. I am indebted here to Jennifer McWeeny's (2021) Beauvoirian-inspired concept of 'figuring'. McWeeny engages in a rich theoretical conversation with de Saint Aubert's suggestion that phenomenological figures are part of a 'carnal vocabulary' (de Saint Aubert, 2020a: 126) that is characterized by 'a poetics of incorporation and intercorporeity' (de Saint Aubert, 2020b: 33; see also de Saint Aubert, 2019). In doing so, she emphasizes how a phenomenological reading of de Beauvoir highlights the fertility of figures as concepts that speak to both an ontological concern with the nature of subjectivity and a refusal to distil or reduce embodied lived experience.

For me, this attention to figures has significant potential for those seeking to undertake empirically focused phenomenological research. 'Figuring-in' as a mode of analytical inquiry orientates the researcher, the research process and the research phenomenon as an embodied and ambivalent undertaking. Figuring-in stands in contrast to the process of figuring 'out' findings that qualitative researchers are often socialized into. Even when engaging with inductive or abductive analyses, accounts refer to coding and organizing data through processes of analytical distillation, enclosure, or working through a metaphorical puzzle to find out more about a phenomenon. In contrast, figuring-in reminds us of how abstract theoretical commitments and embodied data-driven accounts are inextricably connected. It provides a way to maintain a phenomenological integrity when we empirically explore the everyday and mundane acts that constitute ageing at work as a lived experience, disrupting our compulsion to slip into dualist or contained modes of characterizing subjectivity and the bifurcation of answers as discursive/material, exterior/interior, past/present, mind/body, self/other, organizational/individual and so on.

In following a commitment to figuring-in, I thought it would be useful for this chapter to discuss what a phenomenological approach to longitudinal qualitative research might involve in terms of figuring-in research orientations, directions and experiences. The chapter begins by introducing the original site of research and how I began to try and analytically 'get a grip' on ageing at work through the initial and subsequent interactions during fieldwork. From here, I turn to considering the lines of directionality that informed my analysis, before concluding with a discussion of the writing 'up' process as a mode of ekphrasis, articulating the paradox of interpretation and description within the parameters of what constitutes figuring-in findings, which segue ways into introducing the three chapters based on my fieldwork.

Getting a grip? The research context

As with any attempt to comprehend the world, researchers are required to both secure and maintain a 'grip' or coherent hold on the world in ways that also provide a convincing and authentic account that is familiar to participants and those witnessing that world through the research account. The ability to calibrate the 'gearing of the subject into his world' (Merleau-Ponty, 2014 [1945]: 262) as an ontological pursuit is vital for the researcher but also a political endeavour given that accessing a site of work is contingent on gatekeepers and other organizational actors believing that the researcher has the capacity to both blend in and belong in ways that are acceptable to existing organizational members, while not disrupting the business-as-usual of everyday work. Notably, as outlined in the Appendix, getting a grip is often a faulty and contingent process compared to the way in which longitudinal studies are often presented as a systematic and asomatic endeavour.

Taking up my friend's offer to come into his workplace required intensive schooling on my part. He was based in a hedge fund, an organizational entity so named for its employment of various strategies to 'hedge' market risk to forge significant profits. Hedge funds are private financial institutions that can vary in size, composition and investment strategy. While they may not have a high number of employees due to the dominance of electronic trading, the amount of assets that hedge funds manage globally is conservatively estimated to have grown in 15 years from US$1.7 trillion (Maslakovic, 2010) to over US$5 trillion (Statista, 2024). They are part of the financial services sector that use a range of highly quantitative investment strategies that are transformed into trading programmes. These programmes or strategies seek to yield a return on capital by trading across a range of markets with investors' money, with each fund often having its own set of strategies. The UK has witnessed a phenomenal growth in hedge funds and currently has the second-largest concentration of hedge funds in the world after the US. Due to the lack of security around investments, only certain types of investors can engage with hedge funds, such as very wealthy individuals or large financial institutions. Unlike share trading institutions, hedge funds employ aggressive strategies that are often regarded as risky, such as short selling (when shares that are predicted to fall in value are 'borrowed' and sold, hopefully to be bought back at a lower price), that can lead not only to larger returns but also larger losses. Needless to say, this is not a type of financial institution for the masses, with minimum investment often starting at £100,000 (and this would be a very modest amount) and the value of the investment not necessarily determined at a given time (unlike shareholder value).

The high-win-high-lose strategies employed by hedge funds mean that historically they have always been precarious places to work, both in the sense of individual job loss and organizational closure. Early studies of hedge funds pre the rise of automation estimated that only 50 per cent of hedge funds survived longer than 65 months (Gregoriou, 2002; Amin and Kat, 2003). High staff turnover also continues to characterize the industry. Individuals are often invited to leave, with a swift exit encouraged through access to their computers being switched off immediately and an invitation to evacuate the building. Alternatively, people regularly move to different firms for higher bonuses, improved terms and conditions, or to avoid being associated with a company downturn or collapse (Li et al, 2022; Neely, 2022).

However, hedge funds are as much a social actor as an organizational form. I found that there was a tendency for their members to distinguish themselves from other financial institutions such as banks that deal directly with money from members of the public. Yet hedge funds share similar cultural characteristics of the financial sector more broadly, including highly competitive recruitment and development trajectories, long hours and tight professional networks. The market-logics of financial capitalism seep into and shape the way in which these workplaces are designed and organized, how people interact and take up particular spaces, such as through technology, and the way that the bodies of those who work there are shaped, read and understood in the organizational context. Culturally, there is a tendency to ascribe a very high purchase on trust within one's network or 'tribe', partly to offset the risky, unpredictable and often turbulent market conditions in which they operate. This often leads to relatively closed and homogeneous professional circles. In this sense, 'the Market comes to assume the role of master-narrative' around identifies and the nature of the work is central to the way in which people experience themselves and others (Garsten and Jacobsson, 2011: 389). This manifests in a particular occupational 'corporeality, in the sense of the material capacities and limitations of those bodies and brains [that] is critical to how markets function' (MacKenzie, 2008: 11).

Hedge funds also carry the markings of an 'elite' profession that in many cases is imprinted through a gendered or racialized ordering. McDowell's (1997) earlier work in merchant banks highlighted the dual mechanism through which women are systematically excluded, while men are supported, creating conditions through which the city comes to be marked by masculinity. Her retrospective (2010: 657) suggests that while the physical form of markets has changed, the sector is still distinctively marked by a 'specific culture of investment banks and the nature of the system within which they operate gendered, casino or testosterone capitalism'. Ho's (2009) ethnography of Wall Street similarly found that socialization began from hothousing Ivy League graduates, which provided the basis for both the homosocial reproduction of the sector and a hierarchal and spatial location of women and minorities that 'organically' emerged – an order that Neely (2022) considers a process of patrimonialism that is constituted in part, but not exclusively, through the broader landscape of financialized capitalism. However, contemporary accounts of the financial services have for the most part overlooked the importance of ageing beyond the mention of a chronological marker used around aspirations of 'retiring at 30' (Ho, 2009: 288) or McDowell's (1997: 79) discussion of gendered career paths being laid down at an early age. At the same time, the same accounts point to an inverse presence of ageing with references to an agelessness where short-term financial capitalism is itself calibrated on the body of unmarked investment bankers (Ho, 2009: 12).

Intrigued by this absence, I set about replying to a request from HFUK to 'pop in' in a few days' time so that they could find out a bit more about my research. I quickly began to think about what I could offer them in exchange for letting me 'hang out' in their firm, slightly ashamed of my ignorance, as well as my ambivalence about a sector that had in recent months been portrayed in popular media as exemplifying the worst excesses of financial capitalism. Heading into the city, I was buzzed into the building by the HFUK receptionist and then asked to sit next to the abstract art and understated furnishings, before being led through to the boardroom.

The next half an hour was excruciating. Apart from a tertiary understanding of economics from my undergraduate degree, it is fair to say that hedge funds were not something of which I had an intimate knowledge, despite my best efforts at cramming the night before. This is probably reflective of most of the population, despite a significant percentage of people in both the UK and the US indirectly having some form of wealth attached to hedge funds, such as through savings, pensions or insurance institutions who invest via hedge funds. I stumbled through our meeting while trying to justify my ignorance such as suggesting that while I was in a business school, my area was more about people's identities at work. It was possibly the most embarrassing fieldwork experience I have had – my notes from that day still carry the imprints of my clammy fingers as testament to this. However, the next morning, I got an email – short, straight to the point, with no sign off: 'When do you want to come in for your first visit?' I later found out that by failing miserably to answer their questions, I had shown I was no threat: I was clearly a complete ignoramus when it came to financial markets and therefore posed little risk or inconvenience to the core business. Months later, I was told that Alan, who held an important gatekeeping role, found me curious: after our initial meeting, I'd been described to staff as a bit of an oddity, but harmless nonetheless. I became a beneficiary of the fact that, according to one employee, 'Alan collects interesting people, look around who he employs in here'. And just like that, I became, in a very partial and contingent way, part of the City.

By 'the City', I am referring to the shorthand for both the material facticity of financial districts or corporate-bound economic areas of an urban geographical centre, and the way in which logics of financial capitalism shapes and seep into bodies, ideas and aspirations within such spaces. They are usually located within a large metropolitan area (a city) and when walking through them feel like transient places; shiny, slick and smooth in terms of architecture, transport links and walkways, as if no one could 'stick' to them, even if they wanted to. And generally, people do not stick around the City, unless they are there for economic reasons or perhaps the odd tourist. In the relatively small square miles of financial districts, very few people 'live' there as such, although some 'sleep-in commuters' may have a flat close by as a place to stay during the week. Others might live there at the beginning of their career when they have little need for lifestyle amenities that cannot be located in multistorey buildings.

At the same time, the City is a forcefield through which things are orientated: commuter trails pull people into them from significant distances and, with them, businesses come to service their needs: sandwich bars and delis, early morning coffee outlets and gift shops with expensive cards. If you walk around financial districts across a range of cities – London, Frankfurt, Hong Kong, Sydney and New York – all of them are strangely contained epicentres of wealth making and losing. They are logistically very easy to get to, inhabited by a 'global elite' whose movements can be predicted around hours of various financial markets and whose bodies may differ in terms of race and ethnicity, but are usually all well-manicured and mainly male and able-bodied. During weekends, the same City lies dormant, with the coffee shops closed and escalators on go slow; steely ghost towns taken over by the pigeons, waiting for Monday, or perhaps longer as we saw in deserted corporate buildings that became an iconic metaphor for the world stopping during the COVID-19 pandemic. The longer-term impact of COVID-19 on these spaces highlighted how the City changes depending on need, and during my final period of fieldwork, it was noticeable how many bijou takeaways had their shutters permanently down, as well as the odd clean large square on the pavements in boulevards that marked the ghoulish absence of former food trucks.

The City is not just a set of emotional and economic registers contained to a geographical area, but a logic and way of organizing that stretches into other spaces. In London, many hedge funds are traditionally based around an area in the City called Mayfair, once described as 'a latticework of elegant streets immediately east of the hyper-expensive expanses of Hyde Park' (Shaxson, 2013: 30). The area is steeped in indulgence and money that historically 'offered a gentleman's every delight' (Porter, 1998: 109) and this geographical heritage has carried through to today, serving as a centripetal force for money and those pursuing or purging it. As such, it is a natural habitat for the discreet gold-plaqued hedge funds and their customers: individuals or institutions with significant sums of capital looking to make more. Hedge funds serve to reproduce this implanted logic of the City, although what makes hedge funds so powerful has been their ability to make returns that outstrip other forms of investment. However, what makes them so *successful* is a more complex question. A common answer has attributed their success to their agility and flexibility, enabled through a freedom around different regulatory frameworks compared to mainstream financial institutions. It may also be the speed and ability to quickly respond to trends and events. Yet there may also be a performative element to their success where 'financial economics succeeds because it has been able to shape the world' (MacKenzie, 2008: 31). In other words, as one employee from HFUK suggested, the reasons for the success of financial capitalism as the force underpinning hedge funds may be self-generating through wealth, power, attracting brilliant minds and a brain drain from other occupations as it is to do with being the most efficient way to run an economy.

My temporary visitation rights into the City showed that others were aware of this performative element. Many expressed an ambivalence about private investment firms taking away the intellectual capital from other parts of the economy that could perhaps use it to better ends. Nathan spoke about how he had reflected on whether it was 'a waste' that the best and brightest were becoming concentrated in the financial services, while Ollie, who originally trained in science and eventually went back to a science, technology, engineering and mathematics (STEM) career, said:

> There's a lot of smoke and mirrors in this world, most people with half a brain could pick it up. And there are some very very smart people here. But the majority get somewhere through a mixture of bullshit, working their absolutely arses off and knowing the right people, either through family, university or rabid networking. For some, their job is keeping their job and making sure they have a job in the future, rather than any substance. (Ollie, 2010, Y0)

Harry similarly referred to how the city was predicated upon a 'black box' of complicating what were basic economic tenets, mystifying practices and creating a veneer of exclusivity and complexity. One evening during my first period of fieldwork, I spent a 15-hour shift watching different groups trading in various markets. During this shift, Harry referred to how easy trading was, in later years discussing how 'anyone can do it, seriously, you could learn how to do it in a week' (Harry, 2014, Y4).

When I began observing at HFUK, the financial services were still recovering from a Global Financial Crisis, with hedge funds experiencing negative cultural and media ascriptions: over the years, participants would refer to this stigma of working in finance, or the 'barometer of public hatred for finance', as Finn (2014, Y4) put it. This was in part one reason why HFUK and its employees liked to differentiate themselves from the 'normal image' of hedge funds. In my first month of being there, I was told several times that the key senior leaders and their pastimes, interests, backgrounds and political alliances were unusual in financial services. The physical setting of HFUK also provided a valuable way to differentiate or distinguish themselves from 'the others' as it had been deliberately located outside of Mayfair and filled with colourful and offbeat modern furniture. This also helped to support differentiation in other way too, such as their trading strategies:

> You don't get a day go by without some newspaper bashing the banks ... I feel very removed from it, probably because we're not one of the big organizations that were involved in the problem. We never traded mortgage-based assets or anything – we've always traded stuff which is fairly vanilla and fairly liquid – so I tend to feel not connected to that. (Gavin, 2012, Y2)

Similarly, the individuals that made up the firm collectively viewed themselves as a more eclectic group than the typical composite of other hedge funds and banks. Again, this played into early discussions around ageing, where I was told that there was a far broader age range here than in other hedge funds. Several employees had come from studying economics or had STEM masters and PhD qualifications, but there were also others who had a liberal arts education and not necessarily from elite universities such as Oxford and Cambridge. Similar to other hedge funds, HFUK was composed of not just a trading desk, but also people working in operations, client relations, programming and research, marketing administration and operations. Each group had slightly different trajectories into the City and the differences between these groups was mirrored the spatial configuration of the office, which was split over office floors. In some levels were the traders, brokers and operations teams, as well as the receptionists and support staff such as marketing and client relations team. The other floors were taken up by 'back end' operators such as researchers and programmers, as well as the information technology (IT) support.

Access to HFUK, like any research setting, particularly over a long period of time, is invariably an ongoing process rather than a one-time door opening by senior members of an organization. The original plan was that I would undertake 12 visits there over a few months and interview people 'as long as I didn't get in the way', to quote one of the staff. When I arrived on the work floor, people asked what I was doing, having either ignored the internal memo about my arrival or forgotten about it among the deluge of daily emails. I spent a few days a week in various parts of the company, talking to people, being inconspicuous by not have a computer but a notebook and moving about the different groups within the fund. I sometimes came in early to sit with those working on Asian markets and stayed on several evenings with the 'US' team. When the 12 visits were up, I decided that rather than move on to another setting, I would try to stay around a bit longer to work out what was happening in terms of ageing dynamics. I tentatively approached Alan's personal assistant (PA) about staying for longer: 'sure, fine', she said kindly but dismissively.

I continued to watch, talk and interview people over the course of six months. People did not notice when I was there, but also did not notice when I was absent, such as when I went away on holiday for two weeks. I was rather incidental to their lives; a nice distraction, but nothing they needed to take note of. I was also marked out as different: I did not wear a suit or corporate uniform of sorts and I was moving about different parts of the office and up and down the two floors, in comparison to the employees who generally stayed fixed and siloed in their work groups. I was invited out for drinks and lunches, and employees often used me to talk about some of the more tumultuous events or workplace politics happening in the firm at the time. They appeared to do so without fear of retribution or implications; I was viewed as a 'neutral container' to talk about office gripes or worries and someone who knew the people involved, but was one step removed, plus conveniently bound by confidentiality through my university, as many would remind me about during the course of my time there.

Studying the man (*sic*) who wasn't there

The challenges of researching ageing in this environment quickly became clear: the dynamics that surround ageing were not something that are necessarily or immediately perceptible – the impossibilities of 'figuring out' were clear. The only immediate evidence employees pointed me towards was loose generational splits where the traders and brokers in their 40s were more likely to have come straight from high school into the London International Financial Futures and Options Exchange (LIFFE) market: the open trading floor or 'pit' often imagined when discussing stockbroking. By comparison, those who were younger were university educated and often had some international background or experience. This mixture of bodies from global elites and local areas rubbed alongside each other for the most part and while there sometimes appeared to be tensions in terms of certain ways of working, these were often aligned with departments rather than the intergenerational tensions that are so often the focus of popular or media commentaries around ageing workforces.

For the most part, people rarely talked about ageing compared to gender-based discussions. It was even more challenging to explore given much of the informal 'chat' was undertaken online. Instant messages were used and were often encouraged as they were portrayed as evidencing transparency around what is being said and done, reflecting a broader sector climate that was under increasing scrutiny. My early fieldnotes were as informed by permission to read the text chat on people's computer screens as by what I heard and who I talked with, although ageing per se was still rather miasmic.

A month into my visits, some staff at HRUK began asking if I was finding anything, revelling in my reply 'not yet'. Laughing about me 'not being able to find any old people', Ollie (2010, Y0) jested that my study of ageing in this particular workplace might be a bit futile: 'It's like that rhyme isn't it 'when I was going up the stair, I met a man who wasn't there, he wasn't there again today, oh how, I wish he'd go away' That's who you are trying to meet, isn't it?'

This stuck with me and, contrary to its intentions in the banter-led chat of HFUK, made me feel better in realizing there was no one or nothing to find per se that was going to help me 'figure out' ageing; rather, in order to understand ageing in work and how ageing at work was experienced, I needed to become more attuned to the way in which different spaces, bodies and relations came to be stitched together. Figuring in ageing meant re-adjusting the focus of research away from 'looking' for something and towards an embodied and reciprocal engagement that invariably situated my own experience of ageing with that of others.

A few months after my six-month stay, I submitted a short report and did a presentation to staff and management about this initial phase of figuring at an office drinks event after work one Friday. It was met with a supportive and kind response, and some surprise that I had attuned to the cultural dynamics in such a short time. Some years later, Charles told me that 'one of the more cynical members of my team who's cynical and tends to – well, cynical is a good description – said, "This is interesting. We could have paid £650,000 to a consultant to have this"' (Charles, 2014, Y4). The truth was that while an interesting experience, it had been too difficult to get any grip on how ageing constituted an experiential system of relating in and to the world of work. So, 18 months later, I dropped the hedge fund manager's personal assistant an email asking if I could come back to see how people were getting on and subsequently spent another few days a week over the next four months at HFUK.

At that point, the company's fortunes had taken a downward turn and several people had left, with the whole company having downsized and occupying a smaller premises. While I re-interviewed those who were still there, I also got in touch with those who had left or moved on to different jobs. In many ways, this helped me realize that I was not interested in the organizational aspects that more traditional longitudinal case research is often concerned with, such as business processes or operational and strategic change (for example, Burgelman, 2010); rather, I was keen to look at how work experiences were parcelled up with the expressions and identities of those involved, even if they were no longer in the same organization. While the setting of financial services was central to how people had initially made sense of their ageing experiences, I became more and more interested in how people lived through their own working trajectories rather than the life of a particular organization as enacted through people.

What started out in HFUK became a project involving contacting original respondents every two years over a ten-year period. This decision to 'follow-the-people' in organizational research is central to embracing how to figure-in ageing as involving a corporeal fidelity over time that is often threatened or dismissed within normative frameworks and contemporary discourses or work. It recognizes the facticity of context, but does not presuppose that a particular organization has some epistemic priority that serves as the main orientation device for how people make sense of work. My follow-the-people approach held an ethos of walking alongside people to inform my understanding of those I was researching, not simply metaphorically but also as a mode of embodied companionship that began to emerge over time. Catching up every two years was often a pleasurable experience – an enjoyable, if relatively momentary, reconnection.

At the same time, the idea of a 'catching up' with people to develop a longitudinal study implies a casual easiness to arranging these interactions that undermines the labour involved. In practice, my biannual ritual of tracking people down was a bit more harried and unpredictable, feeling more akin to running behind them. Time was spent many evenings and weekends in tracking them down, grabbing their attention, appealing to their kindness through emails and texts, contacting them through other participants, nudging them on social media – all the while trying to ensure my persistence was not received as annoyance or too tinged with desperation.

This practical experience of a follow-the-people approach in longitudinal research is rarely discussed. Research that has a temporal element is either framed as ethnographic within the same field or site, or part of a large quantitative study that draws on panel data. As such, there is little discussion of the experiential dimensions of qualitative longitudinal work in and around organizations. However, following-the-people over time can be inherently sensate, but also potentially bewildering. It is a process that makes it impossible to ignore the cycles and patterns that overlap across spaces, across the cohort and across your own life. It calls attention to the expressive relations and receptions that form the basis of the connections between researchers and participants, and it is often these bonds that provide the momentum to keep going over several years. This speaks to a very practical sense of dependency that we all have as empirical researchers: the best social scientists fully recognize that 'being able to admit the interconnected vulnerability of human existence', as Lynne Segal (2023: 214) astutely acknowledges, is as much a methodological statement for researchers as a theoretical commitment more generally. It requires an openness to the world that takes seriously the expressive relations within research methods in terms of a 'dialogic engagement through feeling' (Freiman, 2017). Surrendering to such a vulnerability comes from accepting that an uneven and somewhat unpredictable reciprocity of research relations patterned over time also means acknowledging the possibilities of losing direction. It points to a tension, in producing such research that is without promise (or, at least, more risky than other research approaches) and is undertaken within a higher education landscape that is increasingly marked by short-termism and precarious employment conditions. Yet these manifold embodied experiences of qualitative longitudinal research are either suppressed or ignored within many practical accounts of research, even if they are incumbent on researchers to think about, as I discuss further in the Appendix of this book.

Calling to attention: figuring-in analysis

Phenomenologically, empirical analysis involves understanding analytical attention as intention. This involves considering how the researcher comes to be orientated to the field we engage with and how this shapes our relationship with related objects, such as our 'data'. It also requires a critical eye on how our own embodied experience comes to connect and orchestrate these objects. This happen while trying to tolerate a compulsion to be too premature in trying to say what is happening and stitch up the world through a neat analysis. Analysis should therefore take seriously not only how we come to work into data produced through immediate research encounters, but also how we constitute our own sociality as researchers by virtue of our own dynamic situated positionality. Elements such as fieldnotes, interview transcripts and the collation of documents and artefacts do not just involve labour in skilfully manoeuvring the demands of producing an 'output'; they also shape the way we orientate ourselves to research and the people it involves, influencing how we come to know the phenomenon itself over time.

A range of elements are part of this process, and any mode of analysis is heavily influenced by an analytical gaze that plots or propels us in different ways. Yet figuring in as a methodological imperative sensitises us to a tension between how to undertake qualitative data analysis in a way that speaks to a phenomenological ethos of avoiding deduction or enclosure through opening into the world, while still producing coherent research accounts. Leaning into step-based accounts of qualitative data analysis is recognized as good practice but also holds the danger of 'analysis washing' – a sanitation of research through creating a veneer of transparent practices. This can particularly be the case when researchers seek to employ template analysis or approaches such as the Gioia methodology; a common qualitative approach for analysing data developed by former engineer and management professor Denny Gioia (Gioia, Corley and Hamilton, 2013). Attending to such a system of analysis is often derived from a need to quickly secure recognition from academic peers or reviewers that is needed to maintain the viability of our work and our careers more broadly. Even for research not requiring external financial support, institutional ethical approval compel us to give an account of transparent and predictable analysis that rely on stencilled modes of engaging with data.

Choosing not to follow these approaches does not mean an imperfect or faulty analytical process; rather, it is to give oneself a permission field to consider analysis as constitutive of both my own and my respondents' negotiations of the One/Other, dynamic situatedness, and dis-ease as part of the ageing experience. Echoing feminist accounts of data analysis and reflexive practice, the corpus forming the basis of this study is both the product of a directed attention to ageing and what shapes the directed analytical attention during data analysis. This is particularly important given that when it comes from ageing, like other modes of living, 'we do not have pure experiences' (Skeggs, 1997: 28) or modes of escaping our own experience of growing older, and this can have a number of consequences. On the one hand, we may recognize ageing as a profoundly human experience that binds us and those we research in some way. On the other hand, to suggest that my occupational, corporeal and socially situated experiences of ageing are 'universal enough' is a gross misapprehension of the complex fabric of ageing. My own mundane trajectory when analysing this data in time is part of moving from a healthy 30-year-old with a partner, no children and relatively young parents to become a 45-year-old professor with two children and a perimenopausal body invariably draws me towards different ideas of familiarity or distance in relation to ageing. But it also charges the reciprocal dynamics that emerge in how I 'meet and greet' myself and my respondents as I encounter them on the page over time. At the same time, those concerned with reflexive dynamics would of course note the danger of placing ourselves into the study of ageing without acknowledging the full extent of the creep of inadvertent biographicalizing our analysis. I am very aware I am the least interesting person in this analytical story, even if I am invariably part of the plot.

In figuring-in through our data analysis, the classical distinctions between what we do and the experience of analysis are invariably corrupted. The dynamics of power and recognition that rebound in and around the topic on which we are focussing require analytical attention that is not simply technical through a systematic order of coding, but experiential as well. Ray (1996: 679) suggests that this is particularly important when exploring something which we ourselves experience first hand, such as ageing, given that 'our research often says as much about our own biases and preconceptions about aging as it does about the experiences and perceptions of elders'. This also means that the identification of themes, ideas or processes involves a calling to attention that simultaneously carries more profound epistemological consequences, as suggested by Merleau-Ponty:

> Attention, then is neither an association of ideas nor the return to itself of a thought that is already the master of its objects; rather attention is the active constitution of a new object that developed and thematises what was until then only offered as an indeterminate horizon. At the same time that it sets attention to work, the object is recaptures by attention ... the object only gives rise to the 'knowing event' that will transform it through the still ambiguous sense that is offers to attention as needing-to-be-determined. (Merleau-Ponty (2014 [1945]: 33)

Attention as an imperative in phenomenological data analysis is thus intertwined with intention and analysis as central to findings as having an 'appearance': something that resembles but does not mirror or fully reflect. To take this into account, I entered the analysis considering how my own modes of attention disclosed patterns or codes, understanding these are neither definitive nor neutral containers, but rather holding devices that enable different ways of moving around the data.

In practice, attention to appearance was supported by NVivo, a computer-aided data analysis programme, which I mainly used to help organize and render visible my own thoughts as I worked through the large number of interviews and data I had: over 200 transcripts from in-depth interviews and thousands of pages of fieldnotes. Being able to electronically mix up and corrupt different configurations or appearances of my analysis that had happened over the course of a decade also helped me to consider people's experience across and over time, playing with different groupings or themes and noting when I engaged with this analysis. In addition, I also printed extracts off and scribbled possible ways of looking at their ideas in the margins. I created booklets for each of my participants with their transcripts over time, as well as printing out many exchanges we had shared, gradually developing my own little key that would allow me, through glancing, to return to certain expressions or resemblances.

Through a network of variegated nodes appearing, what I call ageing resemblances began to emerge through being intervolved in overlapping similarities and differences. I broadly considered these analytical resemblances as sympathetic to Wittgenstein's (2001 [1953]) conceptual metaphor of 'family resemblance'. In part, this was feeling of 'resemblance' in empirical accounts, such as how embodied experiences of ageing came to be known through relations. There may be commonalities or even generalities that cut across individuals that speak to an ageing experience, but these are by no means monolithic or universal truisms. Resemblances call to attention how respondents reached out towards the world from their embodied, situated position, described by virtue of a partial strangeness but interconnectedness of different ideas across interviews. They also remind the researcher that the analysis is not simply forged through spontaneous practices which emerge organically. Rather, analytical attention is bound up with intention in ways that demand researchers stay in the openness of this experience rather than try to distil or contain it to an individual's action. For me, it slowly shaped and morphed into an analytical origami of findings while attempting to avoid disintegrating the unique lived experiences of participants.

Discussion: writing 'up' as an ekphrastic pursuit

In considering how a phenomenological pursuit manifests in longitudinal qualitative research, I have sought to explore how figuring-in ageing is central to the research process. However, before entering into the empirical accounts, it feels important to provide a short reflection regarding translating this research process into a writing of findings for the reader that assumes a finality or superiority in the subsequent chapters. The 'up' element of 'writing up' inherently assumes – or even demands – some abstraction or shift away from the lushness of the field and moves towards something more transcendent and untouchable. In many ways, the tensions involved in writing about empirical findings speak to the paradox of seeking to contain the uncontainable through description within a phenomenological system. As de Saint Aubert (2020a: 127) suggests, we 'cannot describe what leads to the formation of boundaries without employing schemas whose meaning depends on the existence of boundaries; without evoking parthood, suggesting the transgression of an established boundary, or even reference to the bipartition of inside and outside'.

Pursuing this tension as potentially generative suggests that the 'up' in writing phenomenological accounts requires different parameters that operate in the hinterland of the emotional, embodied experience of the research process, the experience being called to account, and the practical demands of producing an output. While findings should seek to uphold the epistemic ambiguity of a postdualist theoretical commitment that informed the analysis, phenomenological research accounts should also invite the reader to vicariously 'be there', creating something that is impossible to read without tugging on their own embodied experiences. It is not about the possibility of simply describing what emerged, but evoking and enacting, hoping to connect with or affect the audience through calling them into actively feeling something towards the person or the textual artefact that carries them, while always recognizing that this is ultimately a reduction of the lived experience of ageing.

To appeal to this, the next three chapters follow this figuring-in methodology through committing to writing as a mode of ekphrasis. Ekphrasis speaks to a concern around the vivid descriptions of an image or object (usually a work of art) or conferred in language (such as literature) where the audience do not merely read an account through the textual description, but also become affectively involved in this interpretation. This encourages an embodied, multimodal or emotional experience through 'describing their subjects in such vivid detail that the reader does seem to "see" them' (Webb, 2009: 2). The predominant medium associated with ekphrasis has been poetry, with authors focusing on a particular piece of art or object. Here the focus on ekphrasis as 'the verbal representation of graphic representation' (Heffernan, 1993: 29) is marked by an intensity emerging from the paradoxical pursuit of collapsing one mode of experience into another, while recognizing the inability to do so in a complete or whole fashion. Ekphrastic texts are not only marked through vibrant portrayals, but also garner momentum through an underlying acceptance of the impossibility of any task that tries to fully 'capture' an object or another form. For example, Keats' 'Ode on a Grecian Urn' (2000 [1819]: 20) explores the ambivalence of meanings that orbit the urn and its pictorial representations, suggesting: 'What leaf-fring'd legend haunts about thy shape/Of deities or mortals, or of both.'

In helping to think about what we do deliberately or inadvertently when we 'write up' research, ekphrasis points to a concern with invoking an intersubjective moment between the text as purveyor of the experience and the audience, while fully acknowledging the multiplicity of interpretations that constitute experience. Each one of these elements is partial and incomplete, leading to some commentaries suggesting that ekphrasis is a 'metaphenomenology in its own right' (Horstkotte, 2017: 161) through the way in which it questions the contingency and embeddedness of multimodal practices concerned with witnessing, visualization and representation. To write up in this way rests on an intersubjective acceptance of audiences troubling and dwelling in their own contingent lived experience of ageing.

This curates a connection between the research account and the reader's own ageing subjectivity as a sensate and open experience through which the 'audience should be able to recognize what they hear, even if that recognition is partial' (Webb, 2009: 109). In doing so, the integrity of the empirical account moves away from normative concerns surrounding a classical notion of rigour towards situating an account of a phenomenon that hinges as much on the thoughts, ideas and experiences of ageing as on the research accounts themselves. In other words, ekphrasis brings relationality to the fore of writing in terms of both its communal and disruptive potential.

With this in mind, the following chapters are accounts that will invariably be read through the reader's own ageing experience while deliberately seeking to provide ways of trying to avoid a subliminal collapse into universalizing experiences of ageing. Attention is made to texture ageing representations and re-representations through the simultaneity of sharing a social world and the multiplicity of representations, while acknowledging the inability to directly translate or collapse working through ageing into a diminutive account. Committing to dialogic engagement with the reader through feeling requires a craft that remains open, maintaining a richness for the affective dynamics and re-representations to gather ground in the act of being read. In part, this is through the temporal intervention that ekphrasis pursues in:

> its capacity to make the audience feel present at past and future events, this effect is also called 'translatio temporum' or, in Greek, metastasis or metathesis (a 'transference [of time]') ... to transport his audience in imagination back or forward to the events in questions, making use of the ability of enargeia to make them feel 'as if' they were present. (Webb, 2009: 100–101)

To speak to this, writing as ekphrastic pursuit means that the following chapters deliberately avoid a structure that might subsume the ageing experience into chronological accounts that document the decade of study. What I hope is that in these accounts the reader can not only read but also feel how ageing is simultaneously an ontological and practical project through an enargeia that evokes a vivacity and liveliness. To support this, each chapter draws on a different phenomenological figure as an analytic intervention to speak simultaneously to the practical and experiential and the phenomenological moments that fold into each other when working through ageing. In emphasizing the situated, embodied and postdualistic quality of world making in terms of our consciousness and subjectivity in growing up and older, they explore how we work through ageing as simultaneously an ontological and practical project. The next chapter focuses on disclosure to explore how moments of curiosity, politeness and spectacularity constitute ageing as a relational phenomenon. Chapter 5 then attends to the figure of grasping in order to discuss working through ageing as a project of the self. This is followed by Chapter 6, which introduces anchoring as a way of considering the way in which the world and the self meld with an inhabited spatiality.

4

Disclosing Ageing:
Revealing the World
in Working Relations

On the Thursday before Christmas in 2016, I met with one of the former traders who had come into London for an annual catch up with old friends from his market days. James was one of the original archetypical city traders who populated the City in the 1990s. From a working-class background, he had started working straight from school when trading was like the Wall Street images that populate the public imagination: shouting trades, gobby masculinity, extravagant client hospitality and promises of a moneyed lifestyle. James had enjoyed many parts of this and still felt close to those who had shared his formative years of work. But he had also been prudent when others had not and had been described affectionately by others as 'keeping his head about him'. He'd saved, carefully managed assets, maintained healthy relationships with his wife and children, and was now financial independent in his 50s.

We ordered our coffee just outside Mayfair and James shared his recent experience of retraining in compliance and starting a new job. For many, moving from 'front' to 'back' office would be a confronting shift. I had been told by others people in the City that compliance was viewed by many as a bureaucratic distraction, while some even dismissed it as a parasitic function within their businesses, given that it did not directly make money – a necessary but derided inconvenience, like taxes. Yet there had been a recent shift in power across the financial services caused in part by new regulatory measures and expectations brought in after the 2008 Global Financial Crisis alongside the increase in automation that was killing traditional modes of trading and brokering. This has meant that in some ways, compliance as a profession was changing in terms of its role and importance. Having gone back to study for his compliance exams, James saw himself in a strong position and quickly received offers from within his established network. He shared how:

> An old friend of mine – a guy I knew from the futures markets – he's a director and he just said: 'Look, a guy in one of my departments, he needs somebody with some market experience. He's got bundles of compliance experience but he's just a little bit edgy around some of the traders.' So he said: 'Come and interview. It might be my decision.'

James subsequently got the job, but in 'just under a year and a half I just decided it wasn't for me, I just couldn't connect'. I was surprised to hear this: compared to some of the more abrasive characters in the City, James was a 'good guy'. He carried all the normative accoutrements desirable in the City, and I'd seen first hand that he was generally well liked, thoughtful and conscientious. When I asked why, he briefly mentioned the frustrating workplace structures and bureaucratic hurdles before moving our conversation on, giving me the feeling that I should not ask again. As we finished up our coffees and he headed out for something stronger with his friends, he came back to this experience in what he'd termed his 'new short-lived career':

> A little bit of my ego as well – you can't … you have to be careful what you say and how you fit in, you don't want to come across as this old know-it-all. Rightly so, I had to come in at a more junior role than I'm used to because you have to take steps back because you're in a new vocation. And there's all this regress. You've still got to do your time. But also, with my age as well, and the age or other people around you, which was younger here, you know that where you can go is going to be capped: 'he's the old boy over there'. And you have to learn politics and play the game and that wasn't me. I like things out in the open, having honest relationships.

A few years later, we caught up again, this time in the pub, and James had not gone back into compliance. There was not much financial need for him to work, but in discussing his recent experiences of growing older, he returned to the difficulty in relating to people in compliance, particularly with some of his younger colleagues who he saw had been successful by 'playing a game I didn't want to play' that required you to be as detached as possible. This was explained by him recounting a younger acquaintance who was 'obviously a very sharp guy. He said to a friend of mine, "Oh, I've been an authorized signatory of this place for eight years. Do you know how many documents I've signed? None". So the idea is, if you don't have your name on that document, nothing can stick to you'. This was both bemusing and troubling for James at a point when he was enjoying not having to perform 'doing his time' in a new career, but was also reflecting on his own recently graduated son about to move into a similar workplace environment.

James' account of deliberately (un)relating highlights ageing as coming to us through other people as part of a dynamic that sits in a precarious zone between connection and disconnection. We are nestled in the everyday relations and interactions of people in and around our work, striving to secure ourselves in a particular point in time through connections. However, doing so we run the risk of being confronted by a vulnerability that we are 'read' by others through expectations and assumptions that are not of our making. While the way in which James spent his career may seem like a world away from de Beauvoir's life, both recognized how formative moments in ageing are revealed in and across relations. For de Beauvoir, her fictional work too is 'interested less in the characters themselves than in their relationships' (de Beauvoir, 2006 [1965]: 10). For example, *The Inseparables* (de Beauvoir, 2021 [1954]) biographically marks the dyadic social and intellectual expectations and aspirations of two friends, André and Sylvie, as they grow older. A more agnostic relational account provides the backdrop to *Misunderstanding in Moscow* (de Beauvoir, 2023 [1992], where a couple called Nicole and André visit Russia and navigate midlife in and through the ambivalence of youth in the embodied form of André's young adult daughter Macha. And just as James' account appeals to the actions, presence and perceptions of others to mark his own age-based experiences, for de Beauvoir, it is in the presence and interactions with the protagonist Macha that age is revealed for the couple, most intensely for Nicole:

> Macha had taken her arm. 'Come on! You're so young, both of you' … Macha said 'You're young'. But she had taken Nicole's arm … they were peers. And then all of a sudden, a gesture, an inflection of Macha's voice, a considerate action reminded her that there was an age difference of twenty years between them – and that she was sixty. (de Beauvoir, 2023 [1992]: 40–41)

These ubiquitous interactions, innocuous exchanges and everyday relations, whether in the workplace or between close family members compel an opening of ourselves to the world in ways that can make us sharply – and sometimes cruelly – aware of ageing. The reveal is not simply about appearing as a mode of consciousness, but about a disclosure – an embodied way of understanding and comprehending ageing that always happens in symphony (but not necessarily in synchronicity) with others.

To explore this revealing-in-relations as a central component of working through ageing, I focus on disclosure as a phenomenological figure. Disclosure refers to the embodied experience of revealing when we engage with people and the world around us. It simultaneously involves revealing ourselves to the world, how the world and those around us are revealed to us, and how the world reveals us to ourselves. While such a process is underpinned by an ontological demand and is a necessary requirement for being and doing in the world, it is also part of the mundane pastiche of being in work. Encounters and relations take shape in the everyday, presenting possibilities or preferences that can be validating or comforting, or likewise make us feel uncomfortable or 'not for me' and subsequently compel of constrain our experience of working through ageing as viable or otherwise. Yet disclosure also carries high stakes in the context of work relations where the easy flow or connections within our organizational tribes is central to being perceived as an asset in the workplace, as well as connected to systems of valuation and a range of material rewards relating to recognition, pay and promotion. As I will show, the organizational dynamics and vulnerabilities engendered in disclosing ageing are not simply an outcome of growing older, but rather make up the ontological building blocks of ageing as a lived experience that is contextually situated within the social and economic landscape of work. Employees do so through attempts to negotiate age-ful subjectivities that hold the possibility for intelligible and multifaceted ways of being and relating as we grow up and older, but such work is undertaken within the 'aged' systems of organizing I described earlier that often create uneven processes that reproduce normative expectations regarding chronology, bodies and biographies.

The first section of this chapter explores disclosure as a mode of curiosity, considering how the desire to connect in the context of work both feeds an apart-ness through distancing ageing and reveals a vulnerability around one's own embodied parameters and boundaries. I then explore a second element of disclosure, deferral, in which a compromising or leaning into normative aged, organized relations is desired but often frustrated through the dynamic situatedness of ageing relations. Next, I explore the operation of disclosure through politeness, considering how generational relations are corporeally experienced and bounded through modes of benevolent Othering, and the costs and consequences of breaching these relational ties. Finally, I consider the being and doing of spectacularity in disclosure, exploring how it relies upon the simultaneous presence and absence of bodies shaped by gender-aged aspirations that are rarely possible to achieve. By tracing the dialectics of disclosure and enclosure in the context of work, the chapter closes by reflecting on what compels and constrains our experience of working through ageing with and alongside others as experienced through simultaneously being a subject and an object.

Disclosure through curiosity: reaching out and connecting across the working life course

Curiosity speaks to the compulsion for disclosure as an ontological necessity stitched into the organizational fabric that makes up everyday experiences and professional interactions. From the very early observations in HFUK, it felt that being able to read the consensual and relational economy of corporate success relative to one's life course positioning was important for conferring legitimacy when connecting with others. For those in the earlier stages of their careers, such curiosity was an embodied expression of both absorbing ideas from exchanges with others while also performing one's connection to the world of paid labour. For others who were further along in their working life course, curiosity governed how to perform a connectedness even when they were perceived as 'incredibly old', as Luke imagined his young teammates saw him. Luke, a programmer and popular member of staff with colleagues, held a similar status to Charles, who oversaw one of the trading programmes. Their colleagues' descriptions of both of them were hallmarked by respect for their wizened seniority, legitimized by their time served in competitive corporate environments and cumulated achievements. Central to this was the cumulation of networks that in practice made one's job and career easier, 'given that a lot of your ability to get things done stems from your informal networks' (Liam, 2010, Y0) and provided a cumulative cluster of colleagues or alumni relations who could 'vouch' for each other. But it also required an organizational performance of being 'still interested, even now' (Archie, 2016, Y6), maintaining an inquiring mind as to how things work in the face of bureaucratic hurdles or changing managerial demands. This formed a key part of their successful public project of ageing in an environment where most colleagues were around a decade younger than them. Charles reflected on his *openness to new ideas* shortly after a restructure at his firm that had provided a good opportunity to retire: 'I'm still fascinated in how markets work, but also how other people work in markets. Just when you have the measure of people, something comes up that you have to work through in your team, and I find that immensely pleasurable' (Charles, 2018, Y8).

Yet negotiating an inquisitive opening into the world was sanctioned by position and expectations, as Thomas' (2010, Y0) experience at HFUK highlighted. His role was commensurate to a middle manager, both in terms of hierarchy and vertical boundary spanning across different functions, which he framed as a rite of passage, accepting that you must be *bloodied* at this 'age and stage of my career' to enable moving into executive roles later in life. Central to Thomas' conviction was that he might 'be unpopular and ask everyone the awkward questions that will make us better'. But such interactions also carried the danger of double reception: demonstrating his credibility and work required him to show his own competence and a desire for success, but not to come across as driven by a naked ambition at the expense of others. In his interactions to probe different elements of the business, trying to seesaw between individualism and relatability was further challenged by team members who suggested that 'anyone at his age' who got satisfaction from a generic management role should be viewed with suspicion. His sudden departure one afternoon felt the inevitable consequence of Thomas's failure to calibrate his age and role with the 'right' kind of curiosity.

Similarly, lines of curiosity were central to the professional gender-crafting that many women undertook. Lucy was keen to emphasize how her own career was kept 'very clean', through being careful about who and how she asked about work-related matters, even though this delimited opportunities that may help her advance:

> I like knowing how people got the jobs they're in, especially as I come from a different country, and a lot of the time it helps as you get to know how people get their jobs or what skills they have. But then some people might start whispering about why you are pursuing him? Do you think he can get you a better job? (Lucy, 2014, Y4)

Accepting the labour of making sure one's relations were calibrated with a concern 'to make people comfortable with you' (Ava, 2012, Y2) often involved women explicitly framing relationships in asexual normative parameters. For example, Willow, who sat on one of the trading desks, used the trope of a big brother or little sister and both her and Lucy often referred to relationships with senior men on their teams in father–daughter terms where 'he always looked out for me, asking how I was, showing me where I might have went wrong but not doing it in a way that was embarrassing, like a father figure' (Lucy, 2012, Y2). For others, such as Ollie, reaching out appeared to be more fluent:

> I enjoy learning about new things, but when you come across someone who doesn't think like you and they are a bit different, perhaps a different generation, or have come a different route into the job, like the old school traders, it's easy to be defensive or arrogant. I think I was far more like that when I was younger, and definitely the market brought out that arrogance. But I would still reach out and ask a lot of questions. (Ollie, 2016, Y6)

Ollie's 'reaching out' was accepted in HFUK, with other traders noting how he could 'just tag along to things' based on the shared similarities he had with many around him in work. This contrasted with Ivy, who began in a similar team, but felt her ability to curiously extend herself into discussions or work activities was marked through being a young woman:

> Yes. The thing I've noticed is, you know Ollie is also young? But they treat him as kind of like, you know, like they'll treat him as you would expect to treat someone younger. Like 'Alright son', they call him and with me it's just 'Hi' ... See, I never had the initiation thing. Although, of course I did in a way, but it was never, like I never had nicknames or anything. You know the way they have nicknames for him? And even if they may be bad, it's still a nickname. Any nickname is good – do you know what I mean? (Ivy, 2010, Y0)

Ivy's perception that Ollie's team were inherently more interested in him played out in a variety of ways around the informal socialization. He was often the butt of jokes and was castigated when he did things incorrectly. At the same time, such derogatory exchanges or actions operated as a form of recognition where he appeared to be accepted by a larger group of colleagues who had all worked together for several years. In comparison, Freya (2012, Y2) was clear that 'you can't come across as an annoying girl who can't make any of her own decisions', while Ivy was always mindful of positioning herself during work-related discussions. She reflected that:

> you have to show vulnerability in a team of women, or they'll be like 'Who the hell does she think she is?' Whereas with men, if you do, they'll just think you're weak. The guys on the other side. I want to ask more questions than I do. I'm worried about just bothering them. (Ivy, 2010, Y0)

In a masculine-dominated sector and at a relatively early point in her working life, Ivy already recognized a need to orientate herself to different people in ways that did not breach expectations of her as a young female colleague. At the same time, Sophie (2020, Y10) shared how her friends increasingly discussed being less likely to be the subject of unwanted sexualized attention as they grew older and that this allowed for 'more authentic and assertive relationships when we are at work'. Sebastian, a researcher with a wife who worked in the same industry and a young daughter, also felt that becoming older and entering the 'dad zone' made it possible to have closer relationships with colleagues. While aware that others viewing him as primarily a parent or a husband could be confronting in juxtaposing his own perceptions of still being 'quite young', it did bring about the potential for more comfortable workplace relationship: 'I'm getting to the stage now where I have sufficient age gap between adult women that there's no complicated gender dynamics because I'm so much older than them, which is a good thing. It makes life a lot easier, actually' (Sebastian, 2014, Y4).

Such age configurations were drawn upon as safeguarding devices against unwarranted or misrecognized attributions relating to sexual harassment, but invariably sanctioned male–female aged relations in relatively narrow terms. Without a plurality of archetypical relationships to draw upon, relations at work that traversed gender-aged distinctions– and offered the opportunity for multiple sources of information, mentorship, or sponsorship opportunities to advance careers or gain knowledge – were often difficult to maintain.

Breaching established and hardened dyadic relations around age could also result in being misrecognized as an object of curiosity. The compromises required to avoid becoming a 'curious object' were often precipitated in a work-related transition. As markets automated and changed the employment landscape, those who moved jobs or professions discussed their sudden awareness of being looked at a different way, as if they were an 'old guy, an alien from outer space' (James, 2016, Y6). Nathan, who moved from financial services into tourism, referred to himself as 'not exactly the most mature person in the world'. Even though he described how working with predominantly younger people was not an issue, at the same time, he was aware of his being cast as 'a dirty old man', which was sensitised through his experience of others around him:

Because we've got 30 positions on the programme, so every two months you get 30 new trainees – kids, anything from 17/18. But one of them at the moment is 55 – he's just a weird, ex-cult member, trying to find himself. Yes, it's mainly sort of mid-20s. It's a strange place to live and work, because you don't feel like there's an age gap at all, apart from relationship-wise – I'm not getting involved with people who are that young. No. No way. God. To start with I'd be like a dirty old man. I know Sam (his boss) will pick me up straight away with 'Dirty old man'. (Nathan, 2014; Y4)

Nathan's keenness to distance himself from other 'weird' age-asynchronous people while in his early 40s highlighted a compulsion to navigate the necessity of relations, while also becoming aware of how they were changing over time 'in the face' of those around them, so to speak. Such embodied experience of growing older contributed to the disruptive or disorientating potential around a threat of becoming objectified, as suggested by Henry. Henry, who had worked on a trading desk since leaving school at 16, was one of the former HFUK employees who had changed sectors completely. As part of the cohort of the City who had joined the LIFFE markets straight from school, Henry accepted that the 'job's not got a long lifespan' and felt that 'things were now too different in the City'. In becoming uncomfortable with stretching his own risk parameters when trading, he decided to walk away from it all, downsizing properties and staying at home while his wife completed her degree. During this time, he got heavily involved in coaching a girl's football team, something that 'would not have been possible when I was younger' as it required 'knowing girls' in a way that he felt could be socially problematic, especially when he did not have a daughter:

> It just seems a lot of male coaches feel that coaching girls is like too many risks involved, from a safeguarding point of view and child welfare. It is different. You've got a kit bag and you've got like hairbands in there and sanitary towels and stuff. Knowing girls, I could probably tell parents when their daughters are pre-menstrual more so than they could. They come and their energy levels are low and their moods [are] slightly different. They might be quite red after 5 or 10 minutes where they wouldn't normally be. They're not ill, it is to do with their cycle. Other men are like, 'I don't want to know about that'. I think as a coach, it becomes like: 'How are you going to get most of them?' (Henry, 2020, Y10)

For Henry, this work took place while negotiating how he was made to feel 'a bit odd' in his new role in the post office. Sitting in his uniform in a coffee shop one afternoon after he finished work, we discussed how the experience of his new role had been initially marked by colleagues asking questions and being friendly, However, curiosity had quickly turned to suspicion about his motives for joining in his 40s when colleagues found out he had previously worked in the financial sector in the City:

> Ten per cent of the workforce have been there 25 years. I don't know if that's common or not. Then they thought I was Royal Mail police as in I was in there spying on them because apparently, they do send people in. I think that's just paranoia. Yes. There's a bit of a chit-chat: 'Henry Shaw, doesn't make sense, I don't know why he's here.' I'm here because obviously, I want to work ... Managers started being really, really nice to me. Like strangely nice to me. They're above me and someone said to me: 'Oh yes' ... Dennis said: 'Yes I can't work Henry Shaw out - why he's really here. He could be just like one of ... the Royal Mail will employ those people who to go from office to office to see how it's run.' I'm like: 'Well, OK. I'm a part of that'. (Laughs). (Henry, 2018, Y8)

This experience of becoming a curiosity contrasted with Henry's initial assumptions that the similarities he shared with colleagues in terms of working-class upbringing, accent and passion for football would make for easy relationships. While the suspicion and distancing eventually 'settled down', Henry latterly discussed a lingering conditionality. For example, given his relative fitness, he finished his rounds far more quickly, which his colleagues felt had implications within a unionized setting. Henry also became aware of when to offer or not to offer help, as this could often raise suspicions, given that he was clear that he did *not* want to progress or be promoted. He 'discussed thinking carefully about what I might or say' and the frustration at his attempts to be a decent colleague: 'You know what, like because I am a team player type person. They questioned it: "This guy's a bit helpful and friendly and comes in with a smile on his face every day. What's going on?"' (Henry, 2020, Y10).

The creeping sense of becoming a curious object was also part of a journey into senior organizational positions when others began to talk to you 'as if you knew what you were doing' (Ollie, 2018, Y8). For Ollie, becoming an object through authority was synonymous with being seen 'purely as a manager that could do things for them, rather than a person' and was a necessary deferral that aligned with 'being at the stage where you have your own shit together', as Harry (2016, Y6) put it. For Archie, whose career had progressed towards more strategic positions in economic forecasting, becoming both older and more senior was marked by a qualitative difference in deferring his own interests, having to avoid personality clashes and making it 'not all about me'. Freya also discussed how career progression was accompanied by having to have an interest in people's 'messy lives' while not disclosing one's own:

I've become acutely aware because of a couple of situations at work that the more senior you get, it really becomes less about the work that you do or the quality that of course, that matters, right? It builds your credibility, but you spend a lot more of your time ... You realize that a lot of it is about personality and politics and holding back, navigating that and being hyper-aware of people's sensitivities and how to have conversations and not having outright arguments with each other, which has happened. It's like I'm at the point where I have to deal with people's messy lives. (Freya, 2020, Y10)

The 'holding back' these positions required was rewarded with advancement that brought financial security and a wider recognition of professional accomplishments and achievements, as well as harvesting the rewards of a curiosity-driven modus operandi earlier on in ones career. Yet it also required an acceptance that one's work persona was revealed through being as an object of authority or care and curiosity *for* others rather than having a reciprocal relationship *with* others. This uneven mode of relating meant that some, such as Luke (2012, Y2), had sought to avoid positions of seniority if they did not nurture the work relationships in which he flourished, instead choosing jobs 'where I felt I wasn't being treated like an economic unit, I was being treated like a person'. Similarly, for Flo, who was a highly skilled researcher and programmer, this brought an uneasy sense that the seniority expected 'at her age' was too much of a compromise as it prevented a choice to 'work with good people how I want to work. Because I can learn something somehow, but (when you are a manager), you see people are too caught up in other things to really be interested in learning, there's too many other things you have to deal with when you are their manager'. This was one reason why she had actively opted out of moving into leadership positions, until she felt it was not possible to avoid doing so:

> So I got promoted last year after having tried to fight against it for about the last 15 years and it had good effects in many ways but I hate it. I never want to be a manager. I have to manage two minions. They're alright, it's just the management upwards and downwards that I can't stand. I feel like I'm caught in the middle. I really don't care about being senior. I still want to be what they call a technical expert, so someone who's good at their job and is senior because they're good at their job. I am hardly coding these days, I have to fight with idiots who don't like our ideas just because they want to change and I don't have time for this. (Flo, 2018, Y8)

Ava also found that the scrutiny that came from being a manager was expected as part of a 'natural progression as you got older if you are good at your job', but found it challenging presenting as all things to all people and 'not really what I want to be':

> I think that's one of the issues I have to struggle with, even applying for jobs. They're always talking about we want people who can be part of a team, blah, blah, blah, whatever. In some ways I'm not very authentic, I feel as though I'm just doing it to go through the motions, to kind of – you know, the real me is that I like working with people I like, a small group of people I trust and usually it's on the projects that I like doing. (Ava, 2018, Y8)

Mia felt more comfortable with the new level of scrutiny about her life and a different sense of dependence on others when she took on a high-profile leadership position. Compared to our previous conversations, which revolved around technical aspects of her work, in our last meeting she described being comfortable in terms of how her career decisions had forced her to recalibrate how she connected with other people and connected with her own professional persona, reflecting that:

I really have to trust them [her team] and empower them to deliver things themselves. It's a changed mindset. I think it's in many ways very good because it moves me into a different future, but I find it in some ways quite disempowering and a bit unnerving ... I think it's a very natural progression but my work doesn't feel like home. (Mia, 2020, Y10)

Herein lies the ambivalence of a curiosity that underpins relations. Curiosity across the working life course opened up career opportunities and the possibility of financial reward and recognition, but also created systems that encouraged a deferral to normative expectations or constriction of ways of relating. At the same time, modes of organizing either based on age-based normative expectations or stage-based linear career norms were part of the fabric through which ageing relations were normatively cohered into working lives and career trajectories more generally. Together this could shape, obscure or thwart the ability to disclose the temporally situated self in relations, making curiosity a desirable but conditional possibility.

Generational politeness as a social emotion

One of the advantages of spending time on the work floor of HFUK was that I saw first hand the extent to which many interactions are implicitly shaped by a corporate acceptability governed by age-based norms. This is in part unsurprising given the relatively formal work setting and that a sheen of politeness has often been central to commercial society. After all, it is no coincidence that industrialization happened at the same time as the creation of an eighteenth-century normative 'civilized' elite that together organized and distinguished market relations and positions. However, its presence in HFUK felt more active: it not only lubricated talk but also had an ability to organize through a veneer of unspoken acceptability that underpinned everyday talk. In this context, while older age as pejorative may have been present, it was obscured by proxy measures that served to 'explain away' different ways in which groups or teams were aligned. The most enduring forms of polite short hand that aided this was 'generations'. In HFUK this was a term used to acknowledge the fallacy of age-based identities, while also employed to justify relationships with others as being 'more natural', in the words of Thomas. That others did not seem to worry about the slipperiness of generation's linguistic manoeuvres made me a little petulant:

Generations is still coming up – in the same breath people say they don't believe in it but then draw on it as proof of what they are trying to say. And always so politely, I'm still not sure why this civility is always hovering around ageing when some people previously played fast and

lose around gender and other attributes, even though there is even
more gallows humour here than when I was here [in 2010]. Why is
there so much politeness around ageing? (Fieldnotes, October 2012)

At first, I had assumed that any highly litigious environment leads to sanitized
talk when discussing age or other legally protected characteristics. Yet
I began to see this approach as safely boxing in difference through civility
in a way that also served a broader ontological purpose, mainly through
attempting to stabilize people and the world they sought to connect with.
The endurance of generations as a key relational interlocutor not only shaped
the conditions around disclosing ageing but was also predicated on complex
counterpositions. These operate through arrangements and associations that
drain ageing as a mode of intentionality.

'Generations' was not exclusively understood as referring to socially or
historically bounded groups, but rather considered as a clustering of people
according to their direction and experience in the labour market. People
placed both themselves and others in this way, such as describing colleagues as
'between my generation and my dad's' (James, 2012, Y2) or Jack's description
of different cohorts who joined the city at various points in time: 'I was one
of the first generation of Essex boys. I was in that generation where you
either become a trader or you become a broker, or you become a mechanic
or something like that' (Jack, 2020, Y10).

Such accounts were not simply about chronological essentialism around
certain ages, but were aligned with more affective modes of connecting.
When I mentioned this to Gen, who had worked within the banking sector
throughout her life and dealt with a 'variety of colourful characters', she
reflected that it felt important to think about why she had a greater affinity
with some colleagues over others, suggesting 'maybe generations is more
where you feel closer to people' (Gen, 2018, Y8), while during field work
in 2012 one of the programming team, Kieran, discussed generations around
'where I would expect to find people'. Generations as a charge or feeling of
closeness was conditional on proximity or distance to other people, but also
to objects, ideas or beliefs and values. James discussed this as not oppositional,
but a matter of priorities that were often dormant and then surfaced in
moments of tension or disagreement. He reflected that:

It's a quite patronising term for some of the younger generation, but
yeah, the snowflake, it's basically they melt quite quickly. They have
some wonderfully social ideal principles, the kids, about this and that
and you can't really argue back with these. But they're not always
pragmatic, it's a bit like we'd all love a better education system, we'd all
love a better health service, we'd all love whatever, but nobody wants
to pay 70 per cent tax, nobody wants to do whatever it is, it's just

the way the world works ... They spend a lot of time thinking about things like that but then when their own shit hits the fan, it all goes wrong. My generation apparently now they're called the gammon. The angry old white man who suddenly gets angry and turns red, so he looks like gammon. (James, 2018, Y8)

Being 'a gammon' was part of a corporeal representation that distinguished one generational body from another. For example, Dylan discussed who ordered heavy IPAs, wheat beer or alcohol-free lager in after works drinks as 'a predictable pattern', while Henry talked about younger generations having an awareness of sun protection rather than coming back from holidays 'looking red and still a bit burnt'. Such innocuous references were also overlayed by expectations of a generational body whereby attention to fitness and sporting activities, diet or lifestyle could quickly mark out how certain groups of bodies were expected to look and how these bodies grew into a situated ageing aesthetic over time.

Generational civility as part of an age-oriented modality also informed work-based behaviours. Thomas, who had previously worked in a large consulting firm before moving into the financial services, suggested that generations were a 'shortcut when you must form a team quickly', as was his experience when moving to troubleshoot in different organizations. Elsewhere, Harry suggested that generations help with 'shortcuts [and] mean you are cutting out all the bullshit and just trying to find out what you have in common, both of you realize it's not perfect'.

However, how such shortcuts were realized or recognized, and under what conditions, remained rather miasmic. In practice, generational shortcuts often led to the subsequent setting up or closing down of relations. They could be employed to quickly justify any breaches due to their 'imperfect' nature, establishing what assumptions or biases could be socially endured or viewed as legitimate within the etiquette of the broader corporate environment, while also excusing behaviour or inconsistent practices. This was even the case when people situated themselves as within the group potentially marginalized or compromised in a benign way through a generational attribution. Leo, who continued to work in financial markets over the years of the study, described how the market structure demanded newer cohorts that were more 'natural' in terms of their orientation to technology:

We're not of that generation. You reach an age where your skill set isn't there anymore or just younger people are – people know it already: 25 year-olds exhale computer skills that are going to be significantly better than mine. Even just using the functionality on an iPhone and probably still more towards calls and a few apps, whereas you, I don't know, half the functionality of the phone. These are the people you work with. And I think you are probably aware a little bit of their skills being better matched, certainly in the financial sector, as you mentioned, the automation's gone exponential and if I lost my job, how much more difficult it would be to find another one. (Leo, 2020, Y10)

This seizure of technology and one's situated embodied ability to 'exhale' capacity, to cite Leo, valorized the notion of generational distinction. Elsewhere, Jack, who worked with both older and younger colleagues, confided that 'I don't really understand the younger generation any more than they understand the older generation' (Jack, 2020, Y10). However, self-identifying as part of a generation could also legitimize ascribing generational foibles to others, essentializing and reifying difference in a palatable way. For example, Isla (2020, Y10) suggested that the 'older generation tend to be more loyal I think, but have got these weird ideas about the workplace', while Sebastian discussed how 'my workplace culture is it is very, very recycling friendly. The young millennial people I work with are very into that idea and it propagates out'. However, the value of generations being brought together in a way that allows value to 'propagate out', around learning for example, could also explain away 'these sort of people':

He came to [name of previous company] as a junior. He's good at talking himself up. He's good, yes. I mean, a lot of people have learned from him. But the sort of people that came in to where we were, it was like 'oh my God, he's a bit ... He's like the next generation'. (Henry, 2012, Y2)

Generational politeness involved a simultaneous disclosure of the self and a distancing through grouping together different bodies. Yet it also highlighted the ease at which slipping into generations as a mode of difference occurred, even for Archie, who was one of the milder mannered of the group I spoke to. His reflections post-lockdown were notable in situating COVID-19 as a 'stress test' between different generations – and a possible breach: 'I do think governments, they found that magic money tree following lockdown and the costs behind it but all you're really doing is passing on a burden to the next generation' (Archie, 2020, Y10).

The idea of an intergenerational contract also fuelled the engines of social emotion around ageing, often through the taking on of responsibility or accountability. For example, Ollie (Y10, 2020), when discussing one formative relationship in his career, mentioned how his old boss 'had a vision to try and build the company and sustain the company and safeguard the company for the next generation. I think he regarded himself as the guardian of the site for that period of time'. Elsewhere, Flo (2016, Y6), a programmer, suggested that despite the conditions of work as being so busy as to occlude a moment to pause on future sustainability or planetary dangers, 'I do worry about the younger generation and what they will face'.

However, the affective pulse supporting this 'passing on' contract also set up a terrain to frame or call out possible violations of norms, often when industry or economic trends were seen as aggravating or disrupting normative aged relations. For example, many referred to the multigenerational workforce and the need for this to be balanced. This balance was not clearly articulated in terms of equal ratios, for example, but rather was fractured or stressed through a perceived excess of, for instance, older bodies, as Liam suggested:

> You've got lots of old boomer-y types expecting to do management and there are millions of them. All these young people never get promoted because there isn't any room, because these people never leave. If all of a sudden people started living longer, then they'd like, they'd never leave for even longer. (Liam, 2014, Y4)

Other political and social events also operated as moments of breach. When the referendum for the UK to leave the European Union was announced, media headlines in the UK focused on a sway in voting patterns for a Brexit 'leave' among those aged over 45. Many discussions I had during this period revolved around rising tensions between different age groups in respondents' workplaces. Ollie's evocative use of temporal unevenness as dispossessing an even terrain of consequences was notable: 'it was of course a democratic vote, but it wasn't really, given that those deciding do not have to live as long with the mess' (2016, Y6). Harry was more forthright in his views:

> The worst thing was when it happened [the Brexit vote] I was so angry and one of the things I thought was when I get back was how to discuss it with people around work. Your generation have had it so fucking good compared with our generation and now our jobs are going to be harder, careers are going to be harder, the world is a harder place than it was. You had everything. You missed the war, you've got lifetime pensions, guaranteed employment and you couldn't resist fucking it up one more time for the rest of us, could you? (Harry, 2016, Y6)

In many ways, Brexit showcased the limited generative potential of generations as a concept to hold difference, exposing the fragility of politeness I had initially witnessed. Generations afforded a 'soft ageism'; a palatable explanation through which an unequal distribution of value (and accountability) could mark out age-based relations in a spirit of benevolence. Yet the flexible ambivalence of generations as a trope was not simply a linguistic display, but also a way of reifying, protecting and reproducing a normative corporeal apparatus informing how people *should* relate to each other, imprinted into the organizing of corporate aged bodies. As both a relational concept and a structuring trope, 'generation' works through being 'in the ballpark' of age, but not so definitively aligned that it disrupts one's own age positionality. In doing so, the aged relations constituted in generations reveal how age (mis)recognition affectively marks out borders between the self and other, and forecloses a need to trouble existing normative relations or question possible bias.

Spectacularity in ageing: relating in gendered ageism

Over my time in the City, the various hedge funds, banks and other corporate firms I visited had one thing in common: they valorized and expected brilliance. In reproducing expectations on how to perform, look, or signal both success and the promise of future success over the working life course, a patina of meritocracy ensues as if brilliance is both aspirational and democratic. The gendered landscape of the financial services sat awkwardly with this claim and participants regularly described a how women were not only in the minority of senior positions in their organizations, but also that women over 45 were conspicuous by their absence. Women were also likely to be disproportionately represented in more junior or supporting functions, including back-office roles.

When I brought this up, asking people about the absence of middle-aged women, a variety of reasons were given, but that question itself was rarely seen as requiring further thought. Some suggested that the growing maturity of the sector itself meant that there should be women growing older soon (although this timeframe for a temporal spillover effect was rather vague), while others discussed how they seemed to 'gradually disappear', in Charles' words. The exception to this evaporation was one senior figure in my early days with HFUK, Margo. Margo was in her 50s and was an impressive presence. She had a wealth of experience in financial services and was a high-profile figure in the City, appearing in international lists of 'top women' and featuring regularly in the media. Some saw her as a role model for women in the firm and the sector more broadly: she appeared on industry panels and spoke at a range of corporate events, and many discussed how she continued to provide them with valuable support and advice long after they left HFUK. However, there were also the standard gender-based tropes around her as setting an impossible benchmark for others, or discussion around the choices she had made regarding her career and family. Margo herself discussed her high standards in terms of work around performance, saying 'That's what I'm paid for. I'm paid to take responsibility. And I'm quite good at it! And I wouldn't be any good if I weren't prepared to take responsibility.' This was not simply responsibility relating to job roles, but how one presented to others as a woman in industry. These expectations became clear when she was reflecting on her school reunion:

> I felt like saying to some of them 'What's the matter with your hairdresser?', you know. It's not immoral to dye your hair, you know! And nor is it immoral to put make-up on and not get fat and wear nice clothes, you know. I mean I thought that all, I mean not all, there's some exceptions but there was a huge tendency for women to just not care. (Margo, 2010, Y0)

The accounts both from Margo and about her resonate with McRobbie's (2009) notion of the 'spectacular feminine' in consumer culture – the young woman who is marked by her unflinching brilliance and is central to the idealized subject of "girl". However, for those I spoke to, luminosity emerged not only in or through youth; indeed, reference to 'rising stars' was solely attached to young men. Rather, it emerged through the positionality of gendered ageing as an aspirational project. Margo was the embodied proof that women could succeed in accomplishing all the career-based, social, familial and physical accoutrements of adulthood, succeeding while denying an appearance of accumulative stress or strain. Yet this was an inherently ambivalent position. Early on in the study, Margo as the 'only' middle-aged woman present and visible was important to the company at the time and served a particular role in not challenging the male-dominated hierarchy in HFUK. This was not necessarily a position celebrated by others and it felt like many of the negative cultural attributes were not only attributed to her by others, but also carried a sticky resinous quality that had a gendered-aged hue. During my time at HFUK, I began to see how Margo's presence also enabled the hedge fund manager to maintain his role as the benign patriarch who would look after them. This was central to employees believing that their jobs were safe, despite performance evidence to the contrary and the eventual closure of the firm a few years later. Meanwhile, Margo often took on less palatable discussions on performance or standards, doing dirty but necessary work. This position was untenable and when I returned two years later, Margo had left by mutual agreement. While I lost touch with Margo, over the years I often heard descriptions of other women in similar workplaces dotted across interviews that bore an uncanny resemblance to how Margo had been positioned all those years ago.

To explore this further, I turn to a discussion of spectacularity as a mode of aged disclosure that refers to an illuminated but precarious presence that orientates relations and perceptions, particularly for women at work. It exaggerates a gendered ageing subject who is representative or aspirational based on projections towards an effervescent and unbounded futurity. In doing so, it undermines or displaces discussions of broader cultural or structural barriers that constrain women's lived experiences of work. At the same time, embodying spectacularity is itself an ambivalent experience, with gendered aged footprints providing the conditions through which certain bodies are recognized through the past ascriptions and future trajectories bestowed upon women by others. In other words, spectacularity goes beyond the notion of professional middle-aged older women as either hypervisible and problematic, or invisible. Rather, it suggests that through normative expectations of growing older, gender relations set up unattainable and unsteady trajectories for those who are beyond the dominant embodied form of a masculine, white corporate worker.

Like Margo, other 'spectaculates' – those who partially align with but can never fully or permanently embody luminescent perfection – were repeatedly mentioned in the narratives of respondents. In general, they were women over the age of 45 who had succeeded within male-dominated or masculine industries. Spectaculates operated as embodied evidence of a meritocracy even when statistically the sectors in which many respondents were working were still heavily dominated by white men in senior positions. As an inflation of proof, spectacularity had two outcomes. The first was that it displaced a broader discussion of how women seemed to simply 'disappear' from the city as they grew older. Women's presence was magnified through specificity rather than highlighted as an absence in general. Contrary to this being problematic, being an ageing woman was presented as providing a positive point of difference. Eleanor provided the example of this marked differentiation:

When you are pitching to clients, you need to stand out from the usual men in suits and one way that firms can do this is to have different people involved ... Yes, it can mean you are remembered, but it can also make them think 'that fund might have a different approach'. (Eleanor, 2016, Y6)

Others spoke of how being an older woman could provide some kind of labour market advantage for individuals, focusing on how their scarcity created opportunities in different ways that were not available to men. This was often supported through accounts of leaving the City as being an active, positive choice for women:

What's happening now, of course, if you want to have a decent amount of women at the senior level on board, that the area you can pick from, the pool to pick from is relatively narrow. A good friend of mine, his mother is a very prominent financial person and she gets offers to be a non-executive director every month. Lots of women drop out of the financial industry, both because they find it ... I mean, I recruited a lot of women in my world, actually more than most departments. We were more representative women than other parts of the City and several of them chose to leave the City, even though I thought they had a very good career ahead of them, because they preferred to do something else. (Charles, 2020, Y10)

While there was an acknowledgement of 'that horrible, terrible tension in the City, which there often is, where women are put down appallingly' (Charles, 2012, Y2), such behaviour was rarely discussed as participants' own direct experience. Bad behaviour was always located elsewhere; beyond their own teams or organizations or distanced as something happening within the sector more generally. It was as if there was a paradoxical atmosphere where women, as they grew older, appeared to both evaporate in numbers from the organizations in which respondents worked, but were still prominent enough to show a purported meritocracy in the sector. In this context, spectacularity functioned as providing a veneer of possibilities while still propagating gendered-aged parameters.

Spectacularity revolved around a set of relations that obscured opportunities to recognize women as growing older in a way that was ubiquitous, habitual and non-eventful. This was notable given that the middle-management positions described repeatedly as diverse were often the locus of white and predominantly middle-class men. Across the testimonies, both men and women discussed instances where promising women had 'lost their shine' as well as some rather damning indictments, including references to 'mumsy brain', 'losing their drive' or 'being unable to fully commit', all of which was used as a means of shattering a possibility of either securing spectacularity or embodying a futurity marked by spectacularity:

Men on the other hand can just go sailing through, even if they've just become a dad. It's hard but that's typically how it is. I think it does, ageing, affects people in the workplace differently ... women that I've worked with in the past, who have been really great to work with, really smart people and they suddenly decided to become a full-time mum or just give it in and let their husband take up the slack and lost their own identity and just binned it all. I think it affects the ageing thing, how it affects people, different sexes at different ages in their career. (Jack, 2016, Y6)

Against these perceptions, women recognized they 'had to be better just to be even' (Ivy, fieldnotes, 2012), but also that competing with 'mediocre men' was made more difficult given their alignment with feminized roles in the workplace that involved looking after people in ways that detracted from potential spectacularity. For example, many discussed how women were often asked to undertake discretionary 'office housework' tasks that had few career benefits, and any goodwill attached to these endeavours was quickly forgotten in organizational memory. Gen also highlighted how the short-term impact of organizational memory detracted from the potential of being afforded a promising futurity in other ways after having a baby. Willow, who worked on longer-term trading programmes, similarly discussed how, during a period when she was working four days, she felt that colleagues thought 'I'm just permanently pregnant', which made it feel impossible to live up to the brilliance required to progress in the financial services. During one of our conversations, even though she had a young child, her tiredness was not attributed to children, but the increased stress of avoiding being overlooked and 'just feeling my world's changed' in her failure to chase the professional image she knew others would value:

> Basically what happens is I have to catch up over the weekend, on what's happened on Friday. So every Sunday I spend a couple of hours just reading and going through emails, but I still think it's better that way than being in the office five days. But yes, it's just because of the nature of what I do. I can't just say 'oh, I have no idea what happened on Friday because I wasn't there'. You know, it's my problem. (Willow, 2012, Y2)

In later discussions, she did retrospectively reflect that: 'Part of me thinks, actually, I did work over the weekend, so if you're then going to lose twenty per cent of your income, you've got to question it' (Willow, 2020, Y10). At the same time, others recognized an inherent paradox of maternity and work. Here maternity allowance was often based on past 'time served' (how long you had worked for the company for), but any postmaternal career promise was rendered impossible in a sector governed by the supremacy of the immediate, which meant that by the time they return from maternity leave, they were insignificant. When we first met, Freya had discussed how she saw colleagues as taking a 'gentlemanly' approach and giving women with young children an easier time at work, but in later years returned to reflect on the consequences of being the recipient of these actions:

> I don't think it's just about sexism. It is sometimes, but I think it's more complex than that, I think, in society ... A friend of mine, the one that was about 31 when she had a child, she went back to the bank after she had it and obviously there's no open sexism, they're not going to sack you or say you can't go back there ... I remember she said to me at the time, she said that you come back and have a harder job than you had before, because somebody else has been doing it and that person has messed it up and she just said: 'It's not overt. You don't get your

job back. You always end up two or three rungs lower down the scale.' She said: 'You don't go back to where you were before. Yes. You grab all the benefits you're supposed to have.' But she said: 'When you come back to do your job, your clients have gone because somebody else has been looking after them and they don't want to give them back to you, even though they were your clients.' She said: 'You've got half the job that you had before. It's always different.' She said: 'There's nothing you can really do. You can't take them to court. There's nothing that you can really do.' And she said it's not possible to have a baby and a career. It's one or the other, really. (Freya, 2012, Y2)

In comparison, it was notable that men's testimonies also discussed how their career had not progressed in the way they expected, and yet their presence in the labour market was both assumed and tolerated: to simply 'be'. For example, Harry (2018, Y8), on having reached his mid-40s, described his career stage as secure in terms of 'being in anonymous mediocrity'. Sebastian (2012, Y2) also discussed how 'in terms of the career trajectory, in that I think in my mind, say, if I get this job with [multinational bank], I was thinking it would kind of establish myself as a kind of middle-ranking nobody rather than someone who has command – he says, with a sweeping hand gesture!'. While these positions may be challenging to their own ambitions or normative masculine expectations, they were not connected to an indictment of failure in organizational terms.

Sebastian contrasted his experience to that of his own wife, who also worked in financial services. He discussed in detail the pressure as she became a more senior woman in her sector, including meeting dignitaries and having an increasingly public profile, such as being interviewed on Bloomberg Television or quoted in the *Financial Times*. This was not an incidental feature of gendered-aged careers: more often than not, as a woman, maintaining a career over time in the City required one to continuously excel and overachieve relative to peers just to stay present. Such an endeavour was experienced through ambivalent benchmarks that spectacularity reproduced, producing a feeling of exposure that was double-edged. It was a requirement for advancement, but, as one of a limited modes of ambitious narratives available to women, also left women vulnerable to unfair and often sexist criticism. In other words, the credentials of spectaculates made it difficult to question their *competency* but did not prevent others from questioning their *authenticity*.

The archetypal spectacular ageing trajectory felt clearly marked out for women. It was a narration of a spectaulate subject position with a certain pedigree, schooled in elite institutions and universities, followed by an induction period at a prestigious banking firm and then a more solitary leadership position, for which they had often received industry recognition or awards. They also required evidence of 'having it all' through the feminine accoutrements of marriage and children, often buttressed by outsourcing domestic care that enabled the Speculate to further shine. Many men were aware of this double standard. For example, Liam (2014, Y4) mentioned how 'professional success defines men to themselves more, and the success of the family, the children and the professional success defines women more. I think that's changing and I think that's a good thing, but I think the reality of the situation is that for people of my generation, that's still the case'. Others recognised achieving a speculate status over time in terms of achievement and authenticity was elusive. The choices Spectaculates made to continue being professional women as they grew older was up for scrutiny by colleagues; one participant described an inspirational female leader in her field as having 'a nanny for each of her children, so she didn't have much to do with ... they went to boarding school' (Gen, 2012, Y2). Others discussed the successful older female leaders in their companies or networks as 'not the warm and fuzzy types' (Jack, 2014, Y4).

The sting of inauthenticity was intensive, but contrasted with high achieving women's own accounts that often referred to leaving the gendered gaze of youth as they grew older. Sophie suggested that not being viewed as young allowed her to be her 'true self', even though this was difficult to reconcile with the demands of female seniority in a corporate career. Isla, who had moved into away from the financial sector, discussed how she felt that the ability to be successful and yourself as an older women was more possible in the arts sector compared to jobs associated with the City:

> I could do a more normal job, but it's important to me that you're proud of ... your work and your personality and your life and to present yourself to someone in an authentic way, in a supportive way. I want to say, the complex that I talk about not fitting in, every now and then, I still feel like I have to prove myself to people. I still feel underestimated sometimes, but the nice thing about this sector is that you can work on it and you can know yourself. (Isla, 2020, Y10)

At the same time, Isla reflected on the danger of being asked to be yourself while also expected to look up to other women within a corporate landscape, reflecting that 'I don't see any of my male friends having to talk about role models or mentors'. Mia made a similar point, but from the perspective of being expected to be a role model, suggesting that this was an additional form of labour above continually proving one can do the job. Mia, who had used her technical expertise to move across different sectors, attributed her fitness to providing her with a presence and confidence that impacted how others related to her, feeling that others perceived that the solitary nature of her sport provided a certain strength and endurance. At the same time, even though appearing to fulfil the accoutrements of a spectacular trajectory, she suggested that women were often left behind:

> There's a slight sense of I should show people that you can do this, challenging this horrible narrative that only young people can achieve things. It only matters when young people achieve things. If you do well when you are older as a woman, no one particularly cares. In this job, it's the rising stars or they're only such and such an age and they've achieved this. What does that give the rest of us? (Mia, 2020, Y10)

Mia was also conscious of sidestepping other feminized expectations through connecting an element of her success around being 'fairly blunt and not that tactful. I wouldn't have said that people skills are one of my strongest areas'. This was reminiscent of Lily's (2016, Y6) description of one of her mentors as 'an amazing woman, but not high in emotional intelligence'. In fact, it felt that a relational authenticity for women as they grew older required being conscious of how and what to disclose: where authenticity was about balancing a partial and conditional revealing of their 'best self'. Freya, for example, discussed how her route to seniority had mirrored being viewed as 'more mid-life' and meant actively not coming across as more distant, while maintaining a credibility and authenticity:

> When I was at that mid-level, oh my God, there's like 50 people you can make bitch with and banter with …. Now, I was actually finally talking to a colleague about it this week, there's literally only two people that I would feel comfortable joking around with, bantering with, or even having a tantrum in front of, that know me well enough. (Freya, 2020, Y10)

As such, the spectacularity around ageing women was incumbent on sacrificing a familial quality, or not being perceived as having normative feminine attributes to begin with. Yet even if this balance was achieved, where Spectaculates were located was highly gendered. Harry (2016, Y6) discussed the disproportionate number of senior women with prestigious careers who had been given 'shit jobs to clear up companies that would be impossible for anyone to do and end up unemployable', while others discussed how women had been brought into high-profile jobs in the sector after the Global Financial Crash that set them up for failure. Similarly, Mia mentioned her boss' warning about actively stepping into public positions that were difficult to retreat from and could leave her vulnerable:

> I was very senior. I won some awards and stuff. I'm in a place now where I can be quite impactful and I'm intending to end up visible.

I'm already getting to the point where I've been asked to do the keynote speech at various industry events. My boss won't let me. I'm arguing that at the moment with the old boss, not the new one. He's like, 'Stay under the radar. You don't want anyone to know you exist'. (Mia, 2020, Y10)

Age-embedded spectacular relations as providing relational parameters for a professional woman were simultaneously an impossible standard and a desiring position. They seduced through providing a kind of hyper-real caricature of a subject position that correlated all kinds of effects with an expectation of how women age, from a promising futurity in youth to an unending source of 'shiny' presentation as women progressed and grew older. Spectacularity in this sense became a means through which gendered ageing relations are experienced in and through a valorization of unending potential or impossible positioning, but also a contingency that echoed the gendered demand to feel both grateful for the affirmation and acutely vulnerable, never able to take for granted 'just being' in the being and doing of ageing.

Discussion: the dialectics of disclosure and enclosure in ageing relations

Working through ageing as a process of disclosure highlights how different relations cluster in and around ageing in ways that organize and mark out different bodies, organizational positions, objects and cultures in the context of work. What I've sought to show in this chapter is that disclosure is both an obligatory way of socially performing professional relationships and an ontologically necessary mode of connection; a 'stretching out' to the world that in many ways was required for maintaining legitimate relations and legitimacy in the (working) world as one grew older. Across interviews, ageing relations were neatly stitched into attractive professional qualities that not only carried value but also suggested a certain elasticity of the self to always uphold these qualities. However, while such relations were central to demonstrating a commitment to one's workplace and career, they usually required a compromise. In order to continue being part of the connective tissue of corporate life that governed these relations, individuals must relinquish themselves in certain ways that displaces their experiences of changing bodies and positions, and their perceptions about themselves over the life course.

Such relations emerge through a comprehension of ageing founded in the presence or the spectre of a second person receiving and perceiving us. It is in the moments of connectedness and differentiation with other people that ageing feels partially revealed. This helps inform and solidify dynamically situated lives, how they are ordered or organized, and the possibilities and consequences for breaching expectations over the working life course. If our own 'personal' or individual experience of growing up and older carries an inherently ambiguous character, and therefore a shaky ontological reference point, we seek answers in the seemingly elsewhere, notably in others and the relations we have with them. For these reasons, locating ageing elsewhere appeared to be far more accessible for people to draw on as a means of talking about ageing given it felt like it was 'not-about-them'. Embracing this 'outsideness' as found in relations is central to the phenomenological project of the ageing self as situated in perceptions, circumstances, relationships and interactions that are patterned into our working lives. Of course, the outsideness of age-related perceptions or ideas is never just outside us, and relations mould how we engage, who fits where and when and well, and how we come to be orientated around others and by others. These relational binds coalesce to inform lines of aged recognition in composition with the ageing body, leading de Beauvoir to suggest that 'whether we like it or not, in the end we submit to the outsider's point of view' (1986 [1970]: 323).

Reaching out into the world encompasses an inevitable ontological quid pro quo and carries high stakes, given that modes of ageing disclosure often reverberate with a relational pull towards enclosure and a possible closing down, negating or limiting experience. Attention to the dialectics of disclosure and enclosure highlights how the relational demands of working through ageing often require a publicizing of the self that shatters the myth of a static age-based positionality or apartness of ageing; as de Beauvoir suggests, even 'by uprooting himself from the world, man makes himself present in the world and makes the world present to him' (2018 [1947]: 11). The interdependency required in most work-related tasks often precipitates this experience of relational disclosure experienced as 'a paradoxical operation in that one is always uprooting oneself from the world one remains rooted in' and that this is 'an ongoing process oriented to the future' (Arp, 2005: 398). Central to this is enclosure as a process that territorializes ageing relations, informing us in a palatable way how far we can tolerate difference within modes of relating and forewarning us of the cost and consequences of infringement within our everyday interactions. Enclosure might feel like an 'easier' way of receiving ageing relations and plays out through an organizational sociality that relies on trying to make ageing stable and safe, especially when our embodied experiences indicate change. At the same time, enclosure relies on relations that are contingent upon ideas of aged modes of value and worth. The costs of not complying require people to navigate subtle dynamics around what is allowed or disavowed in aged relations that themselves are connected to the totems of workplace or organizational points of recognition: a point of simultaneous connection or distinction in relations between ourselves, others and the context in which we work and compete.

Ageing relations are of course not passive, but require us to contend with the circulatory dynamics of how we are received, often in ways that hold an affective quality in how we yield *into* others in the context of work. Organizational relations are underpinned by a 'particular attitude toward embodied existence and its social formations/deformations' (Mann, 2012: 201); a delineation of different hierarchies, sociocultural orders or career-based assumptions. Our professional experiences are held together in the nexus of ageing, organizing and other socially sanctioned delineations and markers that we and others take up through choice, chance or compulsion in our working lives, and these are unextractable from the conditions of labour we tacitly accept when we start a job. At the same time, this requires a vulnerability around the possible negation that may come from taking up relations that rely on aged or aged-gendered shortcuts. We take up that new role, promotion or position where engaging and relating are necessary elements of work, but this happens at the expense of becoming an object for the majority of those you work with. This experience often intensifies as we grow older, whether due to the assumption of an age-based hierarchical seniority, or our lack of expected seniority.

For those working in professional settings where financialized capitalism remains the dominant logic, the economic and organizational conditions in which we might engage and relate with others in and around ageing at work mark out possibilities for how we recognize – or fail to recognize – the fecundity of ageing subjectivities within and across relations as intersectional. Relations compel a need to disclose the self under certain conditions that are read and received through age-pocked bodies. But the techniques that constitute ageing relations operate as points of affirmation or difference; they enable or constrain how we experience relations as aged-gendered and aged-classed bodies, *inter alia*. Here we see that 'it is not just that bodies are directed in specific ways, but that the world is shaped by the directions taken by some bodies more than others' (Ahmed, 2006: 159). It can also, of course, delimit opportunities for other more plural or expansive ways to relate to each other. Despite our best intentions, the particularity of our bodies as a public artefact can often delimit possibilities for doing otherwise. Attempts to do otherwise and carve out relations with colleagues that traverse different normative ageing relations are time-consuming, confronting and carry no promise of a fruitful and affirming connection. Even when we perform a relationality that attempts to break down difference – to try to do 'otherwise' in othering – enclosure makes it easy to sidestep confronting difference as a mode of normative disruption. As is the case with generations as a mode of disclosure, it reproduces uneven and value-laden ageing relations, even when that was not our intention.

Our desire to be connected with others as both an ontological necessity and an organizational demand also means we lean into new relations using normative aged patterns even when we know and acknowledge their unfairness, or know that such categories are imperfect in terms of mapping onto our own lived experience. As de Beauvoir suggests, our ageing relations are organized through a matrix of uneven sociality, particularly for women as they grew older. Notably, younger women felt compelled to temper their desire to get to know people and establish corporate relationships in ways they might wish out of fear that these attempts to open up and be intellectually and professionally interested could be misrecognized. In doing so, they were also aware of their own relations being conditional upon making others feel comfortable and not threatened. There is more than a hint of irony that #MeToo has not dismantled a form of emotional labour where young women were required to perform a mode of 'surplus nurturance' (Bartky, 1990: 101) to avoid potential harm to men's reputations. Elsewhere, the spectacular figure of the older woman performatively generated an aspirational position constituted through an 'othering by glorification' (van Dyk, 2016: 10) where midlife women's ability to detract from a norm is simultaneously celebrated and used to undermine evidence of systemic gender inequality, but is also considered inauthentic.

In sum, we can understand that the dialectics of ageing disclosure as 'reaching out' and aged enclosure as 'pushing back in' helps to understand how we experience being an ageing object-subject in relations. Disclosure-enclosure underpins the normative ageing apparatus that often neatly map onto relations of organizational power and hierarchy, which is unsurprising, given that these relations themselves were informed and shaped by life course expectations. Disclosure–enclosure allows difference to be acknowledged, but does so in a way that does not threaten or collapse chrononormative relations. This is particularly important against a corporate landscape in which acknowledging or expressing views on age always carries the danger of being viewed as ageist or discriminatory, and where connections and distinctions between bodies need to be subject to a corporate palatability that itself inscribes normative relations between different aged groups.

The particular power of aged enclosure lies in the way in which relations limit the reflexive potential of interactions and exchanges to become a means for openly exploring a plurality around ageing difference and change. Encouraging a singularity of ageing relations and experience is part of the machinery of temporal acquiescence that exists in organizations where time is a means of 'occluding historically embedded or structural inequalities' (Burke et al, 2023: 273). The ropes of relationality such as curiosity, generations and spectacularity shared by participants are orientated around a formatting of time as 'altered, modified, and differently structured' (Burke et al, 2023: 273) in ways that undermine the possibility of ageing to be anything other than singular, successful and never detracting from broader corporate logics. They become an embodied command; socialized into relations that deny systemic or widespread aged cultures, but set up as pragmatic ways of managing ambiguities around ageing and polite or affable ways for bodies to meet and mingle. They conveniently imprint onto different bodies by virtue of their affinity or relative distance with other bodies, experiences and hierarchies in the context of work. Unfortunately, our responses to disclosure and our desire for a sociality that propels disclosure can often mean we seek out ageing relations in work that carry the double-edge sword of providing a false promise of age-based stability, while sharpening the ontological precarity of being defined or marginalized through these relations, which can result in significant consequences for our careers.

However, unlike the rather fatalistic Beauvoirian idea of submitting 'in the end' to normative aged relations, there is the possibility of disturbing the organizational capture of aged normativity and a possibility for the normative enclosures of these relations to be disrupted or distorted. When we try to express our singularity in ageing relations – our uniqueness, or exceptionalism of being someone not recognized in the ageing relations in which we are initially received – we invariably become entangled and complicit in other people's projects to express the singularity of *their* ageing subjectivity. The tensions in this entanglement between our own and the other person's performative desire to connect while being recognized as a unique 'One' invariably puts a strain on normative ageing scripts. In fact, it may even allow us to recognize the contingency of normative scripts that enclose the dynamic experience of being an ageing subject. In other words, the acknowledgement that emerges in the need for mutual (albeit uneven) bonds has to come from our recognition of the experience of our dependence on the inconvenient singularity of others on the one hand, and, the inconvenience of ourselves as ageing subjects on the other, both of which will change over time. Such inconvenience as an ontological imperative in ageing never fully match makes our own embodied experience and reminds us that at some point, due to our dynamically situated ageing beinghood, we too might not match ourselves. Being in relation with others in working through ageing is about communality but not coevality, and being is agitated but never absolved by the rhythms of disclosure-enclosure as an embodied experience as we grow older in ourselves; a position we take up in the next chapter on working through the ageing self.

5

Grasping Ageing: Working Through the Ageing Self

Just like a parent, a researcher is not supposed to have 'favourites', but there are some people you meet over the course of a decade who you feel more intimately connected with, and whose conversations disrupt a lot of what you thought previously. Isla was one of those people. Despite having moved cities, occupations and lifestyle to work in a different sector far beyond the financial services, she was always the first to get back in touch and was one of the most enthusiastic about being re-interviewed. While our meetings involved dropping in and out of each other's lives every two years, we both enjoyed each other's company and as the years went on, our conversations became more involved about what ageing at work meant to us as women.

One evening in 2016, we met down by Southbank, close to Waterloo Station in London, for some Yum Cha. In some ways it was like a lot of the other interviews I was doing now; often in people's homes, in cafes or bars, or restaurants that were close to their large corporate offices. In comparison to the more formal settings I had been in that day, the relaxed but trendy atmosphere of the restaurant caught me off guard and I looked out of place with cut-off trousers and unstraightened hair dry shampooed into position, apologizing about clearly letting myself go, since we had last spoken. Isla smiled warmly and said: 'People talk about letting yourself go as if it's a catastrophe. But what are we so scared [about] holding on to? There are benefits to letting yourself go.'

Isla's courteous comment was by no means a banal aside, but was an insight into part of a curation of what she later described the 'exciting, weird kind of direction my life's going in'. As we sat down to our meal, we continued to talk about what was lost and found as we became older, zigzagging across in a discussion that meandered its way through reflections on our changing bodies, other people's expectations about our careers and our ongoing experiences of casual sexism. Then, as we went in for the second course, Isla got up for the bathroom, saying: 'Of course, thinking about ageing too much can age you. It's what I saw with this friend. She was just worked up understandably.' As I continued to fiddle with my dumplings, aware that at the age of 36 I still couldn't use chopsticks properly, I wondered if she was right: ageing might be a biological hazard in terms of where it invariably ends, but is it also an existentially dangerous one: so close and intimate to ourselves that to linger or think about it for too long is itself a painful occupation? And in what way might this pain allow or prevent us holding on or let go of ourselves as we grow older in and through work?

To pause and reflect on this feeling of ageing as an ambivalent, ambiguous and sometimes painful experience of the self, this chapter explores how we work through ageing as interpenetrated in the self–other–setting nexus. While we are always part of relations in a given context, as the previous chapter focused on, coming to terms with the ageing self is central to what de Beauvoir (1986 [1970]: 313) calls a 'final synthesis' of the lived experience of ageing. This final synthesis is premised on recognizing oneself as simultaneously being an object of ageing and subject who ages. In other words, our experience of ageing is realized through the interlocking processes of our relationship with our bodies, our experience of time passing, and the corporeal reverberation of how others in the world relate to us melds into us over time.

To pull at the seams of this synthesis, I draw on the figure of 'grasping' to guide a story of working through ageing as a situated project of the self. Grasping is a figure that runs throughout de Beauvoir's account of the phenomenological condition. It seeks to render visible the mutuality of taking up and comprehending the world. The complexity of this term is recognized within broader accounts of phenomenology. For example, Donald Landes, translator of Merleau-Ponty's *Phenomenology of Perception*, discusses his use of terms such as 'l'engrenage' and 'en prise', which literally means 'in gear' and figuratively means 'attuned to'. But is also connected to the verb 'prendre', which means 'to take or hold', with 'la prise meaning to grip or hold' (Landes in Merleau-Ponty, 2014: 497). Like Merleau-Ponty, de Beauvoir emphasizes how a similar sentiment of grasping is fundamental to the melding of the individual and social in the constitution of sociality, stating that 'the individual is conditioned by society's theoretical [in the French edition this is 'ideologique'] and practical attitude towards him' (de Beauvoir, 1986 [1970]: 15). This is not just about empirical perception, as shown in de Beauvoir's discussion of attitude in earlier work such as *The Ethics of Ambiguity* (2018 [1947]), but rather is part of the 'insoluble contradiction' (de Beauvoir, 1986 [1970]: 323) of being an object–subject. As such, grasping as part of the ontological modus operandi of working through ageing speaks to the inextricable and formative connection between self and society. To grasp age is therefore to both state one's intentions and generate a hold on the world that (hopefully) will in turn recognize our legitimacy as an ageing subject in ways we desire. As such, it involves a necessity of the self to 'disclose the world with the purpose of further disclosure', as discussed in the previous chapter, and 'by the same movement try to free men, by means of whom the world takes on meaning' (de Beauvoir, 2018 [1947]: 79).

At the same time, grasping ageing is a very practical project. When we think about ourselves as ageing subjects, we are both reaffirming our own identity and maintaining our own hold on the world in a very concrete sense through the ways we belong to or 'fit in' with the world in a given context. It is a continual process of alignment and calibration of who we feel we are, how the world sees us and receives us, and, importantly, how we are recognized and accepted. This becomes challenging when we consider how ageing plays out through the dynamically situated self and our own temporally charged bodies. The inevitable but unpredictable aspects of change relating to ageing thus mean that grasping is a complex and thoroughly ambivalent experience. On the one hand, ageing as a mode of grasping speaks to a desire for us to 'hold on to' something: as will be discussed later on, this may be staying aligned with favourable age-based aspirations and identifications as valorized in the landscape of working lives. Yet, on the other hand, grasping as one ages sits uneasily with a desire to know 'me' as that older self and the possibilities that accompany this: a 'me' in all its plurality; an older One that may have been previously viewed as Other; or even an 'alien', as suggested by de Beauvoir (1986 [1970]: 321).

To consider the variegated ways in which we grasp ageing, I return to Isla's conundrum about holding on and letting go in order to explore what is it about organizational and economic settings that render working through ageing such a complex project of the self. I begin by discussing how the trope of successful ageing is underpinned by a certain unrealizability in the individual experience, but nonetheless something that enables and constrains the dynamically situated ageing self via different market and social forces. I then turn to consider how the situated self is rendered more or less coherent within work and life course trajectories. The latter part of the chapter then examines the lived experience of grasping ageing as a project of continual recalibration and one that provides insight into the alterity of ageing and its possibilities for affirmative encounters. In particular, I reflect on how the generative potential for grasping ageing moves away from a possessive modality to one of surprise, providing a way for living in and with an ageing 'otherhood' as an ontoepistemological experience in which 'alterity no longer has a hostile character' (de Beauvoir, 2015 [1949]: 678).

Grappling with successful ageing

For many participants, working in the hedge fund sector involved an active socialization into banking being an anti-vocation; hedge fund occupations were by no means a type of work you were vocationally 'destined' to do, nor perceived as having significant currency in terms of societal 'good'. But this did not mean that work at HFUK was devoid of a soul; rather, the main interlocutor for meaning around work was money and this manifested in several ways: profit as immediate performance targets, high remuneration as an expectation and the ability to procure and secure a comfortable future. However, rather than being a brute signifier, financial security was not simply a material aspiration, but was elevated to being central in curating a self that can 'endure'. This enduring self could thrive in the unpredictability of the markets, tolerate the capricious but very wealthy clients, and ride out economic downturns or organizational shocks while maintaining financial, social and individual value: an ever-resilient self that can withstand and continually produce and respond consistently over time to the unrelenting demands of financial capitalism.

Such narratives neatly intertwine with the 'successful ageing' paradigm: a grand narrative emerging from gerontology synonymous with countering and controlling and age-related notion of physical and cognitive decline as informed by a broader 'active ageing' discourse (see Moulaert and Biggs, 2013). Despite this approach being critiqued for occluding structural modes of inequality, successful ageing has stretched into the moral economy of work, and the subsequent professional playbook on 'how to age' is also about succeeding or failing in terms of how we grow older in ways that can be measured both internally and externally.

In the context of the financial services sector, this notion of clear and unambiguous measurement around how to age well sits comfortably with many of those I spoke to, who used chronologically based proxies to consider economic capacity or potential. Discussions included many references to when their own economic capacity was conditional or not conditional on a particular age-based benchmark. Ronnie, who worked on the more technical side of the markets, suggested that passing for neither older nor younger was important in terms of *exposure* during market downturns:

> I'm in an age sweet spot where I'm not young enough so people think 'just get rid of him', but I'm not old enough as well and earning so much money that 'oh, we've got to go for him because he's costing us this much'. I'm in the middle bit and I think that's very fortunate, actually. Maybe the safest place at the moment, where I have experience – I mean, I earn a decent chunk, but I'm not outrageously paid. (Ronnie, 2012, Y2)

Similarly, Jack, an operations expert who we met in the previous chapter, recognized that while everyone ages, there was also a 'sweet spot' where age was not a hindrance to labour market prospects. He returned to this idea over the course of our time together, reflecting on how he was moving further and further away from this spot each time we met:

> We all change as we get older, but I suppose, if you like, the sweet spot, where you're not that old, you know, everything seems to be coming together and you're getting to an age were ... I would say middle to late 30s would be a nice age to stay at. (Jack, 2010, Y0)

In our first follow-up conversation, Harry (2012, Y2) similarly referred to a '"goldilocks age"' where 'you know something but are not old enough to be a bitter twisted divorcee who hates his job'. This moment of chronologically marked privilege was around a number. And Jack's parameters of mid- to late 30s was shared by others, even those who moved out of the financial services and into diverse but still white-collar professional jobs. This moment was pivotal rather than incidental to many men I spoke to, representing a somewhat less risky launchpad for making a big step up in their careers or earning potential. However, apart from Ronnie, people rarely suggested that they themselves were 'living' through a period of age-based security. In other words, while some ages may be associated with having a tighter grip in terms of success and security in the labour market, it was not accompanied by any broader feeling of comfort or security about themselves when located there. When I later suggested this idea of any age being an impossible but always-aspirational 'perfect', Harry associated this with being part of the broader seduction of working in a heavily financially incentivized sector and that to assume that there was a possibility of the perfect job was a myth. He explained as follows:

Harry: I don't think it's about there ever being a lucky time of life. It's more that you are continually made to feel unsteady – there is usually talk of a takeover, a fuck-up in the markets, then problems with parenting, interest rates on mortgages. There's always the feeling that round the corner [there is] something to knock you off balance.

Kat: You mean always the danger of being out of kilter?

Harry: Yeah, I guess you could say so. Not a sense of doom, but more that you need to be aware. And there's a good chance that this is more significant as you get older.

Kat: Why do you say that?

Harry: That's a good question. I'm not sure. Maybe you've just got more skin in the game ... the game of life ... that's why my body's fucked. (Laughs)

Harry is by no means a pessimist, but his reference to 'skin in the game of life' is evocative in terms of recognizing the needling of insecurity endemic in the financial services sector. During the years that followed, Harry explained that 'hanging on' to success became more pressing, altering how he felt about himself as 'your need to work gets more serious' (2018, Y8). This was in material terms, but also regarding a sense of self being a successful employee, partner, homeowner or provider for family members – or at least a 'good enough' one.

Ageing in a sector where good fortunes are expected yet elusive manifested in a low level but constant sense of unease, borne out of an angst concerning financial failure (or lack of financial success). Being 'knocked off kilter', as Harry discussed, is situated in a broader desire to maintain a hold on to a successful sense of self against a backdrop of expecting fewer opportunities or 'diminishing returns', as Ronnie put it, as you get older. This was very clear from my first discussion with Liam, who worked on the more technical side of trading, having started his career at an global financial institution following a private school and university education. This exclusive background as setting down a blueprint for success might be assumed to have provided a cushion or certain degree of biographically-based comfort, but was also central in making Liam very aware of a 'countdown ticking away in terms of securing returns' that diminished as he grew older:

> When you're in your early 20s, all of your earned incomes in the future – the money – is very much a replenishable resource; it felt like you could be reasonably sure you were going to earn a reasonable amount of money in the future. The point is that the fraction of your earnings which are behind you becomes larger and the fraction of your earnings which are ahead of you becomes smaller, and therefore every day money becomes less of a replenishable resource. So basically, your savings – if you suffer some loss, like you crash the car and you have to buy a new one or you spend money on a holiday which is not an asset – it's just gone. Your ability to replenish that money falls every day, whereas when you're in your 20s and 30s, it feels like it grows every day. And now those years are behind me. (Liam, 2012, Y2)

Part of this was borne out of working – and living – by an economic logic that percolated around discussions of risk. Given that much of the technical work in the financial services is built upon developing, profiling and seeking advantages through negotiating various elements of risk, this vocabulary was close to hand when discussing growing older as aligned with a decreasing capacity to take on risk. This was in part due to the structuring of responsibilities and obligations associated with a normative life course trajectory, such as mortgages, children's school fees, becoming the main wage earner in the family or fees for elderly care. Across our discussions, Liam talked about how 'I'm more risk-averse with everything' (2014, Y4) and how 'going through that experience, essentially trying to find a job, finding it rather more difficult than I thought it was going to be, was quite an eye-opening experience. It makes you a bit risk averse' (2016, Y6).

However, this also presented a conundrum. An age-situated disposition to risk sat alongside the need for career progression that required a leap and feeling less secure in one's capability or capacities. Ronnie was one of many people who explained to me that 'in order to be able to leave something worthwhile, you have to take a few risks as well' (2012, Y2). Taking risks could destabilize or slacken one's feeling of safety, security and skill, but could also result in higher pay or better conditions. For example, just over halfway through our decade of conversations, Liam had left a permanent job to collaborate with some people forming a start-up in the hope that it might lead to significant success. Similarly, Riley, who had moved to the UK for his first job subsequently made a move abroad to help solidify success and financial security through relocating where markets were seen as more fruitful and the cost of living afforded a better lifestyle for his children. Taking these kinds of 'leaps' was framed as a riskier career strategy than more gradual or incremental moves but was also seen as likely to have higher returns. Importantly, they needed to be timed against the backdrop of an ageist culture within financial services.

At the same time, these risks were not just about material returns, but were also about curating a career that could last without forsaking other parts of life: growing older was a project that involved calibrating in terms of work-proofing and life-proofing. During our last interview together, Riley reflected on how normatively successful careers paths were beginning to feel incompatible with who he aspired to be as he grew older. At the same time, he felt the need to have a work orientation in order to allow himself to continue feeling valued:

> I think I've matured a bit in the sense that I think when you are younger, you've got all these dreams and things, but you don't actually understand what it means to get to that level and to take on that responsibility. With extra responsibility comes extra time away from your family and things like that and I've just realized like what am I content with? But what is enough? (Riley, 2020, Y10)

Engaging with these typologies of successful, risk-oriented modes of ageing was incumbent on securing a future self that intersected with other important biographical experiences. Compared to Liam, Dylan had a working-class background and had begun his career in IT programming, but then went on to be a contractor as well as build up a property portfolio. He discussed taking risk as commensurate with success, but in our later interviews reflected on how he was aware that he often had to consciously counter his own hesitations around debt to secure what would be recognized as financial success by his peers, even though this involved different standards from those he grew up with:

> If you're not willing to take the risk, or you come from a working-class background or middle class, or whatever the class that it is you're in, most people aren't in a position to take risks and set up their own company and do their own thing. They look at what's the most money I can earn and with the least amount of risk. Financial services is that, that's the thing where you will earn your most money. (Dylan, 2020, Y10)

Ronnie similarly connected his experience of growing older with a decreasing appetite for risk that he equated with a decreasing feeling of 'being immortal', compounded through tragedies and deaths of friends or significant others. In discussing his own career, Ronnie combined sports injuries, illnesses and career setbacks as part of a compounding feeling of being 'more exposed if things go wrong':

> The knocks along the way take their toll and you do start to feel more vulnerable. That is the same as the knocks your body has, colds take a little longer to get over, or you become more aware of not being able to do things or becoming more cautious. And feed into a bit of a hazard in the job as well, where you have to have steel in making decisions. (Ronnie, 2020, Y10)

Becoming more vulnerable or 'exposed' within an occupational environment with an avarice for risk was not simply about balancing time-had and time-to-go in career decisions, but also about feeling connected to the labour market – and ensuring that the labour market wanted to stay connected with you. Many discussed various techniques and strategies around this connection that centred on demonstrating value and relevance as they grew older. However, the career biographies of many of those who stayed within the financial services were often marked by an irresolvable tension. On the one hand, they needed to maintain a strong enough 'hold' on a professional credibility so that they could demonstrate a sustained track record of competence and labour market value. On the other hand, they had to continually show both a potential and a futurity that was not marked or tarnished by the past through, for example, being associated with a firm that went bust or failed. Being able to embody the paradoxical tensions between 'potential versus experience' was even more complicated when experience and potential were mercurial commodities dependent on one's job status, location in the hierarchy or position in the life course.

Recognizing this 'potential-experience' seesaw as lived through an embodied positionality required a dexterity and agility to shift one's position, effectively loosening (but not completely losing) one's previously held 'grip' on the labour market – or, as Liam put it, 'staying relevant' and being recognized as successful felt contingent on 'the amount of grey I have'. Henry similarly experienced this as a juxtaposition of past achievements that led to promotion or specialisms and a closing-off of the potential to do something different in one's career. He felt that each new step into a job or a promotion carried greater weight in terms of being somewhere he wanted to be:

> I've got a career in this field, so what's the point in being stuck in something which I don't know if I like. But do I want to be where I'm not doing what I want to do? And there's a pain that you're getting old, because you haven't thought about it before ... Because you now just think 'oh, that's never going to happen again'. Whereas when you're young, though, it's like 'what's next?' (Henry, 2014, Y4)

Leo, one of the traders who had stayed within the financial services, was more pragmatic, in part because he felt the need to financially support his wife, who was retraining. He discussed this balance between potential and experience as vital when thinking about 'the right time' to make formative career decisions that worked for him:

> As you get older you think about it more, in that what you're looking to achieve, what your experience says and when's the right time to maybe move somewhere else and make a jump or stay here and see what happens and that kind of thing. And obviously as you get older your options traditionally will decrease. (Leo, 2010, Y0)

For Leo, leveraging experience was relative to the context and age make up of a sector rather than a 'fact' of older chronological age, highlighting the fallacy of 'experience' being a catch-all North star of value associated with older workers. Over the years, Leo realized that leveraging his experience required extending into different occupational spaces. For example, thinking about where skills he had learned in the financial services might be viewed as valuable had led to him diversifying into 'thought leadership' more broadly. He discussed this in terms of balancing out 'evidence' of his experience with 'potential' in terms of insight and more general market forecasting rather than the actual 'doing' of trading. Alongside this was negotiating a shapeshifting professional identity across different positions and spaces in the labour market, hoping that he could find a synchronicity between what the market wanted, what he wanted and his own capacities that orientated around an older professional persona.

Others were more circumspect about losing this grip as the result of simultaneously growing older and career moves, or redundancies. James, who had retrained during his late 40s, also spoke about the anxiety that a jump across jobs could bring about in terms of not being able to rely on an assumed, accumulated bundle of job-specific experience, which was exacerbated by 'looking older and as if I should know what I am doing': 'You get the job and of course it's a great thing, but it is a stress. Right, I've got it, I've got to prove myself somewhere else now, in a new career and being this age as well' (James, 2012, Y2).

Situated in a job, company or career that provided normative interlocutors of success relating to salary or status was also conditional on an interplay between an individual's own biographically embodied inhabitation and the way in which it was recognized as a commodity in the labour market. In other words, bodies are read in terms of how much they could give, how strained they become when performing, or how long they have left. For all that short-term results and numerical bottom lines were made to matter as a proxy for performance, the 'product' of labour within financial services is often highly abstracted and nebulous. This makes the ageing body, as a carrier of time and longevity, highly conspicuous – a 'thing' that could be a focus in lieu of the absence of other things. Bodies became objectified; a canvas from which value could be assumed. This was further exacerbated through an aggressive feeling of diminishing opportunity for credibly projecting one's potential.

Such tensions in grasping through the experience of ageing were further foiled through a broader apparatus of complicity that discouraged participants to associate or recognize their own ageing trajectories as neither an inevitability or holding much merit or being important. This was not simply about ageist stereotypes or perceptions, but underpinned expectations of a normative economic rhythm to one's career and expectations around success over the working life course. Yet while this rhythm was assumed to be the norm, it was rarely lived as a personal guarantee. Instead, a variety of common events invariably put people 'off track' and destabilized an expected sense of stability in ageing, leading to individuals questioning themselves and their actions. Such derailments not only required planning to try and mitigate the effects of these episodes, but also required a disposition that could perform an ability to draw on professionally valued resources such as Charles' reference to 'fortitude to weather the storms' in terms of a stoic endurance. However, maintaining integrity and credibility when negotiating this economic rhythm was also contingent on people's experience of being positioned as gendered temporal subjects, as discussed next.

Temporal gaslighting

Time can play tricks on the self. As de Beauvoir (2006 [1965]: 3) herself suggests, 'its very hard to review one's past without cheating a little'.

Such cheating can be seen as a response to a temporally induced destabilization of the self through disconnecting and severing previous or projected modes of recognition, and for participants, this was constituted in particularly gendered forms. For the women I spoke to, time conspired in ways that instilled a sense of gendered mistrust about giving credibility to previous or projected biographies, which manifested in what might be understood as a form of temporal gaslighting. I define 'temporal gaslighting' here as moments or experiences where people are called into questioning their own retrospective (memories or recollections of events, interactions or experiences) or prospective (plans, ambitions, expectations or aspirations) in ways that undermine the possibility or integrity of a coherent ageing subjectivity. Often this manifested through an obligation to comply with how others presented prospective predictions of their future, resulting in a self-questioning or feelings of distrust around their own ideas, subsequently shaping career trajectories.

Willow, who worked for a global financial services firm before coming to HFUK, recounted several times when experiences of such temporal gaslighting sought to undermine her own experiences of interactions or exchanges. Even when she moved to a more senior role in an economic think tank where she felt valued by most of her colleagues, she was often questioned or overlooked by others outside the immediate team. During one conversation, we discussed one meeting with clients:

> They just talked over me or looked bored when I spoke. And about a few months, about six months later, when they came in again, I said to Riley 'I bet that happens again' and he said 'Are you sure? I don't remember that, remember how they took on your idea about xxx'. And then I thought 'did I misread the situation? Was I just overreacting?' (Willow, 2012, Y2)

Willow recognized that Riley was trying to make her feel better and encourage her not to dwell on the interaction, but this also fed into an uncertainty about her capacity to both recall and read situations. Other women also shared times when they had disclosed experiences, only for colleagues to dismiss them as innocuous or incidental. Ivy, who later left the financial services to start her own business, discussed how she was always aware of never fully being trusted, even though she had come from a similar background to other male colleagues, suggesting that 'I think they just think I'm a bit of an idiot, to be honest, I think that's probably my age'. Others were often cautious about publicly discussing being treated differently due to being a woman, but one did share her colleagues' reactions about her memory of an afterwork event: 'You don't want to say anything immediately but it doesn't feel good when it's dismissed as "oh the City's changed so much since then", or "I've never seen that happen". But when you might look back, you did feel uncomfortable and it did happen.'

Similarly, women's formative life course events were often dismissed or erased from discussions about trajectories. At the same time, people had to contend with a contracted organizational lifespan of 'counting' achievements that might carry a memorialized form of capital. For example, Willow discussed how past job successes as well as justifying the impact of other life events such as illness, deaths or childbirth had a noticeably short 'shelf life' for being used to legitimize a deviation from a normative career path. Gen also discussed the noticeable short-term memory of organizations, where the impact for maternity on careers was very quickly forgotten or undermined:

I think the pressure is trying to prove, trying to act as though you haven't had a baby and still do everything exactly the same, as though, you know, it's just … It's like you've got a puppy at home and it's not like any difference … I'm very conscious of not talking about them [her baby] that much. (Gen, 2012, Y2)

In suggesting that there was a 'short window' of time when past experiences could be held as credible reasons for discussing their position at work, Gen shared an exchange where people were describing their experiences of having children. She listened on as men corrected women's accounts, wryly recalling how one woman had shared her experience from a few years back, which was then dismissed by a colleague: 'After she had shared her experience, he said "that's funny because I didn't experience it that way at all". I was like "I bet your wife did"' (Gen, 2018, Y8).

This became even more notable during the COVID-19 pandemic. While both men and women discussed how supportive their workplaces had been in dealing with their need to work around childcare during the pandemic, even when interviewing immediately after lockdown, many women discussed how there was little space to discuss longer-term COVID-19-related challenges that caring responsibilities had brought about, or how their own sense of confidence or ambition might have changed or dwindled in relation to work. Just after the initial COVID-19 lockdowns, Lily discussed how many women around her were having to deal with the aftermath of COVID-19, creating ongoing additional pressures that did not seem to apply to her male colleagues and friends:

It's not just the times of struggling just to do enough to survive at work while home-schooling, but she's [her friend] set back compared to the men around her [who] can just hop back on the career path, but she is still having to deal with children who missed two years of schooling, need extra help, and one is also particularly anxious and is almost a school refuser. It's her dealing with this. (Lily, 2020, Y10)

Discussions around prospective maternity were also a common site for temporal gaslighting. Here, younger women were encouraged to hold a distrust around their own future projections and capacities to predict how they might feel or work in the future. For Flo, this revolved around people suggesting she would want children 'when the time comes'. Even though she remained thoroughly ambivalent about having children over the years I spoke to her, she discussed the constant demand for her choice to be publicly shared and articulated in both personal and professional spaces. It was this constant draw towards being made to think about children rather than the decision itself that shaped her own narrative. During our conversations, she often discussed how she would 'check in with herself' at points to see if the 'feeling' others had suggested she would inevitably have had arrived, only seeming to believe herself in later years. This 'knowing' was both a response to, and a way of countering, temporal gaslighting – confirming you 'believed' yourself and a reminder that she knew best:

> If I never have kids, that's entirely fine. There's plenty to do. Just knowing what makes me happy. And that's why I truly now feel I can take it or leave it. Back then I used to say that and almost didn't quite believe it, but now, looking back on having found all these things to do, it's confirmed – yes, confirmed is the word that I want. You know, when you would normally think, 'yes, I think I think that way', but I've never had any confirmation of it, so how do I really know. (Flo, 2018, Y8)

Others who had discussed having children in earlier interviews and subsequently went on to become parents also discussed the advice colleagues had provided as shaping their own maternity. Lucy, who worked in one of the support functions (sometimes called the 'back-office' roles) at HFUK, had experienced challenges in getting back on a similar career trajectory after having children. In discussing a crisis in confidence around work, she highlighted a tension of feeling that she should appreciate the helpful advice people gave her to 'futureproof' her career, while also making her own decisions about having a child. At the same time, she was adamant that she did not want becoming a stereotypical 'working mum' to be part of a future identity, which also seemed to carry a stigma for others. Given the persistent structural barriers and cultural perceptions relating to working with motherhood, Lucy recognized that much of this pragmatic advice might have been valuable. Yet it also encouraged her and others to make decisions on job changes, promotions and her professional trajectory based primarily on a possible parenthood rather than career ambitions or strategies to increase salary – elements that dominated male participants' discussions at similar levels or stages of their career.

Ava, who moved from professional services into business development, similarly discussed in early interviews how she was irritated, but tried not to show it when people suggested that she did not know how she would feel about her career after children. At the same time, she was also annoyed at herself for letting pressure around a projected maternalism influence how she felt:

I feel as if there's some urgency to reproduce because I'm at that age and a lot of it is also the herd mentality, because a lot of my friends are now with children and I think 'Oh God, have I missed out on something?' and it doesn't really help when you get in that state of mind. Then you're always conscious of your age I think. (Ava, 2010, Y0)

Ava subsequently had a long and complex fertility journey. A few years later, she reflected on having a lack of trust about being able to predict her own future that she connected to how to predict when and where she should be in her career. This compared to her husband's trajectory, which she characterized as 'wholly predictable – almost to the point of being boring', even though he too was part of this fertility experience. Such discussions reflected a broader narrative for women where the public assumption that they would want and could have children was both an ambivalent and unsettling prospect often governed by others suggesting everything changing in their careers (through becoming a parent), or everything changing in their personal lives through nothing changing (in terms of not being able to have children):

There's sometimes no point being so caught up by it [the future]. Because I think it's difficult, as a woman. I don't know how you find it, but it's a case of just this expectation, somehow, that you'll be able to be a mother and that's what you want. And it's the natural assumption that that's what you want. But it may not be the case; you might prefer to be working and you have to think about progressing. And I've spent three hours babysitting someone's baby on Tuesday and I thought, 'Jesus, this is exhausting'. And the thing is, if they're your own, you don't have the option to turn off. You just have to be there. (Ava, 2014, Y4)

Projected or actual maternity as an experiential site of temporal gaslighting for female professionals operated alongside broader experiences of being discouraged to trust themselves and their plans or curation of prior experiences. Isla, who we met at the beginning of the chapter, was very clear that being childless were neither delusional nor about wanting children as part of her life in some way. At the same time, she was frustrated that these views were often misread by colleagues and those around her.

During one interview, she shared how she had sought out a similar community at an event on childlessness:

> I'm childless by choice. I'm not obviously talking about … A lot of the talk I went to, actually, it wasn't what you might think: 'Oh, kids, that's not something for me.' Amazingly, it was quite a bunch of women who were positive about childbearing and the place that that has in society. (Isla, 2014, Y4)

Isla suggested that normative coupling was often assumed in the financial services 'as a conservative work sector', and was underpinned by a projected equality that still had to result in uninterrupted normative biographies. She mentioned that 'you can now be gay – even gay! – as long as you are a cute long-term couple'. The compulsion to be recognized as following a path towards monogamous coupling then children was felt as part of a broader constriction of Isla's own ambition to find out what she wanted to be and do. In describing how she fought hard not to be pushed into a future that was just laid out for her, she discussed how easy it was to slip back into being the 'good girl' and let others assume where she wanted to go or what she should do with her career:

> I feel like my life has been messy, in my part. I mean fortunately there's not been that many shocks to my life, but I think I've kind of been on a journey finding out what I'm really good at and I kind of feel if I'd – I don't mean this in a oh, I really regret … but I kind of feel like women need to have that time when they're growing up to really explore possible avenues to them and find the thing that really makes them tick because then if you have a workforce that found what they're best at then they'll go off and they'll do that job very well and then everyone benefits. And I think that's kind of why – I feel that's why my life has been so pre-planned because I've never had that space to do that. (Isla, 2016, Y6)

Lily similarly suggested that the footprints created by a 'good girl' expectation early on in life had consequences for women being undermined when trying to mark out their career and life paths. This compared with the way in which some men she knew not only assumed they knew best but benefited from not being questioned by others. Flo similarly spoke about how men were afforded more freedom to carve out their future. Across our time together, Flo connected this to part of a fear of women not being liked, which she had witnessed in previous workplace relationships. Yet she also emphasized how 'a healthy way to grow older' for her meant regaining a sense of her own self through rejecting this socialized compulsion.

Shedding a prescriptive good girl narrative was not only an important counter against projective temporal gaslighting, but something that crisscrossed over difference age-based intersections. For example, Isla suggested that her middle-class schooling had been formative in assuming that following a plan was a virtuous approach to life, while Flo discussed how: 'When I was an undergrad, I wanted people to like me. That's an Asian girl thing, very much an Asian girl thing. Maybe it's even a girl thing. Now, I don't give a monkey's.'

In many ways, the gendered undertones upon which temporal gaslighting was modelled relied on a broader mode of experience of women that de Beauvoir (2015 [1949]: 566) terms an anticipated or projected 'future passivity'. Temporal gaslighting demands that women present their own past or future expectations as untrustworthy reference points rather than sources of validity or ontological coherence. This means having to contend with publicly negotiating who they are in ways that undermined attempts to cohere a professional identity over time. Much of the time, this involved a paralysis of becoming viewed as a 'proper' grown up, and instead being deferential, pliable and always open to receiving the views of others, even when those views curtail autonomy, complying with a normative femininity that requires women to 'realise herself as passivity, to accept dependence' (de Beauvoir, 2015 [1949]: 571). An assumption that women hand over authority of what they were in the past or wanted to be in the future was not only tedious but also frustrated the means through which they could explore a sense of coherence in their own ageing identities and venture into opportunities that felt more of their own making.

The anachronism of ageing aftershocks

A lot of the time, talking about the ageing self is subject to the social rituals of small talk that follows a common script. It starts with a joke or casual aside such as 'it's the one thing you can be sure of besides taxes and death', 'the alternative is a lot worse' or 'terrible thing, glad I don't have to worry about it'. It then often evolves into a deflection onto the researcher or second person through, for example, asking why I might be personally interested in ageing given that I was so young (I should note that this is less common now compared to when I was in my 20s). Finally, it usually lands on a 'one-time' story about the perils of ageing: a fable of the unexpected dangers around ageing, but always focusing on that something happening to someone else. The way in which these accounts begin is often as something 'beyond the norm': the exception or the out-of-the-ordinary of what is seen as an otherwise uneventful process of ageing completely separate to their own impervious sense of self. Yet there is always something unfinished, lingering and discomforting left hanging in the air.

It is easy to dismiss these interactions as age-related platitudes: things people say and share as a form of social lubrication or to defer or detract from a 'real' conversation about what ageing is and means to them in all its fecundity. But rather than simply a warm-up to the real business of working through ageing, they are central to the incompleteness of the ageing self that we articulate about ourselves in the everyday. A discussion between the traders one quiet Wednesday afternoon was indicative of this, when they were recalling someone who had been diagnosed with cancer just over six months after retiring: 'He was only about 56 and for that to happen is just a shock/He looked after himself, in the gym, in the last few years you rarely saw him in the pub/It makes you think, you don't have forever/That's the tragedy' (fieldnotes, 2010; new speaker is marked with an oblique symbol).

This is even more important as the events and episodes the traders recall are not the exception. Most people I spoke to over the course of the ten years of the project had a seismic life course event that had signficantly impacted where, how, and the terms under which, they experienced growing up and older. While ageing itself was rarely the initial point of reference in these experiences, it was central in the reverberations of how people began to make sense of life events. These 'ageing aftershocks' triggered significant logistical planning in terms of reflecting on financial, lifestyle or personal circumstances, but also compelled a reckoning with an assumption of a complete and whole self that is expected to remain the same – or even solidify – as we grow older.

In a workplace setting, ageing aftershocks are characterized by an anachronistic modality where one feels 'out of time' in terms of what one's self or others expect. Anachronism as an out-of-timeness takes hold of us through an uncomfortable awareness of our surroundings, relations and how our situated embodiment becomes questionable rather than taken for granted. Living through a feeling of corporeal discrepancy disrupts a perceptual norm that has otherwise leaned towards an epistemological assumption of a static rather than dynamic (ageing) body. Yet it is also constituted in the awareness of an external witnessing of the ageing self as a gaze that we often try to premeditate or deny. For example, when I met people after two-year breaks between interviews, unsolicited comments were common regarding 'getting a little thinner on top' (Ronnie) or 'emulating a silver fox look' (Jack). It was as if the research process itself was part of what was ageing them; holding up a mirror to their bodies and experiences that both demanded justification and compelled them to re-place themselves in the time and place of our current interview vis-à-vis our previous encounters.

Ageing aftershocks as a mode of ontological anachronism were both wholly unexpected but also common. They rarely orbited around explicit age-related event as we might imagine, such as the predictability of a birthday or work anniversary, or even more stereotypical but socially sanctioned totems such as 'mid-life crises'. Rather, it was more likely nestled in health, career or family setbacks, or when other events rendered visible the workplace environment as unsympathetic to their ageing bodies. People were compelled to make sense of both the initial incident, such as the experience of illness or recovery, and to deal with the aftershocks or subsequent impacts that stretched into their lives more broadly. One of the most significant examples of this was Riley, who, two years into the study, was going for blood tests, magnetic resonance imaging (MRIs) and a lumber puncture to try to identify some ongoing health concerns that started suddenly during 'two weeks where I was sick. I couldn't walk. I was like gone' (Riley, 2012, Y2). Symptoms had been on and off for several years and Riley spoke about the disquieting experience of never really knowing what caused them. For example, he discussed how 'they [doctors and specialists] cannot put their finger on it', which was still the case a few years later when he said: 'They [the doctors] know it's neurological, but they cannot pinpoint it' (2016, Y6). This intermingled with becoming more aware of his body than before and capacity to age in the way he desired:

> When I had this illness, I could see in my body that I'm not as toned as I used to be. I don't know if it's related – it is definitely related to the illness – but it's quite difficult to get out of bed in the morning. I know it's the illness and it's getting older, but you feel, especially in wintertime, a bit more stiffness. (Riley, 2020, Y10)

An embodied unknowing altered Riley's approach to work, partly due to physical necessity and limited energy, which prompted him to try and avoid working as though he was 'just wishing for the weekend'. At the same time, there was an undercurrent of comparing himself to the career progression of his peers where 'it feels like I'm being left behind and when I look at my friends I feel that they are going forward. In that same breath, my wife and I say that my friends don't see their kids often'. This comparison was one reason why he downplayed his health experiences to colleagues with what he called a 'normal line' that would prevent further questioning: 'Even walking – sometimes people ask "why are you limping?" I don't feel as if I'm limping, but I know my walking is a bit … But my normal line is everything feels fine. From up here I'm fine. It's just my legs and so on.'

This 'normal line' was important for Riley chronicling his ageing experience as not impinging on work and echoed how other respondents referred to illnesses. Here the need for a standard 'line' became performative in providing some stability or semblance of continuity in everyday encounters against the backdrop of carrying the weight of a more ambiguous health condition. However, even when Riley was reflecting on his illness in the confidence of our interview, he disclosed how important it was for him to 'get something' valuable from the experience. One way he did this was through calling on age-inscribed virtues. For example, he suggested that his health experience had provided him with an intimately felt 'early warning' about looking after your body as you grow older and the opportunity to have a better feeling of serenity about the future:

> I'm a very patient man. It doesn't come naturally yet and I'm struggling with that a lot but I'm now more – I think I was a bit obsessed when I was younger about 'oh will this happen now, will this happen now?' But now I'm a bit – I think I've learned to be calmer because you learn a lot in waiting. You learn so many things in waiting. (Riley, 2020, Y10)

Others felt compelled to feel they had learned something from forced health experiences, or at least had not 'wasted' them as an opportunity to reflect on aspects of their lives that they felt had got lost in the busyness of work and life. For example, losing parents or close relatives could trigger a reassessment their work-life balance or make them more aware of their own mortality. Even when such events were not related to work, they still had the potential to destabilize desires to fall into line with a coherent and consistent professional identity. One participant, who is anonymized here, discussed how his father dying meant having to reckon with different aspects of who he was and how fragmented he had become. Part of this was attributed to his working-class background and how this contrasted with many of those who had worked alongside him in the City. He discussed becoming more comfortable to be himself at work as he grew older and having a sense of pride about his background. At the same time, he deliberately 'kept back' other aspects of himself that others would not associate with the professional persona they had bestowed upon him, which revolved around masculine parameters of sport, drinking and 'being a bit of a lad'.

One afternoon, he discussed the stress of these different elements of this life colliding as a marking a point when he realized he was a 'grown up':

> It was quite a strain, but … He [his father] had his ashes scattered down in the country and I went down there and … I mean, I hope you don't mind me telling you, but my dad was gay, which obviously is a big shock to a lot of people. I didn't share that with anybody either. So when he died, obviously friends and people from work were like 'yes, we'll come to the funeral' and it put me under a lot of pressure. It shouldn't do, to be honest. People that I know are gay and all the rest of it. But when it's your dad, it's quite a strange one … Does it make you less proud of your dad, or it doesn't make any difference? To be honest, now I'm older, it didn't really make a difference … And in the end I thought 'what the fuck am I doing thinking about myself?'

I should be just thinking about my dad at the time – do you know what I mean? So it was definitely a hard thing for me to …I almost had to face up to it. (Anonymous, 2014, Y4)

In practice, though, grappling with the experience of significant and formative events as ageing aftershocks rarely led to long-term transformations in terms of how people felt or what they did, with many reflecting on how seismic a 'shock' would be required to really change people's lives. One quiet Wednesday afternoon in 2012 during my second period at HFUK, the conversation turned to mid-life crises and whether they were a myth or not:

Wednesday afternoon's game was a bit of a repeat from last week where people try to find holes in my research. Today we were talking about mid-life crises. 'But you believe in them don't you?' I replied, 'I'm not sure really.' This caused a bit of laughter: 'Remember Joe [a colleague from a large bank] bought himself a Porsche and then split with his wife: that's pretty expensive evidence.'

Dylan, who had been quiet for much of the conversation, came in: 'But it's not changing anything. You might feel like you have changed, or really want to change and get all the gear to prove it. But you can't bottle the feeling of wanting to change enough to make it happen.'

I tried to resist asking what this meant, waiting for someone else to ask. Sure enough, Kieran came in: 'Yeah, it's like all these … you can't bottle it – you think "I'm never going to forget how this feels, that's it, I'm changing my life" … but you always go back to usual … you have to because things need to get done.'

By this stage, people had started to drift back to their screens, probably a bit bored that I'd made a jokey topic a bit unjokey and boring. But I nudged Kieran a bit more: 'At work you mean?'

'Yeah, definitely work, but also life and also just you – you can make all these promises, but a leopard can't change its spots.' (Fieldnotes, 2012)

The potential of transformation through what one participant call 'bottling the experience' was often undermined by a perceived inflexibility and permanence of work that made changing oneself difficult. This was not always unhelpful: Riley suggested that this inflexibility of work could provide a sense of continuity during times of flux and coming into work in the same way each day was comforting to a certain extent. However, this sameness was difficult to reconcile with the experience of radical bodily or life changes. One participant, who had a significant health episode that resulted in being in hospital followed by a long period of recuperation, also discussed the challenge of 'using' shocks productively:

When you've been that ill you get massive highs but also massive lows. I found that hard, hard to unpick that. There are times when things get on top of me. I think to a large extent I'm OK. But it's sometimes difficult to do anything other than go with the flow of these and that's not compatible with work, with an intensive work environment and also trying to advance your career. I don't want the double highs and double lows in my life anymore, the massive highs and the massive lows, I'd much rather have consistency in what is now the second part of my life. That's scary saying that but this has made me realize it's true. (Anonynmous, 2018, Y8)

Like Riley, they discussed the need to present as a normal functioning body while also at the same time reflecting on having been jolted into considering ageing in a more direct way. For another participant, whose health episode happened in close proximity to being made redundant twice in a short period of time, the experience 'jolted me into feeling I was past it'. But part of the ongoing difficulty was 'holding' the experience of illness in a way that was meaningful, but did not overwhelm or 'get in the way'. This involved not only recognizing that dynamically changing body as a risk to losing our grasp on career aspirations, but also that ageing aftershocks required coming to terms with our own organic corporeality – all while presenting an image of invincibility at work:

At work I have quite a hard front, not angry, but no nonsense. But you can see the pockets of like the scarring. Probably it helps me remember how ill I was. Probably the single most seismic event I've had in my life negative-wise. I mean, losing my parents was one thing but nearly dying in my 40s is another thing. It's this scar here. The tracheostomy scar. It's OK, it's in the past, it's just an event, but I need to do something more about it. I suppose all of that, going back to what we talked about, the work, that all has an impact on how I feel about working now and what I should try to achieve. (Anonymous, 2016, Y6)

Redundancy was one of the most common triggers of ageing aftershocks, and its potential to unsettle and disorientate was profound. Yet while the prevalence of age bias in job loss or hunting was expected, the assumption that these aftershocks produced longer-term feelings of self-doubt or worth varied. For example, Liam had discussed his naivety in being unprepared to negotiate and justify what he had achieved during his career as evidence that he was still employable. Over the years, he often returned to his own experience of coming face to face with an age-hostile labour market that stood in contrast with how he thought of himself: 'I suspected when HFUK closed there were some people who knew they would struggle because of their age or the relevance of their skills and I didn't think I would. And it turned out it was, it was a bit of a struggle' (Liam, 2014, Y4). The lack of cohesion between ones self-position and being received by the labour market required an intense process of calibration for him, as well as significant practical effort to avoid being permanently excluded from the labour market. This was particularly difficult for those who 'associate my identity very much with what I do for a job, rightly or wrongly. Some people say that's a bit shallow ... and in the absence of success, it's a little bit difficult' (Liam, 2012, Y2). For Liam, ageing aftershocks emerged in a disconnectedness and a mode of contagion. When discussing times when he felt particularly old, he shared his experience of networking when looking for a job:

> You go to conferences and you become toxic waste, because it's like people know that you're networking because you need a job. So it's like you get to the stage where someone will have, like at a buffet lunch, they won't sit next to you. It's like it's infectious ... they're people who I've known for years ... it's like being a leper. (Liam, 2014, Y4)

Even though many of those I spoke to had experienced unemployment or redundancy, from early on, they appeared curious to discover that their ability and capacity to recover or reconcile experiences was stifled by perceptions of their age – something they had not thought about before. Liam also reflected that one reason he found job hunting difficult was that he was used to deferring more existential or seismic changes or shifts *into* his work, not emerging *because* of his work life: 'our inner strategies for dealing with concerns around work are doing something else at work, which is a bit constrained, or doing something else to worry about because everything expands to fill the space, doesn't it?' (Liam, 2014, Y4). Similarly, Sebastian discussed the amalgam of a redundancy shock with an underlying dread of perhaps becoming 'too old'. He described this in terms of a self- paralysis associated with a limited agency to move or re-place himself into the labour market. Others described becoming more nervous writing CVs or becoming more worried in interviews than they had in their earlier careers due to the realization that the stakes were higher and a decreasing number of jobs were available 'at this age and stage of career' (Sebastian, 2016, Y6).

This was important, given that ageing aftershocks happened in a world of work that, up until that point, had felt open and inviting and connected. Work had disclosed itself to a lot of male participants as being of their making – a world made for you and one in which you slot in and can grasp easily. Sebastian summed this up as his postredundant ageing self as losing 'autocorrect':

I think leaving [international bank] accelerated what happens anyway as you get older in that you begin to second-guess yourself at work – not publicly such as in meetings dismissing the brilliant point you've made – but more a sense of losing your autocorrect, to just breeze through work and life. This didn't happen the first time when and I lost my job when I was a lot younger. (Sebastian, 2016, Y6)

Sebastian's description of the quality of redundancy experience as temporally situated suggested that ageing shocks meant being confronted by the shadow of a more marginalized identity – what we can understand as the shadow of the Other as the Self. In other words, redundancy could precipitate a confrontation with being categorized as 'too old' or 'not young enough'. In our last interview together, Sebastian described this as a 'queasiness' that was difficult to shake off with the same temerity as previous setbacks. Liam similarly stated that the perceived disconnectedness attributed to his age meant that his 'risk aversion's just shot through the roof': 'A guy I know quit last week and he doesn't have any job to go to, which I now think is very dangerous. Two years ago I would have thought it was courageous; now I think it's ridiculous – I mean he's about 42/43' (Liam, 2014, Y4).

The possibility of being received as on the 'wrong side' of age thus required a recalibration to work that was previously an 'autocorrected' way of being in the world, to use Sebastian's phrase. Yet this autocorrection was often based on an assumption that it was possible to colonize ageing and pull it back into one's control. In looking back on extracts taken from his earlier interviews, Ollie reflected on how talking about ageing had been dominated by attempts not only to control his own body and career, but also those around him from an unknown futurity: 'There's a bigger theme in it, isn't there and it's all about me, like trying to protect me and my friends and family from an unknown future and whether or not I've made the right decisions I don't know' (Ollie, 2016, Y6). His sense of responsibility and sovereignty over his own ageing experience appeared to replicate a more general idea of growing up and older as a moral economy premised on normative expectation of development and control. For him, this meant holding everything together – something he attributed to driving him to success and to judging himself as either successful or unsuccessful. This framing assumed one 'correct' way of growing older that for others triggered a fear or lack of control or prediction about the future. Isaac, a broker who had struggled to find work after the closure of HFUK discussed a broader sense of losing 'track' of himself. Given his working-class background, this was made even more difficult as there were few familial relations or other lucrative career paths to follow, which resulted in him often calling upon broad terms of reference to try and justify what he felt was happening to him such as 'you know, we're just trying to emulate what the baby boomers

[have] done, but it's not possible' (Isaac, 2010, Y0). At the same time, he remained acutely aware that even if there were helpful role models who had experienced similar ageing shocks in the labour market, he would have been unlikely to identify with them: 'You learn, don't you? But you don't learn from history, you learn from what's immediately affected you' (Isaac, 2012, Y2). This was a similar experience for others who retrospectively looked back on their working lives and discussed the benefit of hindsight, while also being unclear about what might have helped them to better negotiate or prepare for age-based labour market vulnerability.

As such, ageing aftershocks were the manifestation of different, alternative contours of ageing that may or may not be taken up depending on economic location and positionality, creating a double consciousness of ageing at work. This involved health and employment as not only formative to practically negotiate work, but fundamentally shaping the sociality of ageing. Ageing aftershocks saw the experience of growing older as moving from the subliminal to the experiential realm and it is this shift, as well as the substantive experience itself, that disorientates, echoing de Beauvoir's (1986 [1970]: 313) reflection that: 'As Goethe said "Age takes hold of us by surprise" ... when it seizes upon our own personal life we are dumfounded.'

Here the identification of being the same as everyone (given that 'everyone' ages) simultaneously marked difference, and produced the feeling of a haunting potential of becoming 'Othered' through events and experiences clearly not of one's making or choice. This was even more intensive if becoming a body marked out by age happened after a long and relatively stable biography of being 'the One': in this setting a centred, normative sovereign (often male) subject who had rarely thought about being questioned, relegated or marginalized in the labour market. In practical terms, this often led to a feeling of paralysis or losing a hold on who they were and how they might navigate the labour market from this new unknown 'older' position. Yet, as will now be explored, there were also instances where coming to terms with the ageing self could foster more generative modes of intentionality within an age-hostile work environment.

Holding ageing together

So far, I have focused on how we encounter the ageing self through fissures in stability, coherence or credibility that emerge in professional and ontological expectations. These often deny or stultify the ageing self, frequently due to a compulsion to 'hang on' to sameness or not changing as a (false) interlocutor of stability, even when considering their perceived present and referencing their imagined futures. However, in the second half of this chapter, I now want to turn to moments where growing older was defined beyond either denial or a desire to control. While this experience could still be alienating in terms of a disruption to the business-as-usual of 'being me', it was not solely conditioned upon 'agedness' as a delimiting consciousness around being dynamically situated in time, or older or younger Beinghood as only a foreign or othering condition. Instead, it involved a more complicated curation of previous encounters that made up the experiential body and sense of self, while at the same time recognizing dynamic embodiment as providing a dexterity to negotiate age-based and aged-intersectional ideals, expectations or positions.

For many, this emerged from broader experiences of being discriminated against or subjected to biased or misperceptions. It was notable that while participants might be wistful about their own conditional acceptance or marginalization in the past, they also suggested that it provided a rich resource to draw upon when growing older. In some cases, female colleagues or friends were viewed as 'better equipped' to navigate work-based ageism, having had to manage the contingency of the lived experience of gender in their earlier lives. The irony of this was noted by Sebastian, who said: 'It's not going to change anything for women if we accept that "Oh, don't worry about growing older, you've already got enough to deal with in terms of sexist comments"' (2016, Y6). However, female participants also discussed how working and occupying the margins of conditional acceptance as women also meant that potentially stepping into the terrain of being viewed as (too) old or (too) young was in practice neither shocking nor paralysing. As Isla put it, ageist perceptions felt like the 'different tune, same dance'. Freya similarly referred to the 'muscle memory' of marginalization, particularly in relation to learning from a previous gendered-age-based positionality:

What does the entirety of the rest of my career look like? Where does it go and what moves do I have to make? Part of it is using muscle memory. Being aware of people pleasing, I think yes, is something to do with it, is to do with age. I think when you are younger, especially women as well. I think women do find it harder to say no, but I think if I look back. I think you're more of a people pleaser and then at some point, you get age or wisdom teaches you that well, you can't please everybody all of the time, so you might as well factor yourself into it a bit. (Freya, 2010, Y10)

Freya, who referred to calling out sexism at work as 'nailing jelly to a wall', used her past experiences of gendered interactions as a way of articulating and making sense of ageism:

I feel that being a certain age is tough. I mean, the problem is that most people think 'who works in the City, who wants to be working there when there older'. So as you get older it [ageism] might happen, but it will, it's hard to nail down. It's like sexism, it's hard to nail down. This is not a sexist company, but I've learned it's more complex than that – I had to manage a client where he thought I was just waiting to be a housewife. That I was pregnant or wanting to be a housewife. There's no other possible reason that a woman of my age would want to change or do something different. And you can't annoy a client, so you learn how to deal with it, and women have to become more skilled, because they have to deal with it all the time. So when I'm older, like I said it will be harder to nail down and call out, but at least I've learned how to deal with these kind of things so I'll be prepared.

Freya suggested that previously experiences she had negotiated helped to absorb and respond productively to the experience of marginalization, as if being the target of sexist attitudes or practices produced a bodily capacity. She reflected on how a high degree of self-awareness was needed to stop sexism 'seeping into you', either through trying – and failing – to be 'one of the boys' or through feeling you were the problem. Other accounts also suggest that strategically negotiating these elements made normative apparatuses visible, whether they be through being connected mainly with age or age intersecting with other aspects such as gender. As such, there was a greater awareness of preparing oneself in advance for when ageist encounters started to impinge on one's own choices or ambitions as one grew older.

Ava reflected on how the competitive conditions borne in certain sectors required women to be agile in terms of how they curated a self through ageing, particular relating to aspects of ambition, such as 'the right to go for an early promotion or ask for more of a bonus'. An embodied memory of mediating the line between acceptable and unacceptable practices led to Ava suggesting that women were able to 'handle' age-based bias better, as well as being more attuned to recognizing it in the first place. In our interview just after she left the financial services sector, she suggested that starting a new career track while being more aware of growing older was not as intimidating as it might be for her male colleagues and peers:

I think women are much, much better as well at accepting and then dealing with volatility and changes. I think most men, really, it's like their identities are so tied up with their work and how they see themselves, and I think women are much more agile in terms of dealing with it. There's no association that 'this is what I'm meant to be, therefore that's it'. (Ava, 2014, Y4)

Ava was not expressing a preference for determinism here, but rather noting that the contingent occupational acceptance which was an ongoing part of her working life did not seem to be the case for her male peers or colleagues.

Acknowledging this did not mean reconciling herself to a secondary or marginalized position; rather, it afforded the opportunity to curate what we might understand as 'coalitional subjectivities' that emerge from past experiences of being on the fringes of acceptance over her working life that in turn constitute part of an ageing subjectivity.

Flo sought to make such coalitional subjectivities even more central to her own identity acts through noting the arbitrariness of her age, sharing that when people asked how old she was, 'I just say I'm 80'. Instances of being asked to 'out' oneself via a chronological age often coincided with changes to work teams, jobs, or sectors. For Flo, this happened when she returned to study in a cohort of noticeably younger students. She discussed how intent they were on 'marking me' through age:

> They couldn't get their head around it. I have actually tried to get in sooner rather than later, tell people that, I don't want them to think that I am trying to be young. They ask what age I am and I just say, 'I'm old', and then they can deal with any – they can see anything stupid I say in that light. (Petra, 2016, Y6)

Here Flo sums up a common identity contradiction that arose from the age-based social inflections of others. She was keen to avoid being viewed inauthentically through 'trying to be young', but at the same time used a foil of being 'old' to caricature the desire of others to age-place her and explain her away on account of a number. At other times Flo was also aware that colleagues found it disquieting around 'how unobsessed I am about age', even though she was keen to stress how she looked after her health through diet and exercise. In contrast, she discussed how many men around her had a fear of time running out in work that seemed to be central to their own sense of identity:

> I'll tell you something about my partner and his work. Sometimes we do talk about 'well why are you doing this', so he says, 'I think it's a really good idea but more than that, me and my colleague just want to make shitloads of money before age x just to prove that it can be done' and I don't know whether this is a guy thing or not. They both seem to be pretty focused on it. It's like a computer game is the way I think they see it, against the clock. Have you ever met any women who think like this? I'm curious to know. (Flo, 2016, Y6)

Understanding one's own ageing as contained through dichotomous interlocutors of unsuccessful/successful or rich/poor echoes earlier ideas of an illusion of being able to demarcate and completely control both one's ageing as a sovereign subject in the world. Freya and Flo also noted a gender-based difference regarding one's age as a point of self-reference or distinction. Both were aware that other people sought to mark them out – in Freya's case, this was due to not carrying the traditional feminine accoutrements in her workplace style, while for Flo, it was not following a standard chrononormative trajectory of job–partner–marriage–children. In contrast, they described their own experience of growing older as signatured by increasingly curating moments for being themselves, recognizing these as fleeting and difficult to capture or crystalize. This mode of ageing was aligned with a self-understanding emerging from an experience where 'you see the end point and you see the sort of definitely black and the definitely white, but in between you only see shades of grey of someone becoming more and more settled' (Freya, 2020, Y10).

Similarly, Isla, when discussing her own career path early on in our conversations, emphasised the importance of trying not to expunge – or at least tolerate – ambiguity over the course of one's career:

> I think if I did think – like if you think about planning five years or ten years, I think that's actually quite restrictive, because you're saying 'I've definitely got to be here'; you won't necessarily open yourself up to alternatives. I think this is the way my career has gone and how I now think. (Isla, 2014, Y4)

'Opening yourself up' could be an orbicular experience. Flo shared that while others related to her 'as if I was old', the experience of returning to study was recovering (but not replicating) part of who she had been as a child. For example, a period of study coincided with Flo picking up activities and pastimes that she had previously enjoyed, but that had been neglected due to other demands in her life. In her discussions of her changing nodal points of self-definition over the years of our interviews, these activities became part of regaining who she was and were central to being more 'comfortable in my own skin'. Part of this carried the spectre of who she used to be, but also how being successful in her career enabled a point of 'knowing herself with the hindsight of experience'. This came to the fore when reflecting on her working style:

> I think that I've become more myself, so in some ways I think that the way I am now is how I was when I was young, really young, I mean like 13 when I used to get told off for everything, so speaking my mind and things. But also, after everything that's happened since that, now I really know myself. I'm pleased. (Flo, 2016, Y6)

Isla also shared the sense that growing older was in part about a recovery – or at least a reverberation with parts of herself that had been forgotten or deferred due to competing demands on her time and expectations from others. She felt that moving into a different sector from the one she had been inducted into as a young professional afforded her a growing affection and intimacy with becoming older, as her sense of self shifted away from 'workspaces that are tightly controlled … that constrict you'. At the same time, she was acutely aware that this was contrary to the way in which women are more normatively perceived as they grow older:

I think a lot of women, a lot of my friends at least, recognize the irony that as they become more, more comfortable with themselves, everyone else gets more uncomfortable, you become less noticed in work, perhaps overlooked a bit more, at least in some settings. (Isla, 2018, Y8)

For Isla, this was 'a puzzle' of growing older that she returned to across our time together, something that wavered between 'wanting to be something younger but we can't go there' and that 'it would be wonderful if I was always able to recognize all the good in becoming older'. For her, ageing meant reclaiming affirming parts of her previous self and curating these with her current positionality, especially around how she felt about herself in terms of her body and sense of identity. However, for Isla, work could also be a space that potentially stifled this process of puzzling out, given that a lot of the time, workplace relations were predicated on having to negotiate a lack of acceptance from others rather than finding out ways to tolerate and enjoy who she was:

I am still sometimes thrown off balance with things that might happen, if I don't get offered work over someone else or these little things. Some people, you want to seek their approval and it takes you a while to accept that you might not ever get it, and you have to work out why that might be. Is it a legitimate reason that you might want to work on, or not? That can take up a lot of energy, (Isla, 2020, Y10)

For Isla, recovering from being 'thrown off balance' was not about denying her own age-based positionality, but rather making an assessment while remembering how much of her early career has been underpinned by a contingent acceptance based not on 'her', but on gendered and aged-conditional modes of recognition. The effort this negotiation took was only felt retrospectively when she found a place within the arts sector that culturally acknowledged and better recognized a plurality around bodies and age 'where it's about your practice in how you play, not what you look like'.

In reflecting on extracts from our earliest interviews, Isla suggested a differing axis of self-understanding or self-reference point had seeded in her early career decisions, but these rarely shaped actions until later on in her life:

I'm still that same attitude of working but I think, you know, I've become more finely tuned. I think I was probably a little bit like that at that time when younger, but as I get older, I feel a little bit more comfortable about saying no to things if I get a gut feeling that's bad. (Isla, 2016, Y6)

Others found that engaging with the manifesting 'old self' could be a more ambivalent experience in terms of exposing the increasing distance they felt from the professional ambitions that had once been such an intimate part of themselves. When asked what she hoped for as she grew older, Ava said:

I hope I will just regain some of my old self back. I've just realized that I've spent so much of the time since I've met you really worrying about starting a family and now that I have one, really worrying about how do I get back to work. It haunts me, there's always something really big I worry about, and I wish I could just enjoy the present, it's just not a lot of fun, really. (Ava, 2018, Y8)

Trying to hold ageing together between inward-directed and outward-facing dynamics in a changing body was hard work, especially when one was within thick histories of work-related patterns of inequality. The labour of fitting in and styling oneself as acceptable could be intense. It may require always adjusting, always monitoring, reassessing while using the past as a recitational litmus test of whether they still felt 'like themselves'. At the same time, this process may also hold a promise not only around growing *up* but a growing *into* themselves in a generative sense. Building on coalitional subjectivities facilitated a negotiation – or even resistance to aged conditions of recognition by providing techniques that could be used to 'bounce back' from more negating interactions and encounters. There is always the possibility of experiencing some kind of identity whiplash from these regressive aged attributions that may 'stop us in our tracks' for a moment. But there is also a more generative potential held in embodied ways of knowing that can help to stabilize and hold out against a possible rupture of how we think of ourselves.

Chapter discussion: colonization and the ageing Other in ourselves

At the heart of de Beauvoir's (1986 [1970]: 315) consideration of ageing lies a deceptively simple question: 'Can I have become a different being while I still remain myself?'

The ageing self is constituted in organic, social and temporal experiences. Yet what we learn from the accounts in this chapter is that the ontological challenges old age brings according to de Beauvoir also speaks to an ontological reckoning across the life course more broadly. Through focusing on the figure of grasping as an experiential process of disruption-calibration, we witness working through ageing as a project of the dynamically situated self marked by processes of disruption-recalibration. These shape the ontological dynamics of ageing at work and manifest in a variety of practical acts. The examples from men and women of all ages highlight how we contend with the 'loosening' of our ontological grip on the world that a sovereign, career-focused worker is expected to have. Subsequent attempts to regain a feeling of equilibrium of course coalesces with bodily and professional demands, and different changes morph and meander as we move across our working lives.

What becomes clear is that in the context of work, the multiplicity of our ageing experiences contends with being seduced into thinking there is a compelling singularity around how to become older. Moments of a professional loosening oscillate around profound events when our bodies appear to prevent 'business as usual'. In such accounts, we come face to face with the 'Other to myself' that de Beauvoir discusses as part of becoming old. However, this is not just about the dynamics of a 'successful ageing' agenda as percolating contemporary professions and workplaces, but more that ageing as a mode of grasping highlights more nuanced and complex ways that the shadow of an aged Other comes into our everyday working lives. Our own sense of integrity is devolved from trajectories or pasts through being undermined by colleagues. Similarly, asynchronous collisions between ourselves and normative labour market desires and demands emerged in mundane conversations that shaped the terms of engagement as an age-situated subject. These are all interwoven into the experience of apart-ness from our ageing selves that prevents reckoning with what it means to grow older rather than assume we are an immutable, static and ever-labouring body. However, when confronted by identity ruptures during the working life course, the habitual ways of working are replaced by a more uncanny realm that bends us away from what had previously been considered as the 'I'. This presents a challenge particular to the ageing self, in that in order to keep an ontological grip, we 'have to recover its equilibrium every time it is upset; it has to defend itself from outside attack; and it must take the widest and strongest possible grip on the world' (de Beauvoir, 1986 [1970]: 18). Striving to maintain an ontological equilibrium while ageing is even more significant at work during one's career, given that organizational lives are already demarcated through an undercurrent of ever-potential disruption, such as losing one's job, not fulfilling one's own expected trajectory or being marginalized, excluded and undermined in work settings.

Grasping is a necessary intervention that operates in combination with the pursuit of embodying the subject de rigueur of financialized capitalism that populates organizational and institutional practices. The need to recalibrate our ageing selves is not simply an ornamental pursuit that happens alongside professional discourses, but is critical to maintaining one's place in an unforgiving and ever-demanding labour market. It is impossible to escape the organizing elements that make up professional work, from how financial rewards are calibrated or promised to the way in which biographical-based trajectories are normalized and valued. Even those who do not find themselves deeply invested in these trajectories are nonetheless exposed to the totems of normative ageing regimes, given that they are inculcated into how professional success or failure is measured in a broader project of life.

Ageing as ontological disruption was often at its most profound when a lurking feeling of something being out of place became verified through a social response. To use one participant's term, certain episodes 'jolt' into an unknown ontological terrain that had not been experienced or even conceived of previously. Returning to these over time points to the importance of trying to restitch experience back together a coherent sense of self. In some ways, time passing is a valuable salve for reflecting on how the profound rabbit-in-the-headlights moments are invariably part of the ageing experience itself. But even years later, there was still a desire for participants to entrap the self into a normative ageing trajectory that one could control or master if one tries hard enough.

In reflecting on the above accounts, I could not help but find something deeply unsettling in hearing how people – smart, successful professionals who were often thoughtful and reflective in many ways – pursued an ageing trajectory that all too often was conditional on becoming entrapped by a singularity of the self. In other words, they become bound by a selfhood where recognition is contingent on remaining immune to any loosening of the grip of aged normative positions, and at the same time must fall prey to the illusion of an ageing singularity. This often hardened the resolve of ageist structures and systems. Singularity still enables us to acknowledge the 'Other' of ageing: we can identify other people who have grown older and who we might classify as older. In fact, this recognition of, say, an 'older' person' as the 'Other' – always the second person rather than us – is a necessary corollary in our own experience where we accept we might change, but not to the extent of being 'too old'. However, we often strive to ensure that this older-ness, 'young-ness or middle-aged-ness does not penetrate the self. The 'aged' Other is still present, relegated through duality and distancing to a lesser object, dissolved of much generative agency or affirming modes of subjectivity. This is precarious as it means we reproduce a perpetual duality between, for example, old/other and not-old/self. Doing so makes it impossible to explore the shades of grey, as Freya described, in between self and otherness. For me, this colonization of the singularity of the aged subject is one of the biggest and most violent achievements of contemporary culture.

At the same time, we cannot downplay how calibrating the ageing self is invariably a gendered project. I am hesitant to so crudely delineate agedness as coming together with gendered points of orientation in ways that undermine other intersectional axes of power. However, understanding the aged Other-in-us as a central component of a gendered ontological repertoire is vital. De Beauvoir reminds us that there is no universalized structure shaping the conditions in which we find ourselves; rather, the world as it is taken up is dependent on one's situation. A colonization of situation felt particularly pointed for men or those who had previously not had formative experiences of being marginalized. Many men's experiences of living through assumed privilege, or 'Oneness' in de Beauvoir's terms, mean that a misrecognition around ageing is confronting in terms of being uncomfortable, as well as a mourning and destabilizing of loss of the 'One' – a position they were never aware of occupying until it became threatened. De Beauvoir emphasises the potential for the ontological devastation that may occur in the collapse of duality when the intertwined self and Others is realised through embodiment, as is often the case with ageing, as described in her account of the paradox in men's sexual experiences, but which equally might speak to other intersubjective corporeal experiences such as ageing:

> As a subject he posits the world, and, remaining outside the universe he posits, he makes himself the lord of it; if he grasps himself as flesh, as sex, he is no longer autonomous consciousness, transparent freedom: he is engaged in the world, a limited and perishable object; and it is undoubtedly true that the generative act goes beyond the body's limits: but he constitutes them at the very same instant. (de Beauvoir, 2015 [1949]: 310)

While the men I interviewed were in the world and connected to others, in many ways, experiencing ageing in its fullness required moments when they could 'grasp' the interdependency of their own dynamic situatedness as flesh, either through health-related incidences or being affectively touched by vulnerability and fear of being rendered useless in the labour market. Such episodes disorientated a sense of being an independent, separate subject. This is not a result of any individual's action or behaviour, but rather the consequences of a dialectical chrononormative masculinity that still underpins large swathes of professional and vocational work, and the ways in which we assume our lives should play out over the course of our career. It highlights how chrononormative masculinity, or chronophallism, becomes imprinted into contemporary work and how it stymies the parameters and possibilities for contouring how we come to identify with the 'I' in growing older.

In comparison, for women, the squeeze towards colonization of an aged subjectivity felt familiar and nestled into their accumulated lived experiences of subjectification. It underpinned previous instances where they were pulled into doubting their capacity to foster their own trajectories – what de Beauvoir refers to as *'a divorce between her properly human condition and her feminine vocation'* (2015 [1949]: 577). Part of this was an embodied experience of contingency that the women I spoke to had experienced from an earlier age; a 'seeing myself seen' through a gendered aged gaze that seeks to colonize the subject in the object–subject conundrum (de Beauvoir, 2015 [1949]: 529). For those I spoke to, these often circulated around instances where they had been undermined in workplace encounters, subjected to abusive or violent experiences of age-situated gaslighting, or given unsolicited advice they were expected to take on – all akin to women becoming 'grasped by others as a thing' (2015 [1949]: 529). In other words, their own temporal integrity as a dynamic subject was compromised through gendered structures that encouraged them to distrust their own pasts and/ or to doubt their capacity to curate their own futures.

However, part of the alterity of ageing was a thirst for what ageing could afford the self rather than simply preclude. Working through ageing as a mode of grasping also provides glimpses of how we might foster a closer and more intimate relationship with our ever-ageing selves. The destabilizing effects of ageing and gender-based misrecognition provide both an ontological canvas and a bodily repertoire through which to negotiate how to 'grasp' ageing from a point of disorientation in the world. That is not to say that their experiences of being othered was identical to gender-based experiences of bias or marginalization; rather, the quality of experiencing alterity, of being an embodied site of otherness, reverberates around experiences of ageing and offers the possibility of a more affirming mode of being and doing in working through ageing.

This suggests that there is something ontologically profound about ageing subjectivity that affords certain embodied capacities. Acknowledging the impossibility of the ageing subject as having a stability or continual 'harmony between what we aim at and what is given, between the intention and the performance' (Merleau-Ponty, 2014 [1945]: 144) provides the opportunity to explore what it means to be a temporally dynamic self in a world which often confines different or plural modes of subjectivity to an Other. In practice, it might emerge through a part-recovery, part-renewal of a sociality not so confined to strictures and expectations that had sought to colonize the self previously. This is powerful, given that despite the competing, constraining and occluding patterns of work that push us towards decrying or denying ageing, working through ageing might also provide a possibility for ways to explore and connect with the ageing self. By this I mean that there still remains the possibility for exploring different, alternative curations of the self that resist dismissing the 'Other' of the ageing experience.

While not akin to her own accounts of growing older, this potential of an ageing subjectivity as beyond singularity and towards an embodied, expansive ontological sentiment builds on de Beauvoir's (2018 [1947]: 47) early accounts of passion as a relational dynamic. Here, she suggests that 'the cause of the passionate man's torment is his distance from the object; but he must accept it instead of trying to eliminate it'. In the torment of his distance, which resembles the dis-ease that is part of a phenomenology of apartness as outlined in Chapter 2, she is predominantly concerned with our relations with another physical person as the Other rather than the 'Other within':

> It is only as something strange, forbidden, as something free, that the other is revealed as an other. And to love him genuinely is to love him in his otherness and in that freedom by which he escapes. Love is then renunciation of all possession, of all confusion One renounces being in order that there may be that being which one is not. (de Beauvoir, 2018 [1947]: 72)

Read through the lens of ageing, I would suggest that such dynamics serve as a valuable device to articulate the self–other relationship we encounter in ageing as part of a temporal corporeality. It suggests that rather than renouncing the demand to possess ageing, to entrap or colonize it, working through ageing is also about recognizing the generative possibilities of holding the ambivalence or ambiguity of the ageing experience. Doing so requires balancing an ability to lose or renounce some elements or aspects of our selves, while still maintaining enough of a credible semblance to be recognized. To try and successfully achieve this requires recognition of what institutional or organizational conditions enable or constrain, as discussed in the previous chapter. Yet it also requires choreographing how one is situated in and across settings and contexts as a dynamically situated self, as we will explore next.

6

Anchoring Ageing: Chronochoreography in Space and Setting

Luke, one of the programming team in HFUK, wryly called commuting 'the most democratic thing about London', in that public transport is by far the easiest way to make your way around the city. And at first, it seems a democratic space where anyone can potentially temporarily inhabit or move through a train, bus, tube, road or pavement. However, after travelling to an interview from a friend's flat on the outskirts of London, my naivety as to where, when and how labouring bodies occupy such spaces became clear. By 6.03 am, I was at the station at the start of one of the main underground lines into London. This was early for me, but hours later than the first shift of service and domestic workers who had already travelled in to prepare the city for others. I boarded the train, half noticing I was the only women there, then that I was the only person that looked under 50. By the second stop into London, a majority of the seats were already taken by people, again mostly older than me and certainly looking more tired.

As we moved into the zones closer to London, I witnessed each stop populating the carriage with younger and younger passengers, until the carriage was a patchwork of suited bodies of all ages. People bunched together, but usually making sure to do so next to similar bodies, with men's and women's bodies sometimes contorted to make a gap between them, or likewise, women turning towards other women when (more) men piled on at another stop. Occasionally seats were offered to older 'civilians' such as tourists, but rarely to fellow 'suits'. By the time it was my turn to twist my way out of the train, my carriage was full of people, all seemingly sharing the same uncomfortable but necessary experience, despite coming from very different lives in flatshares, parent's homes, other cohabited spaces or perhaps even their own houses if they were rich enough or lived far enough away from the city.

Commuting is one of the more explicit sites where working through ageing as ordered and organized is so visible. Some see this commercial pilgrimage as an incidental or a nonplace: what Augé views as 'spaces of circulation, communication and consumption, where solitudes coexist without creating any social bond or even a social emotion' (Augé, 1996: 178). They are not places where people choose to dwell, but rather find themselves as a means to an end: a way to reach or leave a more desirable place. Yet for those who continued to work in urban areas, even after the so-called hybrid working revolution associated with the COVID-19 pandemic, commuting was part of the entanglement of their ageing experiences. It is just one of the many places and spaces that we inhabit or move through due to choice, change or circumstance at various points in our lives that is part of a chronochroreography of labour. By 'chronochoreography', I am speaking of the ways in which the being and doing of ageing is constituted in the commercial rhythms, work spaces, institutional locations, organizing dynamics, and broader histories and politics that constitute economic settings, and subsequently implanted into the material facticity of the environment. This recognizes such elements as ripened through both aged conditions and parameters, and our own inescapable situatedness as we dwell in them.

This chapter explores these experiences of chronochoreography as central to working through ageing, focusing on the phenomenological figure of anchoring. Anchoring emphasizes that working through ageing is neither objectively imposed upon us in mute or neutral spaces, nor entirely subjectively experienced in a space we imagine and curate in isolation. Instead, it is enacted and constituted in webbed configurations and relations that calibrate how comfortably we inhabit a particular commercial or organizational setting, while all the time situated in our own carnal temporality. Through our inhabited spatiality, the world and the self marinade with social, political and historical trajectories, as suggested by de Beauvoir in her review of Merleau-Ponty's *Phenomenology of Perception*, where she suggests that 'the experience of spatiality is the experience of our situation in the world' (de Beauvoir, 2004 [1945]: 161). In considering her sympathies with the idea of subjectivity as always in situ, ageing requires context to be understood as dynamically experienced and revealed through our corporeality as much as we are revealed through being in context. In this sense, anchoring involves a practical doing in the spaces we move in and through as we take up positions in the world that makes certain objects, ideas, and ways of Being appear on our landscape as more or less desirable, relevant to us or possible depending on our own corporeality.

While anchoring is no static achievement, at times it may present as such, and the mirage of its stability can both seduce and derail us. To explore this further, I first turn to the age-indexed sociospatial experience of aged hostility in City work to consider how work, economic and social planes correlate and naturalize the context of work in particular aged or age-biased lines of direction. Here we see that even when not fully physically 'there', such as through remote working, mediators such as resources, routines and rituals govern how and where we seek to situate our ageing selves. Inhabiting occupational, institutional and working space involves recognizing that things that we need in order to claim our place in the world also require us to recalibrate with our surroundings, often facing obstacles or unequal conditions of possibility. With this in mind, I then turn to the spatial negotiation of age-appropriate bodies, where working through ageing requires us to consider anchoring as dynamic in its quality not only in terms of the spaces and relations in which we are situated, but also in terms of our changing corporeality through which we find and take up work-related spaces. The theme of the changing body in situ is reflected in the third section, which explores how the experience of labour intertwines with different spaces of commercial, leisure and familial activity over time. It explores how this can reveal the unexpected pleasures of ageing in settings and an opportunity to explore the wanderlust of ageing experience, but does so against the demand and continual desire to 'drop anchor in some "milieu" that is offered to us' (Merleau-Ponty, 2014 [1945]: 264). In reflecting on how these elements come together, I discuss the dynamic situatedness of ageing as a chronochoreographed experience that manifested in working lives as 'an unstable system in which balance is continually lost and continually recovered' (de Beauvoir, 1986 [1970]: 17) in different spaces, places and modes of dwelling. This is invariably a tensile experience between anchoring and what I term unmooring. Together these produce an ageing situation that is contingent on our aged, gendered and socioeconomic *inter alia* location, but also integral to reflexive possibilities for exploring where and how we inhabit over time.

London: no city for old men?

The city is not a singular place, but the parts of London where I spent time during this study felt made for money. The buildings and immediate surrounding areas of the city where participants work and the easiness of movement within them reminded me of what Seamon (2015: 151) called a 'place ballet': 'the prereflective union of people usually unaware of the whole they help create'. Certain bodies and objects are inherently part of a spatial lubricant that can, for example, assist easy travel or exchanges, but also facilitate an intentional order that enables people to bypass thinking and avoid detracting from the primary organizational task of productivity or creating wealth. A number of participants discussed this as a pleasurable experience;

a mode of City socialization where 'becoming part of this crowd feels grown up' (Sophie, 2012, Y2). Others referred to a familiarity and comfort created through years of taking the same journey meaning the individual gets to know, for example, exactly where to stand on the platform, what carriage to get on or even how to make a 'quick shortcut' through walking on the right part of the pavement. Similarly, Theo discussed moving to a more industrial sector as a shock to the system in terms of navigating grey buildings and uninspiring interior design compared to banking, while Will (2012; Y2) discussed how one of the penalties of moving jobs was 'feeling clumsy' when having to learn a new pathway to work, even though it was a 20-minute shorter commute that was 'giving me back hours of my life each month'.

Together with commuting, long hours, networking or professional events and drinking after work created a density of connections in and around work that absorbed people into the City as a space of commerce and exchange. It provided a bodily experience of belonging to something successful. At the same time, these elements tied together signatures of money-making spaces with an unforgiving precarity around ongoing acceptance. This was not simply indicated through spaces being inaccessible due to security, but in ways that only became apparent to participants when they suffered an injury: polished steps where stairlifts would have ruined the aesthetic of entrances, listed buildings with narrow corridors making the most minor of accommodations difficult, and a population of ever-working bodies where one who had a slight limp or moved slower than a frenetic pace stood out. Against the backdrop of this environment, some such as Charles (2020, Y10) suggested that the pandemic and the ability to work from home for at least part of the week had extended his working life, given that he didn't have to 'face the daily gauntlet' every day. However, moving through commercial spaces also underpinned how the pastiche of different bodies was decadently age-bound, as suggested by James in reflecting on one journey into the office:

James: I was on the way to Oxford Circus, in a pretty busy tube, when a young lad stood up to let someone sit down. Naturally you just look to step out of the way [of] who's wanting to sit there, you know, sometimes those 'baby on board' badges women wear … but there wasn't anyone – it was me he was offering it to! I obviously say 'nah thanks mate', or something like that, so then the two of us are just standing there holding on with an empty seat in front of us that no one else was taking until the next stop.

Kat: How do you think the other guy felt?

James: Probably embarrassed. Or maybe not, not even that bothered probably.

While our discussion quickly moved on, when getting the tube back home that evening, I wondered how that must have felt, 'just standing there' in the lingering aftermath of becoming the object of 'assisted seating'. The synthesis of restricted place, time and mobility in public transport clearly intensified the awkwardness, puncturing James's own perception of 'an older but pretty fit guy that looks after myself'. But it also made it impossible to escape that the person he assumed himself to be and how he fitted into the jigsaw of that space had suddenly dissolved. His older self was there, not sitting on the chair in a crowded underground carriage.

For others, locating and inhabiting more immediate places of labour were experienced by an increasing contingent mode of belonging, overlaid through the conditional hospitality that marked the professional services and banking more broadly. This subsequently required a careful negotiation of how an individualized career that maintained commercial value should be spatially circumscribed as one grew older. For example, over the course of conversations, how and where people moved to in terms of employment was often bounded by an age-oriented capacity: on the one hand, 'bringing in' value from one area to another or diversifying one's skills through moving organizations or sectors could result in faster career progression; on the other hand, this needed to be tempered with a danger of becoming a stranger or outsider, unable to transition back in or tarnished as an 'old dog trying to do new tricks' (James, 2014, Y4). For example, Lily discussed moving into the public sector as a 'going to pasture' while Theo recalled being received as a relative 'foreigner' when looking to move back into financial services after holding a position in the manufacturing sector. While he could personally see the benefits of his experience elsewhere and the job itself was similar in terms of the technical components, others had implied he was too far down a path of another industry: '[I was told] Well, you've been out of this industry for eight years in an unrelated industry. Even though technology-wise you've done some great stuff, it's hard to get traction with certain companies.'

Theo went on to become a contractor and worked remotely for an organization over 100 miles away. He suggested that this made it easier to 'add value' while not fully embedded in the business, allowing him to sidestep some of the age stereotyping at work, while also reaping the benefits of 'seeing yourself as outside of this whole politics and career progression thing' (2020, Y10). At the same time, he was keen to be seen as having expertise in a way that did not occlude his previous experience and negotiated ways of achieving this remotely:

> Maybe this is a sign of ageing, but if I was a company and I was hiring a contractor, I just want that person to tell me everything they know. That's what you get paid for as a contractor. Maybe even more so

than I was 10 years ago, I'm very much comfortable with that role of adding value in that way. (Theo, 2020, Y10)

The balance of placing oneself in a particular location that reaps value, while avoiding others viewing you as sedimented or 'stuck' required an awareness of ensuring that one's bodily capacity was never viewed as 'out of place', even though 'many of my colleagues don't know necessarily how old I am or not. I do notice that the majority of my colleagues are younger than me. That was something that I think, in my own head, I had to deal with it in a way' (Theo, 2020, Y10). For others, the fear of sudden exile from the financial services also required counterbalancing a bodily capacity in a setting that accelerated age-oriented modes of deterioration. Freddie, a long-time trader, emphasized that 'there's a physical element to this work, getting up early, working late on different markets, the stress and high stakes of losing other people's money, that means you have, you could say, a date of expiry' (Freddie, 2010, Y0). In Freddie's accounts, there was evidence of geospatially age-hostile work practices not through what he saw but who was not there given 'you don't really see older people' (Freddie, 2012, Y2). This invisibility of older bodies was also a clear signal to Dylan (2020, Y10) that 'the legacy skillset, or the technology skillset that I have has definitely got an expiry date'. Part of his awareness was ensuring that when onsite in a consultancy role, his own body compared favourably with those around him in the workplace, such as 'making sure your hair's neat, a well-cut suit – and those things can matter when you go somewhere on a daily [rate]'. Others who had undertaken consultancy work or work involving the public sector echoed this, summed up by Henry's (2012, Y2) wry image of 'fat grey-faced old public service workers'. Staying present, both in terms of up-to-date skills and maintaining visibility or employment in commercial spaces, was often described as an endurance sport. Henry went on to discuss how competitive careers required discipline to avoid frequenting spaces of excess too often, even when 'there's always someone going to the pub', and also the need to dedicate time to offset the effects of stress or long hours that may intensify and speed up bodily deterioration or decay.

The geospatial age hostility that mapped city working also led to Finn, who had continued an upward trajectory in the financial services, strategizing a career that helped him succeed financially while 'trying to reduce the chains attaching me to the city as I get older' (Finn, 2016, Y6). In part this was about 'never coasting', such as when his job was restructured after Brexit and put him in physical daily contact with 'so many bright, young grads coding up ideas on the fly' (2018, Y8). He had earlier connected changes to organizational structure and being located in a new team on a different part of the work floor to making him aware of still looking like he belonged:

I've had to learn some new code just to understand how our trading systems work, so I'm moving along that front and then I've had to understand a bit more about the portfolio management side as well in our model of portfolio management where humans don't get to make decisions. So I didn't really have a choice in that but having made that transition I think I've kind of future-proofed myself a bit. (Finn, 2016, Y6)

Around the same time, Finn's family had made a significant move out of London to provide a 'healthier place for the kids to grow up', while he lived in the city during the week. This compared to when we began our conversations in 2010 when he was firmly ensconced in London. Gradually but actively marking out his future was underpinned by a broader aspiration that he could 'get out [of a financial services career] unscathed and on your own terms ideally' (2018, Y8). In this sense, ageing was constituted in part through a simultaneous process of generating wealth, while extracting and replanting friendships, hobbies and family away from a city into a more forgiving and sustainable environment.

The City, as outlined in Chapter 3 as a physical space fermented and organized through logics of financial capitalism, held as much of an ambivalent relationship with people's ageing bodies as people held for the City. However, this did not mean a comfortable acceptance of 'growing out' of the City. Being jolted out or exited through redundancy and job loss was often viewed as a rite of passage, but nonetheless could bring a previously unquestioned belonging into doubt, as suggested in the previous chapter. During one period of redundancy, Russell (2012, Y2), who worked on economic modelling, described being unemployed as not only about financial anxieties, but about missing the aesthetic of a workplace and being part of a daily routine: 'I never thought I'd become homesick for working, not ... the abstract art you know, the monochrome [of corporate buildings] or the horrendous commute. When you have time to think that it might not be a part of what you do, was not, I suppose, very pleasant.'

For Russell, it was not simply the materiality of physically experiencing corporate spaces that was missed, but that being located there was an expression of 'something I was familiar with but without even noticing'. He was conscious of using the enforced time off productively on fitness and catching up with friends and 'work on feeling a bit younger and healthier', but its open-ended nature made it difficult to enjoy, especially given that he was 'not a graduate, being a bit more expensive, and less jobs at that level are around'. Those in employment also pointed to regular reminders of one's peripatetic situatedness. On a local level, this may be in the physical work setting. For example, nearly everyone I spoke had at some point witnessed a 'walk of doom' across an office when a colleague was made redundant and 'escorted out the building with a box of stuff'

(Gen, 2014, Y4). Elsewhere, hot desking, which became the norm for many participants after the COVID-19 pandemic, led Ronnie to suggest that they helped managerial control, in that they 'reminded everyone of their temporary status'. Lily also discussed how post-pandemic working conditions could further mark out bodies as 'older ones', with accounts conflating older bodies with those requiring additional adjustment. For example, when describing her workplace, she namechecked older employees when explaining how 'everyone hot desks, except for a few of the ones who need special chairs or set ups'.

For others, the idea of being extracted from the City was more grounded in a broader patterning through perpetual cycles of economic growth or decline often attributed to economic or geopolitical changes. These cycles mirrored creating older bodies through work intensification, exiting, restructuring and subsequently forgetting about ageing bodies after redundancies as part of periodic 'cleansing' (Sebastian, 2016, Y6), of layers of middle management who were often in their 40s and 50s. At the same time, participants expected to be 'age zoned' at some point, put into a category targeted for restructuring, or removed from the organizational structure. Such moments were important to trigger a more explicit consideration of transitions into retirement or leaving jobs that were at the forefront of financial capitalism. Partly, this involved looking at the path that others had taken out of the City. Archie discussed how COVID-19 had made some people in his network decide to retire due to policy and government messages on vaccination and social distancing, although he suggested in his last interview that this trend has been short-lived. Ronnie (2020, Y10) similarly suggested that the pandemic had operated as a 'sweeper' for older people leaving the City, describing certain conditions that may make accelerate people's decision to stop working:

> I've been thinking a lot about age actually, especially in the current climate where some firms have basically just told their employees right back into the office: 'We don't care that you'd feel uncomfortable getting on public transport or that productivity levels have actually been higher in a lot of jobs. We just want you back in the office.' I think that in bigger places like the Goldman Sachs, the JP Morgans of this world, they're very much like that. They've got this view of presenteeism if you like, or you've got to be present for people to see you. People seeing you actually means nothing in terms of doing your job. As long as you do your job and the numbers are where you expect them to be or better, that's the most important thing in my view.

By comparison, Charles discussed how the cycles in the economy and geopolitical changes made him more curious about market dynamics and encouraged him to keep working, although often became the target of gentle jibes from others in that 'they think that I must have seen absolutely everything before as I am so incredibly old' (Charles, 2018, Y8). At the same time, such comments were bound up in him coming to terms with the fact that in practice you rarely even 'made a scuff on them [workplaces]'. This was in contrast to organizational spaces often being indelibly imprinted onto us, such as through the 'aches and pains of too many hours' or in the 'wonderful or not so wonderful memories of colleagues': 'I like to think I'd made a small mark and that is recognized by those who matter, but I can't guarantee … who knows? Perhaps I'm fooling myself that I really mattered, even though I've spent a majority of my working life in rather influential positions in the City.'

Isaac (2012, Y2) similarly described his experience of leaving a job as akin to being deported from city working and how age may thwart an easy replanting into another job. At the same time, there was a worry that the absence from the City and a workplace might accelerate ageing, or at least shape his experience of feeling 'older and a bit useless'. After being made redundant from HFUK, he emphasized how: 'I miss the jokes and the banter, it was like a family atmosphere, you were part of a crowd, I knew a lot of them from before HFUK and it was a nice atmosphere, to go into everyday. I miss that.'

Daily performances were ensconced into workplaces, such as 'in-jokes', routines or a sense of a collective team atmosphere, and these worked to generate ties despite and share some semblance of growing older together. Despite the sector-wide cultural hostility around older employees, the workplace as a site was characterized by some as a relatively constant place that remained steady in the face of their own personal issues such as marriage breakdowns, acrimonious or fractious family affairs, deaths and illnesses. In other words, there was a desire to believe that being in a workplace held the seductive possibility of a 'resting place' – somewhere consistent amid the flux of moving through life.

Of course, recognising spaces in and around labour as *stable* sites did not mean that they were *permanent* site for participants. Conditions and possibilities of sudden job loss were synonymous with their various sectors as was a simmering intolerance to anything that disrupted the expectations of a commercial body. As such, inhabiting the City also contained the possibility of fragmenting participants' own sense of continuity and biography. Workspaces were characterized as providing a rhythm to life while at the same time, holding a promise of containing ageing through providing enough flickering promise of stable inhabitance to offset the flux of life. But they also reminded those within them of the finitude of their careers and workplaces consumed the bodies that passed through them in ways that often accelerated them towards a 'too old' positionality. This worked in symphony with spatial strictures that were more explicit in creating aged sanctions, as we will now explore.

Anchoring ageing appropriately

In workplaces, ageing bodies are expected to be ordered and organized in certain ways, and also have a corporeal awareness of how they fit into economic spaces over their life course. As experienced by James' experience on the Underground, it was often in the seemingly innocuous everyday interactions relating to commercial and economic spaces that required people to recalibrate how they moved, behaved and connected with others. The sociospatial structures of ageing were particularly sharp in places where there was no buffer to help sustain relationships with others. In such situations, one's body became an object for others to interpret, as discussed by a group on the trading desk one morning. One morning, due to a malfunction on the Victoria underground line that had led to an increase of people on alternative lines, a group in the kitchen at HFUK began to discuss etiquette in the 'commuter crush', such as when to give up your seat on the tube and for whom, such as 'someone older/or if it's a woman and she is standing because she doesn't want an old guy's sweaty crotch in her face' (Fieldnotes, 2012). This moved into the discussion of a moral judgement around the 'need' for seats, such as those not being fit enough to be able to stand and endure the journey. But this was also accompanied by a broader debate that actions intended as chivalrous may lead to being misrecognized as a 'dirty old man'. Isaac shared that he was more wary when he was close to a woman in crowded settings, while James discussed being more aware of how he might be viewed by others, in part due to his teenage daughter now travelling alone. In a later interview in 2018 (Y8), James went back to this concern about his own body being read a particular way now that he was a 'bit older', in his words. This included when in a busy pub or coming back late from the city centre where 'I've become far more aware as I've got older of being in a carriage with just me and a woman in case she felt uncomfortable'.

Bodily vigilance as age positioned was not simply important for those trying to avoid unwanted touching, but also pulled certain bodies into place as potentially likely to 'make contact or 'accidentally touch' in ways that could be chronologically indexed. This was even more explicit in later interviews, in part due to participants becoming older and in more senior management positions, and also with the rise of #MeToo in 2017 that was often mentioned during interviews. In relation to this, one evening shortly after an interview, I received a message from Dylan in front of a billboard campaign on the London Underground, standing next to a sign about 'pressing' against people being a form of sexual harassment. In our subsequent messages he stressed that work or commercially orientated spaces and encounters required ongoing governance of one's own and other aged-marked bodies as sites for and claims about sexual harassment, with claims rather than actual incidences being more of a concern for some. At the same time, our exchange suggested that while awareness of work as a site for sexual harassment might have increased, it also had unintended consequences in creating more conservative and regulated spaces to support women.

To suggest that the ability of a person to be a sexual predator can be indexed by chronological age is a huge simplification of power and predatory behaviour in public or organizational spaces. At the same time, this appeared through an emphasis on the danger of 'claims' rather than 'real incidences', suggesting each held different consequences for younger women and older men. During the study, one participant disclosed an incident of being inappropriately touched by someone she called a 'normal guy', but was keen to stress this did not happen in HFUK and also that she 'didn't want to make a fuss'. She had earlier discussed how 'important it was to have a professional appearance if you are a women developing your career' and from what she had shared about her workplace at the time, I could understand her concern how 'smoothing out' the experience and not 'fussing' was part of this professional expectation: the sensible thing to do. By 'sensible', I not only mean in terms of pragmatically performing an expected way in the workpalce, but also striving for a sensibility that steered her away from disrupting a professional narration of the self, given that the situation was unlikely to ever be 'fixed'. Her awareness of this was clear in not wanting to further expose herself to scrutiny in her workplace by telling anyone, even though she stressed to me that colleagues would not think about 'things like what I had done, where I had been, or wearing, you know, those kind of old-fashioned questions you hear about'. At the same time, her description of sitting at her desk after this traumatic episode emphasised how she wanted to avoid any actions that would situate her as a helpless young female, where even benevolent 'well-meaning support from colleagues would be difficult to handle and make it hard to not cry'.

In negotiating the overlap between different commercial settings, other women shared how growing older could bring a greater sense of being able to make up their own spaces of labour. Mia discussed work flexibility in terms of the freedom to be able to travel to work when she wanted and how the choice around where she worked was correlated with growing older and a seniority in her career. Similarly, Flo discussed having more choice over her roles as she acquired expertise, and that this enabled her to avoid rush hours and working in different ways that avoided long or late nights with certain colleagues if she chose to. For others, such as Gen (2018, Y8), the benefit of growing older was bound up in the benefits of jobs that shortened her commute time so that 'I could be doing far more exciting things with [her daughter] now she's a bit older and there's a short period of time where she's going to enjoy spending time with me'.

At the same time, women were aware that seniority as part of their career progression worked against their own ageing bodies being read as either less normatively desirable or more assertive in taking up space. This had benefits in some ways: for example, they felt less exposed and less likely to witness sexualized behaviour in commercial spaces. This was not to suggest they themselves felt less sexual or to deny sexual violence at work still existed, but rather:

> I'm not a natural target anymore, not that I was before but it was definitely discussed more when I was younger. And also I'm not in those spaces anymore, but more senior meetings that are usually either full of other senior people or meetings where I'm central to the conversation. So you don't see it as much. (Anonymous, 2018, Y8)

In terms of not bearing witness to sexual harassment, Lily similarly reflected how certain safe and unsafe spaces were often coded by the age of bodies present. For example, women were often the main carers and 'had to rush off' rather than attend evening networking events or after-work gatherings that were positioned as potentially predatory spaces, and because of this there were 'less senior and older women around when things might happen'.

In other cases, women discussed growing older as coinciding with being situated in the 'mum zone' in ways that shaped where and how they were expected to occupy spaces at work. This did not necessarily correlate with when they had children themselves, but was more associated with colleagues' behaviours, such as when they began to confide in them. Lucy (2012, Y2) discussed always being the one to remember birthdays and special occasions on her team, as well as how some colleagues had begun to privately share their worries about growing older with her: 'Sometimes you don't even need to ask the question and he's going to come and tell you about all his problems. Including problems [that] you don't really need to know about! So, yes, he mentioned he was worried about getting grey and about having his second child.'

Lucy enjoyed this role and when we spoke in 2014 (Y4) when she was struggling to find another job, she reminisced about being in a place 'where my technical skills were valued, but also how I was an important part of the team in lots of ways'. Other women actively worked against being positioned as emotional caretakers for their colleagues. For example, Flo (2018, Y8) mentioned how there was a danger that 'my space and my time do not become my own' due to younger colleagues continually seeking her out, both for her technical skills and also for assurance. This included other managers putting a disproportionate responsibility on her to influence those at the same level as her in different parts of the organization, even though it was not part of her role, stating that 'I cannot be bothered to be the one to beat them into shape. I find this very tiring. It's not what I'm suited to'. Men also mentioned how their partners had experienced this at work. Harry (2020, Y10) discussed how his wife currently had volunteered at their children's school, but that was 'actually more stressful and consuming than her previous career, she's expected to always be on call'. Nathan (2014, Y4) also reflected that some colleagues think that 'as they [women at work] get older, perhaps they are seen as less of a threat, around competition for promotions or something, so they [men] feel safer telling them stuff? It's insulting, isn't it? And stupid as well, but men can be stupid at times'.

Second sites of work

Second sites of work are spaces that are more loosely connected to financial and other career-related outcomes over the working life course. This is not simply explained through the vocabulary of work-life balance, but rather the experience of biographically recalibrating different spaces that offered different possibilities as one grew older. References to second sites emerged repeatedly when asked about the future. Most participants edging into their 50s did want to continue working, some joking about friends who had retired 'getting under the feet of the Mrs' and the disruption of a gendered territorializing of domestic space. Yet this also hinted at a latent anxiety around ageing and masculinity, and what might happen should they find themselves spending more time at home than at work. Their account mirrored our discussions during lockdown, when many talked about commandeering part of their homes for work, such as a large cupboard or spare bedroom, rather than having to work in 'public' home spaces such as kitchen tables or living room couches as more junior colleagues had to do.

For some, lockdown had been a positive experience for Charles, who discussed feeling 'marooned' between work and home as one reason he might continue working for longer. At the same time, his stories of how 'many of my friends have found new places to spend the week, mainly on the golf course or club house' (2016, Y6) echoed other participants' accounts of their non-working peers avoiding being in the house too much. Across these discussions, it emerged that even if not working, for some men I spoke to, their home remained a space that they provided *for* others rather than one that they fully belonged to themselves. In these accounts, I picked up on a sense of angst around being 'just' at home. However, when I later asked participants if their friends or close colleagues felt the same, all but one said they had never really talked about growing older to anyone, even to their partners. Admitting to ageing was fine, but the more unknown elements about *where* you belonged as you grew older remained unspoken:

Serious stuff like that, it's a bit of a downer isn't it? When you get together, it's usually to do something, play golf, go to the football, celebrating someone's birthday at the pub so you might have a laugh about grey hair, or feeling a bit stiff, but you don't talk about … feeling a bit depressed, or the stress of home life. (Dylan, 2016, Y6)

The activities mentioned by Dylan were common across different participants and often marked by a longevity of group relationships in men's lives that brought a sense of familiarity of doing the same thing with the same people over a number of years. At the same time, the duration of their friendships appeared to make them hesitant to disrupt the established rhythms and routines of interaction through introducing new feelings or experiences; there was a fear of disturbing the points of anchorage that had been laid over time. The prospect of introducing new ideas or feelings about growing older into spaces defined through externally orientated activities felt a more fragile context to pause or dislocate in order to share or discuss growing older. Henry (2014, Y4), who had a well-established friendship group over decades, summed this up by suggesting that 'as you get older, it's becoming more common that someone from around [you or your friends and colleagues] dies or gets ill, you might have a … [conversation] about how sad it is, but then you quickly move onto something like the football or something else'. Others felt little need for an extended analysis of both the persisting sequestration or deflection of death, or the impossibility of successfully containing it. Kieran was well aware of the increasing frequency and creeping intrusion of age-connected health experiences as impacting different activities and spaces where there had previously been no need to think about it. Yet he reflected on the difficulty of negotiating such 'deep discussions' then slotting back into more everyday or banal conversations.

In other words, the sites of relationships, friendships and pastimes, how they were built, and where they were located (such as through football, local pubs or work-related social networks) could be complicit in sequestering a discussion of a more sustained attention to ageing. It felt as though there were certain spaces where the repetitive or ritualistic quality of activities and relations stifled 'airtime' for many age-related conversations or interactions. This compared to my final exchange with Theo, who by comparison has discussed how he had striven to recognize value in changing dynamics more broadly, but also how this took effort:

Maybe sometimes people will suffer or struggle if they don't embrace age … If they still think that the person that you were before you got married or before you became a parent, that's still the person you want to be. In my opinion, anyway, that's something that is almost not possible, not in a fundamental way. You can do little things to make you feel or make it seem like, you still have the same things. You can still go to your pop night on Thursday with your mates and all that. Fine, those are all superficial artifacts of almost clinging onto some habits of how you lived before. (Theo, 2020, Y10)

At first glance, Theo's reference to 'clinging on' certainly does not sound as though it holds the potential for a generative or fertile space where one can explore growing older. Instead, Theo suggests that to 'embrace age' is to try to accept that stability and sameness is 'almost not possible, not in a fundamental way' and later in our conversation he suggested that engaging with ageing on these terms is both valuable and meaningful. Others highlighted this too over the years, showing how ageing was associated with embodied modes of surprise, and that different sites of labour and leisure were central to revealing this possibility. One example was Dylan, the person who had helped me gain initial access to HFUK back in 2010. Having played football and shared the same friendship circles as my partner, over the years we had moved from multiple impromptu nights in pubs with to double dates in nicer restaurants to annual family friendly brunches next to playparks often arranged weeks in advance. During one afternoon, when occupying a large table in the middle of a bar for Sunday lunch with our families, I had joked I found our own ageing trajectories were so predictable and closely intertwined and rather boring that it was not great for my study. In response, Dylan emphasized that he found himself happier in now being able to occupy 'gentler' settings and spaces that were more comfortable for him than when he was younger, suggesting that he enjoyed that 'you feel less judged', given the focus was often on his children rather than just him where 'the places you go at the weekend [such as his children's activities], you often turn up in whatever and all the dads look as casual and tired as you do'. Later, during our interview, one afternoon after he had been to watch one of his children play football, Dylan discussed the 'big divide' he felt between the comfort that growing older as a dad brought compared to the professional and physical demands he increasingly felt in becoming 'one of the more seasoned ones' in the workplace, although he recognized how discomfort in one affected comfort in the other:

Dylan: In south London it's more of an older dad crowd, a nice group you could say, people having kids later, on their second home, a bit more secure.

Kat: So there's less shouting from the dads at the side lines than I remember?

Dylan: Definitely. You always get one shouting his mouth off, but mainly people just clap every so often and I think you also are more likely to talk to them, about work, or about your own football injuries or how the kids are doing without feeling a one upmanships or boasting.

The overlap of social and economic spaces that Dylan later described as shared at the side of the football pitch is no surprise. He was well aware his job allowed him to live in 'a nice area with similar people' and the spilling over of interests, influences and relations between people in these spaces was part of a homosociality around professional biographies. This spilling over was also important for one participant, who left the financial services sector to start a lifestyle company that directly marketed to city workers, successfully melding who she was with her previous city credentials into subsequent branding. However, second sites, while reliant on financial success and different modes of biographically accumulated capital in order to be able to access these spaces (such as living in certain school catchment areas or having certain interests), were also where ageing as a source of pleasure began to emerge more explicitly. For example, Henry (2014, Y4) discussed the 'second job' of football coaching when 'you become the spectator rather than the player' as being a unexpected source of gratification. Going from playing football to passively watching their children was not simply a case of 'giving up and becoming an old man', but an experience of interactions that brought enjoyment and also enabled subsequent reflections about their health, their career and their economic future more broadly.

This is often connected with the potential to recognize and recalibrate their priorities. For example, Dylan similarly talked about the enjoyment found in becoming what he wryly called the household 'chief of staff' during a period of not working and taking on the primary caring role. The affective pleasure of these 'softer spaces' as sites for thinking about ageing also put into sharp focus what workplaces lacked around meaning making. For Sebastian, the transactional nature of work became more stark compared to a pleasure he experienced in the deepening of relationships in other spaces as he grew older. This had been unexpected and always partial given they were also accompanied by many other 'mundane tasks' around caring. At the same time, Sebastian discussed how he was surprised about how much he enjoyed these moments that he contrast to the staccato experience of belonging that had dominated his work environments when he was younger. During our 4th conversation, he gave an intriguing retrospective account of being 'less concerned with relationships' and 'more concerned with what people thought of me' and how this was changing. This compared to interviews with female participants where relationships had been a formative thread of interviews from early in the study. However, for men, this seemed to appear as an experience only discussed later in their lives. For example, Sebastian (2016, Y6) shared that: 'It's [caring for his child] a kind of connection and pleasure that grows rather than just being about a certain objective. Some people might have this in their careers, but I certainly haven't.'

Theo was similarly clear that his own pleasure in ageing was beyond work and instead was found in sites or spaces that prioritized relations rather than transactions. He emphasized that this was not something that could be taken for granted, but emerged as he grew older and more deliberately tended to relationships and life outside work, paying attention to things that 'can affect you deeply':

> I think it's a case of like your wife, your children, your marriage, or being parent, they shape you in ways that you would not have chosen perhaps yourself or chosen as in predicted, but they've done it for the better. They've done it in a way that you would never have you would never have chosen for yourself because the whole point of being a husband or a wife or being a father is it's not about you anymore. It's less about you than it is about other people. By definition, also then you would probably not choose things because you would choose things out of a selfish way normally or a self-centred way ... it's changed me in ways that I would never have imagined would be the case. (Theo, 2020, Y10)

Given these second sites could be precious sources of pleasure in ageing some discussed the need to publicly perform an active territorialization of their separateness from more transactional settings such as workplaces. One reason for this was that second sites often involved deploying effort and energy that had previously been reserved only for work, and participants saw possibilities of this being perceived negatively by 'other alpha males at work' (Jack, 2016, Y6), even if those activities carried all the hallmarks of reproducing a virile masculinity. Others felt that there was a danger that talking about these spaces as enabling different ways of being could conflate with feminized expectations of 'conflicting priorities, or even not coping with work and family ... this is still the assumption of a lot of employers' (Lucy, 2014, Y4). During the later years of interviewing, many women such as Lucy looked back on our previous conversations around expectations of future family life and often felt that: 'One thing that hasn't changed is that there is still a wall between work and life. Men might be more vocal in doing the odd thing or be more likely to take time off, but it's not changed that much.' Similarly, Mia said that the expectations she discussed in 2010 about work becoming more 'family-friendly' had not transpired. While 'family responsibilities' was now a lexicon she heard more at work, it still expected that everything else simply slotted into the rhythm of work. In this regard she referred to as 'all the rest and organizing it all' had to be done 'almost in secret', despite increasing seniority (Mia, 2020, Y10). In particular, she suggested that as a senior woman, there were certain nonwork activities she could be seen as doing and others not so in work: 'Now it seems ok – at least sometimes – to acknowledge you have to leave to pick up the kids, but there is still not a recognition that pick-ups and drop offs are the easiest and most predictable task when you are a mother.' Less acceptable infringements the were more common as children grew older included being called away from work through a phone call or having to take time off for illness, as the unexpected nature of these incidents disrupted the expected flow of working. These ruptures suggest that the person occupying work and second spaces were delineated by a gendered fourth wall:

> When you grow older, you are more likely to be in a high performing team, everything you do is so connected and dependent to other colleagues' work, so when you have someone who is key to decision-making and all of a sudden can't be there, it's hard not to get a bit frustrated. (Mia, 2018, Y8)

Larger social and political changes also led to breaches between commercial and second sites of working through ageing. For example, many discussed how Brexit saw the explicit and public emergence of age-correlated political allegiances. This disrupted previous expectations that 'politics is just something you shouldn't discuss unless with a few close friends. There are so many divergent and surprising political views people hold in professional services that it's not worth getting involved, especially in a client facing industry' (Sebastian, 2010, Y0). Similarly, during fieldwork in 2012 at HFUK I had overheard a conversation suggesting the 'people talk about politics, but they hardly ever talk about their *own* politics'. However, in 2016, when conducting interviews just after the outcome of the EU referendum, many felt unable to avoid discussion of the referendum, despite these norms, and how political conversations in work also revealed backgrounds and biographies 'that up until then, you did not think about or mention', calling into question the maintenance of what Sebastian called his 'neutral facade' at work. For example, Dylan described how conversations on Brexit brought into play different political allegiances that were connected to different age cohorts in his workforce, such as being '80s Thatcher right' or 90s Blair left', although this intersected with other identifies as well: 'even if a different age or generation, if you come from working class or lower middle-class sort of background, then you tend to think like along the same lines about Brexit, not matter where you are working' (2018, Y8).

The spatial emplacement of ageing's intersections with race, gender and class became particularly sharp just after the UK vote to leave Europe, particularly for those who had previously assumed themselves to be global workers and viewed themselves as having an international professional currency. For others who were not UK citizens or had partners who were not UK citizens, it meant having to reckon with the possibility of uprooting themselves. One participant discussed how a member of their team has felt lucky that 'they were still quite young', which they felt gave them more options in whether to stay or move elsewhere given working visas can have age limits. Others discussed the worry of talking to their manager 'to make it clear I might not be as welcomed in this country anymore' if visa or immigration rules changed. For Flo, who was born outside Europe but had spent most of her adult life in the US and the UK, Brexit correlated with discovering their own political capacity as they grew older: 'I suppose it's right to say that at the moment I'm definitely discovering a lot more of a political identity than I ever – I never thought about it, I never cared until 3.00 am on Friday, June the 24th. I'm not sure what I'm going to do about that' (2016, Y6).

While Flo suggested that this might alter how she thought about the sectors in which she worked, Brexit also forced an imagination of a possible future in countries and locations beyond their choosing. Lucy, who was from another EU country, similarly suggested that 'it made me question a lot, not just about work but moving over to the UK and making a life here'. This was about not only supplanting one's expectations of a predictable trajectory with a more questionable future, but also questioning the legitimacy of past and present feelings of comfort and belonging in places and spaces, and whether they had ever 'really' been accepted.

Discussion: unmooring ageing

Space renders visible the irrefutability of how the ageing body is made through a grounded materiality. Being located across different spaces and places make it impossible to deny a situated interdependence and that sites of ageing and participatory exchanges in these sites irrefutably make up the self while also existing beyond the self. The sociospatiality of ageing carries with it a disturbing potential, as it prevents us from speaking to the 'out-thereness' of ageing and the rawness of confronting the idea that we are both ageing subjects and ageing objects within a constellation of other people, objects and things in a given setting. It highlights the power of space in constituting part of how and individual 'grasps, through foreign consciousness, her body and her relation to the world' (de Beauvoir, 2015 [1949]: 761) and is a formative element in de Beauvoir's concept of 'situation'. Location articulates sociality as conditionally anchored through being dynamically situated in a biographical nexus of age, gender and other parameters of recognition. Yet, as Tuan (1986: 11) suggests, space is also a powerful tool in showing that 'outsiders, by implication, belong to a lower order'. Spaces plot and demarcate who is the outsider or who becomes the outsider as they grow up and older, marginalizing without the requirement of words or actions.

The durability of the built commercial environment is central to this, given that it appears as more neutral, enduring and immovable than our own careers or even our own bodies. There is a seduction in presenting work as a space simply 'given' and operates similar to the way de Beauvoir (2018 [1947]: 39) discusses how children escape the 'anguish of freedom'. The context of work can provide a comfort, giving us the feeling that we 'can not make a dent in the serene order of a world which existed before', thus absolving us of weight or responsibility to even try and do otherwise. Being materially located or attached to somewhere, physically attached and corporeally bound, can provide an illusion of fixity and permanence – a mirage that we can hold on to when our own bodies and other events in our life are in flux. However, this offering is already skewed by pre-existing configurations that appear 'just as': ageing bodies are ordered and aligned in particular ways that signal how certain bodies should dwell in spaces of labour and for how long in terms of job role, status or level in the hierarchy or sector. They also carry certain chronochoreographical expectations relating to movement, mobility or career direction. Often these encourage a reproduction of well-trodden paths of who professionally belongs where and when as we grow older. Anchoring ourselves within this landscape can make us complicit in a blueprint for how to inhabit working life across our life course. Even when existential events such as COVID-19 or Brexit happen, or our own affective experiences of joy through familial ties partially reveal the chrononormative commercial faultlines within workspaces, there is a compulsion to return to the assumption that these spaces were themselves external, independent, immutable or unchanging.

Just as commercial spaces provide the possibilities for us to nestle into particular aged locations that feel validating or comfortable, they simultaneously hold the possibility of 'unmooring' us as we grow up and older. Spaces remind us of our own peripatetic limitations, and how changing bodies and lives are consumed within changing sites of labour that have the temerity to exist for a longer time than we ever could. Experiences of anchoring and this corollary of unmooring highlight how indexes of normative age relations are invariably 'riveted together' in space (de Beauvoir, 2015 [1949]: 19), making economic and commercial spaces central to realizing our own bodies are dynamic and changing. This can happen within a seemingly static space of an office, boardroom, shopfloor, classroom or any other context where labour is undertaken, but always does so in time as well, often in ways that bend ageing's perceptual embodiment making 'space seems monstrously swollen [while]... time seems strangely contracted', as de Beauvoir (2004 [1947]: 307) recalled during her travels in America. Ageing hostility is disclosed in these moments given that 'space takes over time's betrayal – places change. But even those that seem to have remain unaltered are not the same for me' (de Beauvoir, 1986 [1970]: 407). On one level this means that bodies in settings are age (in)appropriate through the way in which they are quickly read and interpreted in the eyes of others. However, to complicate this, sites inform and shape our own sense of what ageing may mean. For most of our participants, the rhythms of commercial life in which ageing bodies are cohered were made up of dizzying movement across spaces, transitory exchanges and multiple encounters within settings that pulsate through a jungle drum of financial capitalism. They got used to being carried along in this way, but it meant that any physical or sensational jolt to our own sense of self can be both irrefutable and disorientating. The moments in which we become an aged body-object in space can be so fleeting that they are not supported by expressions, vocabularies or set of epistemic resources that can help us negotiate how we want to be seen as an ageing subject or how we might regain a sense of equilibrium. We are instead left with the lingering sense of discombobulation, feeling a bit lost in a sea of ageing.

Taking up different spaces across our working lives is not simply about an engagement that anchors us, but is constitutive of conditions of ageing in terms of how our temporally situated bodies are cohered in situated relations. The chronochoreography of ageing is constituted in economic and labour market trends, retrospective sense making around sector patterns, and the expectation of linear and upward career trajectories that serve as broader anchorage points and organize bodies in and around work. They provide a sociospatial case in point of how 'my history must be the sequel to a pre-history whose acquired results it uses' (Merleau-Ponty, 2014 [1945]: 265). Participants found that even when their own personal biographies did not reflect gendered life course expectations, an imagined domestic sphere often plotted the spectre of the Other in the workplace. This populated opportunities and spaces to develop one's career and move on and up. However, they were usually contingent on traditional gendered domestic labour seeping into the workplace, functioning, as de Beauvoir suggests, as 'walls [that] block out the horizon' and restrict, shrink or assume the 'whole future in portable form' (de Beauvoir, 2015 [1949]: 762). For example, Ava's and Lucy's colleagues expected a bleeding of care capacities from the imagined familial space into a mode of 'managerial mothering' that Cutcher (2021) also discusses.

Domestication as a site that is attached to women's commercial careers across the life course in particular becomes central to understanding how work-based opportunities and ageing trajectories become laid out. Here spatial configurations are key to an unmooring that operates within normatively accepted discourses, such as narrations of parenting. This appears to have changed only slightly since de Beauvoir suggested that 'One can hardly tell women that washing up saucepans is their divine mission, they are told that bringing up children is their divine mission. But the way things are in the world, bringing up children has a great deal in common with washing up saucepans' (Schawarzer and de Beauvoir, 1984: 114). By comparison, in not being compelled into anchor points of care, some men had the possibility of exploring ageing as a generative mode of surprise in mundane locations of family life that were less plotted. For example, we might think about Sebastian's description of experiencing 'connection and pleasure' of looking after his child once he has stopped being so tied to being youthful masculinities, which points to a pleasure in feeling an attachment not tied to paid labour. This is perhaps not a radical assertion and we should be mindful of romanticising care work in any way, but it does say something about how different forms of ageing masculinities may afford a greater plurality of anchorage points compared to earlier in life. The extent to which such spaces of unpaid practice or care continue to rely on the uneven emplotment of traditional feminine biographies is another matter.

Working through ageing thus demands attention to the chiasmic relationship between our dynamically situated bodies and organizational sites or locations. This is not simply about a duality of being (un)situated, (un)comfortable or (un)welcome in certain commercial contexts or where our jobs demand us to be situated. It is also about recognizing that our preponderance for anchoring and recoiling from feeling unmoored means that attending to the sociospatiality of ageing highlights how ageing subjectivities involve a quality of tensegrity. Tensegrity in this sense is about the integrity of a given structure or project – such as a suspension bridge, or in this case the dynamic body in situ – that relies on experiencing continuous and often invisible tensions and compression points between various components to hold it all together: ourselves, others, our relations and the locations we inhabit. Tensegrity is achieved through different elements appearing to be unconnected, giving the illusion of not touching each other or 'floating'. Such an image highlights the ontological importance of spatiality as setting up, conspiring or opposing forces that disclose ageing. Different spaces can provide the capacity to withstand or endure incremental changes as both the components of the self and the environment shift, whether that be a suspension bridge in a storm or an ageing body in the organizational milieu of financial capitalism. Tensegrity as a quality of ageing is central to our own ongoing sense of self where disclosure itself requires what de Beauvoir calls a 'perpetual tension' in that 'the fact is that the world becomes present by his presences in it. But the disclosure implies a perpetual tension to keep being at a certain distance, to tear oneself from the world and to assert oneself as a freedom' (2018 [1947]: 23).

In this sense, ageing requires a recognition that interdependent elements must hold together across different locations to maintain an integrity of the self, often in ways that are difficult to perceive or consciously connect. In practice, such forces are pre-reflective invisible points of intention that are often worked through in an organizational landscape: continually pulling for the next promotion against craving more leisure time; moving jobs enough times to maintain the credibility in one's careers, but not too much so as to breach it and seem uncommitted; requiring family spaces to be wrested into economic demands for (hopefully) a short period of time; or inhabiting the high stress of commuting or work travel, or the accumulative quivering stress of inconvenient but potentially generative caring demands. It even maps onto the expectation of a professional body that should be consistently capable of performing such endurance, and mirrors the leanness of a frenetic work environment, even though in practice bodily disrepair may be accelerated due to occupying stressful and uncertain sites of labour.

Expectations and experiences of transegrity often compel us to think that it is *our* ageing that is out of kilter rather than these settings being contingent and unstable. We might hold expectations of an orderly and predictable ageing process in seemingly orderly and predictable spaces, but our lived experience often finds that these are lived out in an uncomfortable manner. Being unable to feel completely safe or coherent in certain spaces can in turn compel us to submit or conform to aged expectations time and time again, even when our bodies or our relations with others indicate the strain as time goes on.

However, I would suggest that the tension of tensegrity as manifest in anchoring and unmooring ageing that we saw in participants accounts may also provide more generative opportunities to ponder how a more situated encounter might constitute an ethical potential in situation of ageing in space and place. In her exegesis of Beauvoirian ethics, Sonia Kruks (2012: 8) suggests that 'what she [de Beauvoir] propounds is an account of human existence as intrinsically driven by ambiguities and tensions that precisely are not amenable to a synthetic resolution. These tensions are the very stuff of life itself'. Within ageing, tension is central to how things appear to us as aged individuals, through a situated and sited orientation or disruption to the 'active style of living one's body' in the world (Butler, 1986: 40). However, the body is not essential or fixed but 'a *field of interpretative possibilities*' that invite 'a dialectical process of interpreting anew a historical set of interpretations which have become imprinted in the flesh' (Butler, 1986: 45, emphasis in original). In the visceral experience of somatically inhabiting spaces imbued with a commercial temporality that might clash with our own carnal temporality, these points of tension render visible a bifurcation of ageing as neither autonomously cohered by the invidiously nor socially circumscribed. The strain this creates invites us to recalibrate how we inhabit different spaces, and may serve to break down the de facto apart-ness we have from of our own bodies, even if in doing so we face the risk something snapping or breaking.

However, if our anchorage is never fully accomplished or guaranteed, perhaps recognition of its contingency through the experience of tensegrity can also provide the opportunity to understand unmooring as an important element of the ageing body in space and time. In other words, paying attention to the tensegrity of ageing also provides the possibility for alternative pivot points to come to the fore. This could be an array of speculative futures and how in turn we might set about provisioning spaces that take us there, as well as a consideration of how the carnal echoes of past locations or sites might provide the cinders that help us imagine a different way of growing older. Part of this returns to Kruks' ethical promise and asserts the perceptual capacities of the age-situated self as having a potential to withstand unmooring as much as anchoring; where unmooring is a quality of an ontology of ageing that 'will be lived in both heartbreak and joy [...] since at the moment one releases his hold, he again finds his hands free and ready to stretch out towards a new future' (de Beauvoir, 2018 [1947]: 30).

This is not a universalized experience where chronochoreographies categorize us all the same way to delimit or allow recognition in commercial or economic spaces based beyond the potential to extrapolate labour or value in situ. Rather, the experiential qualities of inhabiting different spaces over our working lives mean that unmooring can be generative in the ongoing experience of ageing and its disturbance or disorientating effects that hold us in sociospatial tension. This is a recognition of how unmooring holds the potential for a more expansive encounter with ageing in situ. To consider if this expansive mode of working through ageing might be possible in the broader theoretical apparatus of ageing, I will now move on in the final chapter to consider the potential of working through ageing as a generative project.

7

Mottling: Surfacing a Generative Experience of Working Through Ageing

While my aim has been to provide new ways of thinking about our experiences of ageing and work through empirical attention to one particular group of people, researching ageing is inevitably an intimate undertaking, as became clear seven years into this study. In 2017 my daughter was born prematurely at 25 weeks gestation in Barcelona on the day after the Catalan Independence Referendum. She was in the wrong place at the wrong time, not only 'hatching' too early to allow my family and I to go back to our lives in Australia but also landing herself in an alien healthcare system and country, given I had only been there for a period of study leave. Crowned by her nurses as 'The Youngest Member of the New Republic' at minus 15 weeks old, she spent 86 days in the neonatal ward with myself and partner doing alternate eight-hour shifts while my own mum flew over from the UK to proxy parent my three-year-old son for three months.

Every few weeks felt like the turn towards transcendence I had been previously reading about where her before-born body was 'moved up': shuffled from one end of the ward, reserved for the earliest or most unwell babies, towards the door, where you eventually got your freedom away from institutional care and towards a projected – though not promised – 'normal' life for all of us. I had an enviable panorama of Barcelona FC's Camp Nou football stadium from my chair in the neonatal ward and spent my days waiting for this view to change as her incubator moved closer to the exit. For a while, the idea of ageing at work was the last thing on my mind and life became caught up in a very different and unexpected series of temporally marked institutional relations, patterned by these little moves. At the same time, repetitive days merged into each other through taking four hourly temperature checks, cutting out tiny nappies from the smallest size available (a task to keep parents busy rather than being useful, admitted one nurse), learning Spanish on the train to and from the hospital so that I could try to make small talk with staff, and hours of 'kangaroo care', holding her while she was connected to machines and monitors that were doing an equal if not more important job than me. It was both banal and stressful, and the monotony of such tasks stood in sharp contrast to the impossible awesomeness of the possible consequences emerging from what can be a life or death situation. At the same time, my response was predictable and mundane for a researcher, continually feeding on any knowledge I could find about what 'works best' during extreme prematurity. I read anything about 'preemies' obsessively, each article stitching together an ontological security blanket of good mothering that did not quite overcome having to leave her in a lab of incubators at the end of each day.

One day, when there was due to be a 'shuffle' of incubator positions, her morning paediatrician raised a query about some mottling on her feet. 'Nothing important', I was told – a rather cryptic message where every indication, every weigh-in, every murmur, stretch or muscular reflex, every hourly check and passing of bodily waste is measured, written down and interpreted. But while I ferociously speed read about mottling, I could not get past its ambiguous parameters mapped out and justified through chronology in ways that allowed my daughter to fit in – the frustration of ageing had dared to bite back at a most inconvenient moment. My armchair research revealed how mottling was a discolouration that occurs as a result of a disruption to blood supply underneath the skin. It often signalled that something was out of kilter, indicated by a bodily flow that we take so much for granted as part of the 'recessive body', as opposed to the ecstatic surface 'where self meets what is other than self' (Leder, 1990: 11). When recessive modes of embodiment surface in some way, such as through mottling, they mark a disruption which commands and demands attention. They become a point of orientation for our relations, perceptions and actions.

However, this depends heavily on whose body is mottled. It can be hereditary and in animals in particular, mottling can be part of a patterning passed on through genetic heritages, manifesting at any point in life and, while sanctioned as normal, can impact the animal's market value and ultimately its trajectory. For humans, when you are terminally ill or considered very old, mottling may be read from your body as a sign of moving towards death, some suggesting that mottling is a '14-day indicator' of mortality (Dumas et al, 2019). Approaches or interpretations also depend on where the mottled body is located. If mottling happens in an acute hospital setting, it is likely to bring about a host of different tests, while in a hospice or gerontology ward, it may trigger more holistic, less interventionalist rituals. Different minority ethnic groups may also experience different patterns and manifestations of mottling as they grow older (Rawlings, 2006). By comparison, mottling in babies is common and often requires no more than the usual unrellenting demands of monitoring through the parental gaze.

But there are some cases in which the pluriverses of space, place, time and bodies mean that the surfacing of mottling holds an ambiguous quality, as was the case with my daughter. She was very premature and was still not supposed to be born for another seven weeks, but had up until now been 'healthy'. Should a specialist be called? Should she be immediately moved back and 'away' from the door and into a more intense care regime? Was it best she be consigned back into incubator isolation or did she need to be held and her temperature and heartbeat regulated by closeness to another body? Could I check if I had experienced mottling as a baby or whether my brother and sister had similar episodes? Was I more worried than usual, had I eaten anything different that could affect my breast milk or changed the brand of my deodorant? Being unable to explain the disruption to the skin is met with disruption to where the she and the we of our lives were located, treated and positioned. Something surfacing on her skin in this context at this moment in time pulled a 780 gram bundle's bodily histories and heritages into a situation where we were never supposed to be in the first place.

In one way, the practical minutiae of mottling felt a world away from the testimonies of ageing and working in financial capitalism that I concerned myself with for years before and after. But when returning to my participants' accounts since, I became aware of mottling representing one of many tips of the experiential iceberg of ageing where attention to our corporeal complexity shows us 'emergence of the flesh as expression' (Merleau-Ponty, 1968: 145). Here, lines of action spring into place and manifest in different ways of relating, being and situating. Ageing as the bodily acts of 'doing' highlight the ontological experiences of being; a profoundly phenomenological project situated in perceptions, circumstances and relations between the self, others and settings. This project manifests in ways that may be innocuous or seismic, transitory or marked, but always felt in and through our body as dynamically situated. It surfaces ageing, if only for a moment, and always too quickly or ambiguously for us to fully grasp. This happens in and through an ever-changing corporeal body: unlike Leder's (1990: 173) suggestion that the body is 'a way that we, as part of the universe, mirror the universe', the ageing body holds no promise of being a steady reflector we perhaps wish it to be. However, could it be that this dynamically situated flesh holds even richer and generative possibilities for being and doing?

In this final chapter, I want to consider how mottling as a figure of ageing speaks to the phenomenological dynamics of surfacing that constitute working through ageing. Surfacing cuts across disclosing, grasping and anchoring in the accounts of people we have previously heard from in this book, and points to how we as ageing subjects and aged objects are revealed through the knotted experiences of the working life course. But it also points to a depth of ageing experience, some of which lies beyond the horizon of our direct perception, but not yet part of a fully recessive corporeality. I explore this through pausing on the ethical, political and psychosocial inflected elements that characterize a rich dynamic interiority that is particular to ageing. In doing so, I am not working towards an indissoluble point of 'truth' of or formula for a good life as we grow older that can be found if we excavate enough; rather, surfacing allows us to recognize the deeply welled constellations of people, relations and contexts that come together to form our experience of being an ageing self that is fundamental to ageing as a corporeal bound 'way of casting oneself into the world and of disclosing being' (de Beauvoir, 2018 [1947]: 44).

As I found in my experience of mottling and the accounts of my respondents in previous chapters, surfacing ageing as a mode of ontopoiesis is both ambiguous and ambivalent. It requires us to disclose, grasp and (re)anchor our selves in ways that are both contingent and disruptive, and deeply grounded in our temporally charged corporeality. Surfacing as a line through which we cast ourselves into the world also opens us up interrogating the ambivalence – or even the belligerence – of the dynamically situated body that is so central to ageing modes of sociality. De Beauvoir herself concedes that:

> Doubtless, every one casts himself onto it [the world] on the basis of his physiological possibilities, but the body itself if not a brute fact. It expresses our relationship to the world, and that is why it is an object of sympathy or repulsion. And on the other hand, it *determines* no behaviour. (de Beauvoir, 2018 [1947]: 44, emphasis in original)

In de Beauvoir's treatise on old age and her novels such as *Misunderstanding in Moscow*, we see is this unresolved tension play out. She recognizes that ageing is not an absolute experience and the specificity of ageing as a situated embodied experience must consider that casting oneself into the world is always differentially experienced. At the same time, while she suggests that the dynamics of subjectivity are temporally orientated, she curiously assigns an almost quantitative value to our positionality on a definitive timeline:

> Because habit confers a certain quality upon the world and a certain charm to the passage of time, at any age we lose something when we give one up. But in youth it is not ourselves that we lose, since it is in the future and in the accomplishment of our projects that our being lies. The old person dreads change because he is afraid that he will not be able to adapt himself to it, and he therefore does not see it as an

opening but only as a break with the past … tearing him from it means removing him from his very being. (de Beauvoir, 1986 [1970]: 521)

Read in isolation, this might imply a rather ontologically determinist stance where our positionality in the life course changes our ontological make-up. Less generous interpretations have suggested that de Beauvoir's own internalized ageism both predominantly shapes ageing subjectivities and informs her personal stance as situated in France at a time when strictures around how women should (not) grow old were part of the cultural fabric. However, considering de Beauvoir's accounts of subjectivity across her work and the complexity of disclosing, grasping and anchoring ageing in the accounts of ageing to which I was privy, I would suggest that while our finitude is invariably acute,[1] *only* paying attention to this can undermine attention to ageing as a phenomenological project. Notably, it ignores the potential for surfacing as a way of holding an invitation to move beyond a simple reverberation of an age-hostile world and instead allows us to consider what other qualities working through ageing might attend to, what modes of mottling might be recognised, and how work as a particular site enables or constrain this.

Bringing together de Beauvoir's reflections in conversation with her contemporary Merleau-Ponty's concern with latency in his later work, surfacing bring together the ideas of ageing as disclosing, grasping and anchoring introduced in previous chapters. To begin this exploration means returning to the context of professional work in financial capitalism. Below I introduce how the invisibility of ageing redolent in accounts is not only sector-specific but also points to a latent or hidden aspect of ageing that is inherent in our sociality as we grow up and older. Exploring this latency as a phenomenological feature of ageing, I then turn to focus on what I term the compostability of ageing, considering how our corporeal experience of ageing is part of an embodied and psychosocial experience of being

---

[1] Finitude is, for de Beauvoir and many others, aligned with death, which has also been synonymous with how ageing has been theorized more generally. Such accounts and ideas around ageing and death are both important and valuable to ageing as realized through the planes of the known and unknown. My own position, as discussed in the preface, is not to dismiss that death might be important to the ageing experience. Indeed, in my conversations with people, there were certainly instances of both near-death experiences and the death of close relations that were formative to people's experiences of ageing, as well as cases of potential ontological death where a mode of recognition central to that person's sense of being was potentially extinguished. However, I have sought to depart from a concern with death to avoid theorizing ageing as predominantly a journey which always presupposes a final destination. As my participants revealed, attending to death is by no means the only or even the most important way in which the phenomenological project of ageing appears to us.

in and through time. Emphasizing how ageing operates through a bodily promiscuity, I further develop the idea of being Other-in-myself introduced in Chapter 5 to consider the ethical claims that ageing might enable through considering different modes of relating and recognition in work and beyond. Finally, I suggest how attention to the phenomenological project of working through ageing underscores the social and political potential to render the dynamic, embodied and ontopoetic experience of ageing intelligible against a contemporary landscape that remains pockmarked with ontological enclosure and epistemic siloes.

The invisibility of ageing in financial services work

While perhaps not the primary objective of financial capitalism, the way in which the ageing experience has been sanitized and relegated into such narrow parameters within economic and corporate landscapes is nonetheless an impressive achievement. Unless discussing the realms of joining or leaving a job, joining the call to prevent age discrimination, or hand-wringing at the stubborn demographic forces and the challenge of longer and healthier working lives, age lingers beneath the surface when talking about work. The ageing experience of work for those I spoke to involved a subtle percolation of cultures and logics of financial and professional services and other professional occupations where performances emphasised short-term measurement and the deferral of the now or past onto the maybe-future. Given our bodies can be seen as dependent on 'historically contingent ways of producing forms of knowledge, truth and identity' [that are...] often beyond our ability to apprehend' (Tidd, 1999: 91), it is unsurprising that market trends, modes of labour, and the historical and cultural trajectories of various professions or sectors were part of the ingredients that could make or break the bodily contours of participants. Existing accounts of city work by scholars such as Daniel Beunza (2019), Melissa Fisher (2012) and Linda McDowell (1997) are testament to this and have provided rich insights into how policies, practices and local actions are desired, sanitized and insisted upon. Just as Ho's (2009: 324) study of Wall Street highlighted how bankers subjectivities 'are enmeshed within the organizational culture of Wall Street', ageing within my own study could rarely be understood as separate from the stratums of commercial and economic market concerns.

My concern with ageing in this setting highlights that uneven but neutralized territories operate over years of working that both benefit some bodies over others and are experienced through our own unsteady corporeality as we grow up and older. An near-impregnable aged ongoing hostility is difficult to challenge when you are ambivalent about being its hostage or have even been its beneficiary. Even individuals who did recognize the systemic and structural fallacies and biases of the sector often found that the logics of the sector encourage a position of the employee to be one of 'detached contemplation; outside of time and far from men, he faces history which he thinks he does not belong to, like a pure beholding' (de Beauvoir, 2018 [1947]: 80). While de Beauvoir could not have predicted that this tendency towards 'impartial interest' would be such a feature of working in financial capitalism, she did warn of the consequences of such a position to labour, notably through her reference to children working in sweatshops in that 'enchanted by the tale, the style, and the images, we forget the horror of the sweatshop or even start admiring it' (de Beauvoir, 2018 [1947]: 83). There is something both stagnant and enduring about modes of production and social production that stymy our ability to connect its success with the harm of others in an enduring or recognizable way. In other words, we see how organizational contexts and cultures are central to deflecting our attention away from the enactment of age-hostile relations, perceptions and locations.

But more significantly, these systems of work lay the groundwork for enabling ageing to be narrated and framed as a curse on one's agential capacity. It shows age to be another convenient interlocutor through which inequalities can thrive and people 'hedged out', to use Neely's (2022: 266) term for 'a form of boundary making around an elite status explicitly tied of masculinity and whiteness'. Even when working in roles where the day-to-day function is not directly working with markets, it is clear that there are embodied expectations and consequences of operating 'at the edge of the present moment, a location of high uncertainty where the authority of knowledge fades as traders try to anticipate slight market movements. With this murky view of the future, traders orient themselves with charts and social knowledge, but the matter that they shape the most assiduously is the self' (Zaloom, 2006: 173). I would argue that the logics that underpin financialization, including the way in which money, value, commodities and productivity drive behaviour and practice, are increasingly setting the playbook beyond the financial sector and bring with them the marksmen for modes of aged hostility that invariably imprint onto the corporeality of the subject.

However, this carries consequences far beyond this sector and informs how we think about working through ageing more broadly. Understanding these dynamics in and through an attention to ageing helps to show the vicarious consequences for growing older in the shadow of the resilient, resistant and autonomous subject that contemporary management discourses thrive on. This is a subjectivity that compels us to displace or deny any sensual or bodily experiences that cannot be captured within the canons of an economy of financial capitalism. Buying into the myth of an organically immune 'ideal worker' subject is in many ways part of the infrastructure that disavows any institutional or social responsibility and accountability for the ageing body.

It is helped along by a working trajectory marked by a fractured engagement with multiple employers, managers and workplaces over the life course who have little incentive to take on a body previously harmed and little incentive not to cumulatively harm a body that is likely to move on to another employer in the future. We can see here how agedness as a systemic practice of inequality is predicated through patterns and modes of working that are assumed to be age-neutral; where different ages may be recognized as more or less affected, but ageing itself is persistently viewed as standing beyond any structure. As we have seen in the previous chapters, this is of course incorrect. Aged practices are not located only in individual bad behaviour or cultural perceptions of weakness or fragility based on chronological or chronobiological attributes and experiences; rather, it is present in the brittleness of the normative institutional apparatus that require us to be ever-productive, ever-infallible economic units, and the interface between aged systems of organizing and the shoring-up of particular corporealities.

In this context, the 'work' in working through ageing does not simply accept 'powering through' the conditions of a highly competitive and intensive trajectory in the shadow of financial capitalism. Rather, it invites our attention to the theoretical apparatus that illuminate the broader ways in which other workers – whose labour and life circumstances may differ dramatically – are also subject to the experiential dynamics of ageing as a way of being and doing in the context of institutional organizing processes of work and the economy. Work is an important way of creating a sense of belonging and connection in the world, and while there are of course other ways, it is particularly powerful, given that it is also expected to provide financial and material sustenance, although recent commentaries on precarious work suggest that this is no longer a given. It is one of the 'persistent social structures that influence our capacity to experience the world, not just in isolated instances, but in a way that is deeply constitutive of who we are and how we make sense of things' (Guenther, 2019: 13).

Organizations are not simply about transactions but interactions, albeit uneven ones, and are also a locus of recognition in an ontological sense: important given that 'none has its real meaning except in its relations with the others ... the individual's relationship with his body and his image during the last years, to his relationship with time, history and his own praxis, and to his relations with others and the outside world each in turn, must be read from the viewpoint of a final synthesis' (de Beauvoir, 1986 [1970]: 313). As shown through attention to ageing subjectivities as relational, experiential and situated, our own understanding of who we are is contingent not only on 'what I think I am', but on 'what you think I am' and 'what you think that I think you think', and this invariably structures the ageing experience. This muddling of the I and you is not simply in everyday experiences, but also in anticipation of the gaze of others and how it is fed back. Such processes are invariably intersectional where the nexus of aged, gendered, racialized or socioeconomic systems of power can either threaten or validate one's ontological integrity and coherence.

In this regard, a phenomenological theory of working through ageing is both a critical intervention and critique to counter how ageing – and by extension, us as ageing subjects – become captured through organizational regimes that seem divorced from our dynamic, situated corporeality. It renders visible how exclusion, marginalization and harm is occluded or belittled when ageing is either displaced, colonized or only recognized through instituted, external canons of knowledge rather than our own corporeal experience. In other words, working through ageing through the experiential canons of disclosing, grasping anchoring and mottling provide broader theoretical inroads to recover the physical, social, socioeconomic and existential struggles and joys that are part of the process of ageing, showing how work is key to how and where ageing take place and plays out in terms of power, agency, capacity, embodied experience and perception.

The generative Other-in-ageing

At the same time, this account of people working through ageing highlights the value of considering how the ageing experience as a process of being in and of the world connects to the formation of the ageing organizational subject as witnessed in the dynamics of disclosing, grasping and anchoring. When I speak about surfacing ageing as part of a dialectics of invisibility, I do not only mean being the opposite of visible as in wilfully hidden by organizational systems, structures or norms, or even a 'de facto invisible', as Merleau-Ponty puts it (1968 [1964a]: 151); rather, it is invisibility as a quality of ageing that is part of 'the invisible of this world, that which inhabits the worlds, sustains it, and renders it visible, its own and interior possibility, the "Being" of this being' (ibid). It is a lining to the visible of ageing experience rather than an opposite, giving ageing shape and depth.

This lining of ageing has ontological consequences for how we work through ageing. For one, a lining is rarely visible, inferred in perfunctory side talk or glimpses in the mirror we walk past, that make attempts to disclose, grasp or anchor the ageing self more challenging or less perceptible, visible, or close to our selves. Its nebulous quality makes the illusion of solid and external markers of normative ageing or aged infrastructure that can be found in the materiality and discourse of everyday lives even more seductive, even when we become privy to their negating effects. And in some ways, this invisibility may be part of the reason for the compulsion many participants expressed for relinquishing their own experiences of ageing to the 'outside' of cultural ascriptions, or alternatively limiting ageing to the manifestation of bodily sensations that they can consciously feel or easily witness. It would be too simplistic to explain this away as internalized ageism; rather, it emphasizes the experiential challenges of ageing as in part located in the flux of a dynamic corporeality. As suggested in Chapter 5, dynamic corporeality orientates us around the One as the absolute subject and Other as the incidental or inessential upon which the One relies for their reification, to use de Beauvoir's reference points. Just as de Beauvoir (2015 [1949]: 516) described how 'complicity is invited' during the early socialization of girls, dis-ease helped participants leaned into ageist tropes while recognizing their own vulnerability. In some ways, participants' accounts mirror de Beauvoir's own analysis of young women's socialization, in that 'accepting her [or their] passivity, she also accepts without resistance, enduring a destiny that is going to be imposed on her from the exterior, and this fatality frightens her'. In other words, the desire for recognition in ageing can mean an exaggeration of socially normative ageing modalities that not only make us mistake the totality of our bodily ageing experience as predominantly conscious and possible to access, but also render us vulnerable to reproducing the Other that we may become.

However, this also throws us into an ethical relationship of the One and the Other as a necessary ontological component of ageing as dynamically situated beings, especially given we are often thrown into ageing from an intersectional 'somewhere'. While I have not focused on class and socioeconomic position in this study (although have done elsewhere – see Riach and Cutcher, 2014 for example), and even less on ethnicity, in part due to preserving issues of anonymity in the relatively small sample, we have been able to see how ageing rarely surfaces through a lining of 'only' ageing. For example, the empirical accounts from many men I interviewed corroborate with de Beauvoir's ontology of gender which suggests that men's early socialization often orientates around practices that refute interdependence, such as through physical altercations, where the 'ordeal the young man overcame in childhood and adolescent fight [that is] to be a thing of flesh on which others have a hold' (de Beauvoir, 2015 [1949]: 647). While the substance of childhood may have changed slightly, refuting interdependence remains, and we can see how this plays out in the roles employees leaned into in work and life. Even when men became subject to age-based misrecognition themselves, they often still sought to cling on to a myth of independence, not recognizing the paradox that 'sovereign solitude' and situated freedoms are encased in the human condition of always being-in-the-world. In other words: 'When the struggle to claim a place in this world gets too much rough, there can be *no question of tearing oneself away* from it; one must first emerge within it in sovereign solitude if one wants to try to grasp it anew' (2015 [1949]: 1188–1189, emphasis added).

For women, this 'tearing' experience is also part of a gendered positionality marked through 'the way she grasps, through foreign consciousnesses, her body and her relation to the world' (2015 [1949]: 1207). While both require a 'bouncing back' of sociality through relations, there are differential experiences of 'Oneness' and 'Otherness' from which the gendered aged subject reaches out and rebounds back in the world. This of course impacts our everyday working lives and is in many ways a persistent feature as we grow up and older more broadly. I remember one participant telling me that the best advice she had received was writing her CV 'as if I was someone else', and the sense of satisfaction when feeling it had been written about someone else; someone clearly better than her, and how this had helped her to negotiate ageism in her later career. Similarly, many female participants repeatedly referred to alliances that were built up over time to enable them to professionally manoeuvre within age-biased systems, albeit with varying degrees of success. Women are encouraged to be aware of their Otherness as inherently part of their own sociality, in ways that became both a practical and ontological tool at their disposal for how to implant themselves in different ways as they grew up and older.

While the preceding point invariably fails to serve as a wrecking ball to a chronophallic aged-orientated patriarchy, it does show the possibility of a more intimate and embodied experience of reciprocity and relationality with the Other that may lean into a generative character that ageing could afford. If relationality as part of the human condition invariably informs our experience of ageing reciprocity, then we might suggest the mottling of ageing as a mode of surfacing has a particular quality that holds an ethical potentiality. This is in many ways an extension of de Beauvoir's concern with early childhood and adolescence that situates a thrownness towards an ethical relation along an ageing trajectory. Indeed, initial references that support this ethics of an 'age-ful' rather than 'aged' subjectivity appear in *The Ambiguity of Ethics* (2018 [1947]). Here de Beauvoir suggests that, compared to infancy when the world is presented 'as a fact' to the child, during adolescence we experience the emergence of conditions of subjectivity and the relations of recognition that constitute a relational Beinghood. It is then that we are bestowed with the obligations of being in the world in relation to others and the inescapable demand and indivisibility of our actions and practices from those around us. This coalesces at the same time as an affirmation of temporality and the possibility of a future that bounds us through co-dependent conditions of sociality. Doing so sets an ethical obligation of our actions in the present in relation to the Other. Elsewhere and prior to *The Second Sex* and *Old Age,* it seems no accident that de Beauvoir set up the 'young man' as the composite character who must 'realise himself morally' beyond mistaking the world as made by him alone:

> If he is reasonable, the young man immediately understands that by taking the world away from me, others also give it to me, since a thing is given to me only by the movement which snatches it from me ...

One can reveal the world only on a basis revealed by other men. No project can be defined except by its interference with other projects. (de Beauvoir (2018 [1947]: 75–76)

In this respect, the ethical relation of ageing emerges from an inherent temporality that is part of an ageing process requiring us to recognize our dependency on the aged Other to secure our own future project. This is because 'what concerns me is the situation of other's situation, as something founded in me', as de Beauvoir (2004 [1944: 126) suggests, and also because who is created 'in me' as part of the relentless temporality of the dynamically situated self. At the same time, while there may be a wanton desire to shed or exile the lining of ageing that begins to feel too close to our selves, the Other-in-us of ageing as an ontological mode of curiosity can surface in ways that are both unexpected and surprising. For the people I spoke to, it flickered in the surprise that they were 'already there' in terms of a seen or seeing themselves a particular way, or perhaps 'still there' at a career crossroads or juncture. It pulsed through moments where they worried about losing their way in their professional lives, in the threats around job security, and was palpable in the shadows cast by different aged-subject positions and totems, whether that be the spectacular businesswoman or the empty seat given up for the absent older commuter. It was echoed in the scars of significant illnesses or health episodes. In many ways, curiosity about this invisible lining of ageing is central to being always but never fully situated in ageing, as de Beauvoir's (1986 [1970]: 323) account of old age suggests:

We must assume a reality that is certainly ourselves although it reaches us from the outside and although we cannot grasp it. There is an insoluble contradiction between the obvious clarity of our inward feeling that guarantees our unchanging quality and the objective certainty of our transformation. All we can do is waver from the one to the other, never managing to hold them both firmly together.

For de Beauvoir, this wavering is a reverberation between being viewed as 'old' from the outside while experiencing an inward feeling that 'guarantees our unchanging quality'. As discussed earlier, she suggests that when it comes to old age 'whether we like it or not, in the end we submit to the outsider's point of view' (1986 [1970]: 323), somewhat undermining her earlier exegesis on the constitution of the subject. In part, this submission may be down to her concern in *Old Age* with its 'arrival' rather than the experience of ageing more broadly. Nonetheless, I would depart from de Beauvoir on the inevitability of a submission to the outsider's view, or at least suggest that it is not as straightforward, linear or deterministic a process of submission as de Beauvoir suggests. I would also refute that ageing must be about either changing or unchanging as she suggests. Rather, attention to ageing as a latent lining upon which surfacing relies points to a more complex inward set of systems informed by our organic and biographic compounding experiences of growing older in different settings in the world. In other words, surfacing ageing reminds us how the Other-in-us of ageing shows ageing as simultaneously a public effigy portrayed through our bodies, and a source of surprise, trickery and betrayal that requires us to contend with nebulous modes of invisibility that are a central part of ageing as an embodied, and possibly psychosocial, subjectivity. Ageing is part of an expressive temporal body, meaning that there is never any 'single witness' to our experiences, to use Merleau-Ponty's (1964b [1948]) term. My participants' accounts bear witness to how corporeal dynamicism can reveal itself at the most inconvenient moments, demanding we pay attention. But *how* this coalesces with a latent depth and makes the ageing experience invites us to consider a particular kind of bodily intentionality that involves the psychosocial dynamics of the ageing self. This means that to understand the ageing experience at work and the way in which we might capitulate or counter the normative aged modalities of work, we should not only think about ourselves as situated subjects who are the sum of the chiasmic intertwining of self and other, but also as involving a third plane: the rich interiority of the ageing self.

The psychosocial promiscuity of the ageing self

Until recently, considering the psychosocial dynamics within accounts of the self has not been a mainstay of ageing research. In part, this has been due to a psychoanalytical heritage bias against older age. Despite Erik Erikson's (1980, 1982) developmental account of psychosocial life stages being commonly cited within gerontology and Pearl King's (2020) careful exploration of mature adulthood and psychoanalysis of the elderly, there is still an enduring hesitance where 'we find in many analysts a deeply rooted, partly unconscious aversion to dealing with what they associate with "old" or "ageing"' (Junkers, 2019: xiv). Woodward (1995: 79) has been more pointed in her critique, suggesting it is older women in particular who are the 'missing person in psychoanalysis'. Others have suggested that ignoring any age-situated unconscious is inevitable due to Freud's assumption of the psyche as becoming too 'hardened' by age for valuable analytic intervention. Indeed, de Beauvoir reflects this ageist position of psychoanalysis through suggesting that 'our unconscious mind knows nothing of old age; it clings to the illusion of perpetual youth' (de Beauvoir, 1986 [1970]: 325). De Beauvoir also holds a broader sceptical light to psychoanalysis more generally, suggesting that:

[The] interiorising the unconscious and all psychic life, the very language of psychoanalysis suggests that the drama of the individual unfolds within him: the terms 'complex', 'tendencies', and so forth imply this. But a life is a relation with the world; the individual defines himself by choosing himself through the world; we must turn to the world to answer the questions that preoccupy us. (de Beauvoir, 2015 [1949]: 122)

In its challenge to free will, she rendered the 'dogmatic symbolism' of psychoanalysis useless 'for exploring a normal human being' (de Beauvoir, 1960 [1965]: 21).

At the same time, a turn towards more psychosocial concerns to consider the beyond-conscious tenets of ageing can suggest that more latent modes of being and doing can be more complementary with social theory than the ambivalent relations psychoanalysis has with traditional phenomenological schools of thought. In no small part, the unconscious realm is less estranged from recent contemporary phenomenological debate thanks to Judith Butler's accounts of subjectivity as an imbrication of psychic and social structures. Here, the 'wavering' of lived experience that is percipient to de Beauvoir's account of subjectivity might also carry a more generative quality through being 'rippled, containing fissures that infer different levels of association' (Butler, 2021: n.p.). Following this concern suggests that ageing is more than a moment solely constituted in the cross-section of self-other-setting, but that it can also 'reach us' in ways that bubble around the level of the unconscious.

In his later work, Merleau-Ponty, as one of de Beauvoir's peers and contemporaries, began to explore the fertility of such ideas informed by Freud and Klein. While much of this thinking appears sketched out in lectures notes rather than published before his sudden death, it does provide an invitation to consider a rich interiority as not simply a part of the phenomenological subject-object ontological paradox, but also that this may speak to a dynamic interiority. In particular, we can see echoes in his work of Melanie Klein's concern with the unconscious anxiety-interpretation responses. For ageing, these feel particularly notable as they point not to a repetition (in that we are destined to repeat the same behaviours or unconscious patterns), but a sequencing, most clearly articulated in her account of infant relations and their interior development as they seek to secure a separate sense of self (Klein 1997 [1932]; 1948 [1940]).

While an extended exegesis of Klein's work is for another time, it is valuable to slightly pause and summarize her system of object relations as relevant to our discussion of an ageing interiority. Object relations theory suggests that development is centred on two competing mental constellations that organize the psyche. The 'paranoid-schizoid position' sees the phantastic splitting of both the self and other objects into good or bad as a coping device to quell anxiety or feelings of persecution. This is most often explained through her example of a child experiencing the same breast as a 'good breast' that nourishes, sustains and comforts, and the 'bad breast' that withholds, frustrates and persecutes (Klein, 1997 [1932]). Gradually, with support and the formation of consistent relationships in the 'external' world, we see an ability emerge to withstand the possibility of recognizing the good and bad object as the same, allowing the individual to move towards the 'depressive position' where this confluence allows the individual to develop reparative and richer modes of engagement about the self and the world.

When using this to help consider a dynamically situated ageing subjectivity, this achievement of the so-called depressive position is never fully accomplished or stable, but is best understood as 'a developmental achievement that must be constantly defended and regained through life' (Alford, 1989: 33). However, in unpublished notes Klein (n.d.: 11) points to an interiority that I would suggest complements the ongoing incompleteness of disclosing, grasping, and anchoring as the interconnected trinity of ontological demands that were described in earlier chapters. She suggests that the 'capacity to detach oneself from the earlier ties has the effect of allowing one to grow up because then new relationships will not simply be built on the pattern of the old one … not just a repetition'. In doing so, I suggest that the patterning that emerges from ongoing experiences of disclosing, grasping and anchoring ageing also reverberate with a psychosocial demand. Here, patterning (rather than repetition) is particularly important for a dynamically situated ageing self to develop, given that interiority cannot simply replicate, but must cumulate and order experience while attending to the changing reception, perception and experiences of the ageing flesh.

This unsteadiness of an interiority of working through ageing further arises from the character of ageing to render visible what Merleau-Ponty terms 'promiscuity'. As Emmanuel de Saint Aubert suggests, body promiscuity involves:

> integrating the promiscuity of space and time into itself – of my past, registered in the body schema, of space as imaginary body, starting with that of others – and haunted by the promiscuity of the body and bodies, the flesh becomes a 'promiscuous body'. This promiscuity, in turn, is inevitably projected onto the world. (De Saint Aubert, 2020: 39)

As part of Merleau-Ponty's later work that became increasing informed by a concern with the depth of the bodily schema involving a psychosocial intent, promiscuity is part of the broader chiasmic experience of flesh and the intertwining, porous condition of corporeality. On this level, it speaks to both the knowing body and our denial and struggle to accept this knowing, or, as de Saint Aubert (2006: 12, my translation) puts it, 'the knowing modality of the flesh, while indicating our resistance to it, our natural ignorance of the flesh as a promiscuous being'.

If, as McWeeny (2016: 215) suggests, promiscuity means that 'subjectivity will be essentially promiscuous rather than merely reversible, moving in and out of bodies, overflowing its own body, taking in the bodies of others, leaking into and absorbing the flesh of the world, at times to the point of indivision', then the idea of promiscuity feels particularly at home with our experience of ageing as informed by more latent psychosocial dynamics. The disruption and unsettling that is part of the ageing experience may not only be about the lack of alignment with the revealing of ageing in the self-other-settings nexus, but also in terms of the inherent promiscuity of the ageing embodied experience that involves anticipatory (but unpredictable) reciprocity and openness and an embodied corruption. On the one hand, it may move us to colonize the Other given that it arouses 'the unbearable of the familiar: the other is so present to me that I enclose him in this presence' (de Saint Aubert, 2006: 23, my translation). On the other hand, the terms of engagement with ourselves and others we have previously curated and absorbed are thrown into potential disarray and demand a more thorough response in terms of a psychosocial calibration.

For this reason, we might see the psychosocial dimension of an ageing subjectivity as invariably bound up with an ethical compulsion. As Arp (2001: 69) suggests, 'to act morally requires not only an ability to grasp the temporal continuity of human life', but also, as de Beauvoir suggests, the willingness to affirm it. Through the virtue of being a future bound subject, we recognize the conditions of recognition and subjectivity as part of an embodied temporal process – an ageing process. The corruption of the One/Other inherent in ageing can thus be seen as part of a political project that echoes the hopes of de Beauvoir and how she 'wondered whether recognising the inevitability of ageing could help us all to reconceptualise our responsibilities to those we are so often inclined to reject' , as Segal (2014: 9–10) elegantly suggests. But on another level, the promiscuity of our ageing bodies also highlights the ongoing unsettling affective textures of reciprocity in ageing subjectivity.

Compostability and the onto-organics of ageing

To bring together working through ageing as intertwinement of this dynamic interiority with the never-ending negotiation of being and doing in the self-other-setting nexus, my final extension to the composition of working through ageing is the concept of compostability. Compostability points to the material facticity of the body as inevitably organic and temporal, but not in terms of a determination or absoluteness. Compostability also points to how this intertwinement is constituted through corporeal folds of time. But this is not a temporal regime synonymous with failure akin to the medicalized 'ageing as decline' master narrative discussed in Chapter 2 that has shaped much of the contemporary debates around growing older in the Global North. While it may invariably involve decay and a breaking down of different elements, it also points to a geminating that demands a series of transformational, fertilizing and generative forms of agentic action. Here I suggest that the corporeal mulch of ageing holds an intentional quality, generating meaning through making a claim in the world. Ageing's compostability is not simply a 'surface' activity of, on or in the body, nor an interiority that drives unaided; instead, it is a embodied practice that relies on layers of situated embodied inhabitation that are often out of the reach of perception, but are nonetheless the result of one's presence in the world.

Compostability oscillates around our own temporal charge akin to an affective pulping that holds a transformative capacity of experience. This ability of time to transform is akin to de Beauvoir's acknowledgement that certain occasions can 'become so charged with significance in retrospect that they stand out from my past as if they had been truly great events' (de Beauvoir, 1965 [1960]: 88). While this past may impress on experience, it does so not only mnemonically but also through a breaking down and building up. Fertilizing experiences and practices can enable both a patterning and near repetition of doing things 'as before' but also allow for an intological 'spring cleaning' of the dynamically situated self. Compostability speaks to the absorption and synthesis of experiences coming together to germinate and generate an ageing sociality. The capacity of an age-ful subjectivity means that we do not simply carry previous experiences in the form of a repository, but that of a living archive that is powerful, even if it is 'not only invisible, implicit and unconscious or latent, it will be always unknown: always un-named, and maybe never nameable' (Stoller, 2013: 22). Here, formative, visceral or profound moments are lived and pattern the self's ongoing constitution. While only ever indirectly experienced, I suggest that compostability is central to the ageing experience and part of the neverending ontological momentum and practical acts involved in working through ageing.

Compostability speaks to the reckoning with the 'Other' discussed earlier. For de Beauvoir, what marks out old age is not only the experience of being Othered, but rather an other-to-myself. To this extent, she suggests the impossibility for anything other than an interior subjective distancing of the self where 'it is the other within us who is old', pointing to an 'unrealisability' of age that does not have any 'inward experience' (de Beauvoir, 1986 [1970]: 324):

For the outsider it is a dialectic relationship between my being as he defines it objectively and the awareness of myself that I acquire by means of him. Within me it is the Other – that is to say the person I am for the outsider who is old: and that Other is myself. (de Beauvoir, 1986 [1970]: 316)

Compostability refutes de Beauvoir's suggestion of an inherent inner denial or infertility of recognizing our older self where 'his inner being does not accept the label that has been stuck to him' (1986 [1970]: 325). In her suggestion that 'the old' picture themselves predominantly through how others view them, she suggests that 'the image itself is not provided in the consciousness: it is a cluster of rays of intentionality' (1986 [1970]: 324). However, if compostability is part of a clustering of rays on intentionality, then 'the inner', as she calls it, may also have the potential to 'hold' the other without fragmenting the self: to hold the other *in* myself as well. There is still a fertility of being in the Other of ageing and this is not simply a possibility, but also a necessary component of our ontological integrity. Experiencing the Other of ageing is never simply 'an operation of thought that would set up before the mind a picture or representation of the world, a world of immanence and of ideality' (Merleau-Ponty, 1964c: 162); rather, it attaches us to the world in part through the amalgam of our psychosocial compostability: the matrices and the latent shards of selves we were, selves we imagine ourselves to be or become, selves we feared or hoped for, selves that were lost and selves that were coherent and felt full or were negated or misrecognized.

The achievement of the ageing self we are outlining here is not just about when 'we try to picture what we are though the vision other have of us' (de Beauvoir, 1986 [1970]: 325). When considered in terms of an ageing, there is a psychosocial intentionality that is composed and composted in and of our own lifetime through the intersubjective embodied demand of situated practices. In many ways this speaks to Linda Fisher's (2014: 113) suggestion that: 'While every situation can be viewed from without and from within, in the case of some situations, the outsider and insider perspectives can co-exist within the individual subject: perhaps juxtaposed, perhaps coinciding and uniting, or perhaps – as with ageing – colliding.' Our psychic compostability enables this coexisting and in many ways prevents us from 'falling apart' in the face of misrecognition in the face of age hostility, even if our material conditions are impacted.

This demand to reimagine that compostability affords is of course vital for the ageing self, but perhaps also for our political potential. Attending to de Beauvoir's (2015 [1949]: 1214) own warning that: 'Let us beware lest our lack of imagination impoverish the future', I am not suggesting an epistemic privilege for 'older people' over 'younger people', but rather a positionality that comes from compostability as enabling an ontoepistemic plurality. The plurality inherent in compostability may even provide a politicising potential to surfacing ageing, part of a broader 'ethical attitude of ageing'; one that 'allows for an open encounter with the other within myself and makes change possible – a transformation that ultimately also shapes and redefines our relationship to the world and to people' (Stoller, 2014: 208). Central to compostability, then, is a creativity constituted through the generative and unpredictable experiences, desires, hurts and achievements as they slowly intermingle and germinate over the ageing process to create new possibilities, subjectivities and connections.

This compostability incarnate in surfacing ageing also suggests a more politicizing potential particular to ageing. As suggested earlier, surfacing is not simply about recognizing the Otherness in ageing, but that the experience of compostability is itself a *participatory exchange*. If we recognize the body as 'being in latency, and a presentation of a certain absence' (Merleau-Ponty, 1968 [1964a]: 136), the compostable character of the ageing body is also generative and could involve the further seeding of an ethical relation that works in confluence with ageing as a mode of embodied difference containing the potential of surprise: a surprise of the flesh as phenomenological and psychosocially imbued to generate 'the capacity to talk back as it were, to surprise us, to explode our horizons, [forming a] paradox of immanence and transcendence' (Yeo, 1992: 40).

Working through ageing: beyond a blueprint

The above theoretical ruminations might feel rather abstract when considering working through ageing as a practical project. To talk about the inner richness of ageing may feel like a weak balm for how our material lives are impacted by aged structures, ageist cultures and age-biased interactions. But an ambition to dismantle these elements entails excavating working through ageing as an experience of dis-ease that requires the dynamically situated self to negotiate the One/Other. Developing a conceptual vocabulaty to do so is vital and involves a deep engagement with figures such as disclosure, grasping, anchoring and mottling as well as corrolories including the other-in-myself, enclosure, mooring, surfacing and compostability as introduced in this book. Gathering these together begins to challenge the continuing schism that has been reproduced when discussing the 'out there' of ageism and the 'in there' of ageing as a situated experience.

However, it also highlights that the age-biased world de Beauvoir discussed in 1970 appears to follow a similar hymn sheet to the one demarcating financial capitalism today, where the parameters of recognition still oscillate around a narrow chrononormative currency. We still see that in many ways, 'society cares about the individual only in so far as he is profitable. The young know this. Their anxiety as they enter in upon social life matches the anxiety of the old as they are excluded from it. Between these two ages, the problem is hidden by routine' (de Beauvoir, 1986 [1970]: 604). As de Beauvoir suggests, ageing is rarely an affectively comfortable place for anyone to inhabit: you either feel that you are excluded from any societal purchase or feel the latent creep of that impending exclusion as you grow older. Empirical attention and policy interventions that seek to address the more immediate instances of ageism will not alone dismantle the broader structural challenges and the Gordian knot of aged inequality in and around work, workforces and the economy. Neither will people be able to tackle this individually: I heard many participant's accounts of profound ageing experiences and moments that carried the potential akin to a possible ontological reckoning, only to find when we spoke again years later that they still absorbed the age-hostile cultures and practices that had scarred them.

But what if working through ageing as an ontological project can also provide a new space to practically pause and explore the more plural modes of being, doing and relating and a possibility for a more generative age-ful subjectivity? Earlier in this chapter, I have suggested the theoretical operationalization of such ambitions, but what might such spaces look like in the realm of the everyday? The likelihood is that they already exist but require a solidaric kaleidoscopic twist to fully realize their form. This book exposes the depth, porosity and complexity of the ageing experience through a new theoretical lens, but this is not an alien or otherworldly set of possibilities devoid from the everyday innocuous experience of ageing we all have. The processes through which ageing is experienced are always intimately entwined with the world of policy, age management practices and age-based systems of organizing that exist in organizational and institutional settings, and a theoretical understanding of these can help to reexamine and transform practice. The phenomenological project of working through ageing can furnish us with different systems of thinking about and experiencing ageing within contemporary spheres that govern economic lives. For one, it might critically critique the modalities of difference used as a shorthand in the business case for diversity, instead transplanting a better account of how plurality affords different modes of relating (rather than simply 'age') as fundamental to organizational successes and does not require workers to be anatomized into a single monolithic economic unit. Alternatively, working through ageing could show how a focus on intergroup conflict, such as a concern with intergenerational relations, is often treating the symptoms of agedness rather than addressing the more systemic causes and ontological compulsions that underpin how and why we might be compelled to distance, deny or decry ageing. It could even suggest that while a focus on outward discrimination is important, interventions also require attention to the ways in which age-biased workplace dynamics not only rely on a malevolent organizing ethos but also operate through conditions set by a more benign politeness of othering.

This questioning of who is invited to step into, or not step out of, aged or chrononormative relations, and the reverberations of submitting or resisting this invitation in an workplace setting, helps to nuance our understanding of the terms under which people become 'object and prey' as they grow older, to borrow from de Beauvoir (2015 [1949]: 1149). For one, it can help to move on the conversations around unconscious bias or internalized ageism towards interventions that consider processes of interdependence, relating and unrelating, and expose the institutional and policy-orientated contradictions and discrepancies that reproduce certain dynamics. And it could invite a move away from a focus on targets around keeping different chronologically-defined cohorts in work or out of unemployment towards an exploration of how compostable subjectivities emerge in unpredictable and surprising ways that can transform how we think about the long-term sustainability of working lives across a range of organizational practices, from career development to occupational health and wellbeing.

This of course is not just about a commercial concern or policy intervention, but a political call to recgonise the unevenness of ageing trajectories and enable us all to age and work in a more democratic way. If our freedom and future sociality is inherently tied to the second person of ageing, the Other-in-us, there is a clear ethical imperative underpinning why we should dismantle and better interrogate aged systems and practices. This is not simply about showing ageism is wrong or that we seek to acknowledge 'other' ageing subject positions, but rather we provide a means to see how one's actions are always tied to us. But working through ageing may also attend to how we can more effectively explore ageing hostility when it surfaces rather than simply seize or displace more complex discussions.

In over 20 years of asking managers, leaders and employees about where ageing is discussed in their organizations, I find that after their accounts of celebrating groups through national awareness days or professional workplace accreditations, they concede that the primary space where age-related workplace conversations take place formally are usually connected age discrimination and a fear of employment tribunals. While this is often justified in terms of reputational and financial cost, I gently question this, and not only because everyday ageist systems and cultures are more likely to represent a bigger financial loss through people leaving the workplace and workforce. In tribunal courts over the last decade, there is a yearly average of 13 sucessful age discrimination cases finding in favour of the claimant (UK Government, 2023). Yet tribunal rulings are an example where age-related public documents become inflated, narrated in professional magazines and subsequently ventriloquized through expert practitioner commentaries or Human Resource managers and employment lawyers. Such practices amplify the talk of ageing as concerned with avoiding punishment rather than more explicitly considering ageing as part of the daily processes and practices that constitute work. To look at these documents may be professionally important but can also make us assume that ageism 'happens elsewhere': beyond our teams, organizations or responsibility. It might even validate our own sense of righteousness in that the 'bad employer' has been appropriately dealt with and sanctioned, fulfilling a desire that might feel good on some level, as de Beauvoir's (2012 [1946]: 248) account of punishment suggests. But they ultimately fail to change anything about the ongoing persistence of aged organizing. I provide this example to invite readers to imagine how working through ageing as a critical intervention may help to better understand and render visible the ageing experience in the commercial world beyond these narrow parameters, even providing a counterpoint to broader systems and processes that censure ways of relating more broadly.

Such interventions are needed now more than ever given that the ageing in work and beyond is increasing impacted by broader rejections of engagement, connection and inequality. During the 15-year gestation of this book, the Global North has witnessed a significant swelling of partitions of difference at a local, national and international level. Unfortunately, I am sure that the divisive commentaries that have become entrenched in political and cultural practice have also taken their toll on how we experience ageing. The potential for us to enjoy the dynamic embodied changes in and over the life course are likely to be thwarted in any world that encourages epistemic breaks and a siloing of relating into the lowest denominators of perfunctory belonging. Binary identity politics is never a generative way of curating a fullness of the self, and yet we still cut up age-related experiences into me and them, victim or perpetrator, old or young, all replicating a hope that it will give us a sense of control. The ageism in hate speech might not be as explicit or centre stage as other experiential sites such as gender or race, but there is still an inherent cruelty towards ageing in society; a graffitiing of how different cohorts of people are entitled to live; a corrupting and gaslighting of temporal social contracts that underpin pension schemes, and an anatomizing of leisure activities that are coded through cohort, to name but a few. Despite claims on four-generational workplaces and communities, there feels like fewer spaces than ever to engage and relate to people positioned as too distant from us according to aged markers. We see the performative power of such divisions where accounts of age-based voting patterns or criticisms of a generational hoarding of wealth operate, seeming to confirm our suspicions that age is fundamentally an impassable ravine of difference, even when this myth of separation breaks down when taking into account our own experiences of our compostable bodies. All of this hurts both others and us, but invariably has differential consequences for different bodies. The participants who informed this study mostly carry the bundles of socioeconomic privilege that afforded them a certain level of material security, and yet even then they struggled to claim a stake for greater plurality regarding the ageing experience. It is likely that others are even more vulnerable to the challenges of seeking economic, social and psychic security while trying to recognize and enjoy a dynamic multiplicity that can be a part of ageing.

I am aware that any extended account of ageing is in danger of making it sound like a rather bewildering and hostile experience that is unsympathetic in the way in which it shakes and jolts us with abandon. But maybe this shaking and jolting is the point, as one of participants, Theo, reflected in our final conversation: 'if I knew exactly ten years ago how I would be, then it's like, there's almost no point in this journey, this being human and learning from things that happen to you'. Ageing can never be the main occupation of our lives: to age with a constancy of concern around ageing would undermine or even occlude those moments of potential or generative surfacing. But at the same time, it might be that simply an invitation to consider how we think, feel and relate to age as part of our everyday experience of work is itself one way to begin working through ageing.

This is at once a simple and awesome task, given that it guarantees no answers, as I was reminded during an email exchange with one participant asking for some work-related advice that led to a chat about when they would receive a copy of the book. 'Of course I won't read it', they said, 'but I might look at a few pages at the end' adding, tongue-in-cheek, 'hopefully in there you'll be able to give us the answer to what ageing at work is all about!' I am guessing they will be infinitely disappointed about the impossibility of providing some blueprint for working through ageing. But in the spirit of reciprocity, I would say this: ageing is not something you can buy or power your way out of, as if it is a logistical problem to overcome. It is not about a singularity of doing something successfully or better or worse than someone else or an accentuated benchmark. There is no single witness to ageing, but it is also not a spectator sport or something that we can do in isolation or away from relations or a second person. It is not about prioritizing transactions over interactions, even though the former make the most noise and are always in the headlight of our economic lives. Ageing is not about looking for a definitive statement because the right questions on working through ageing do not have an immediate or perceptible answer. Instead, it is an invitation to consider, query, disrupt and engage with life; an opportunity to explore how different apertures and ways of thinking and doing might make working through ageing a more generative experience for all.

Undertaking Longitudinal Qualitative Research Through a Phenomenological Lens

When presenting parts of this study at conferences, seminars and workshops, one of the most common questions I was asked is how a phenomenological approach might practically inform how we undertake qualitative longitudinal research. As such, it feels disingenuous not to disclose some of the more applied aspects of this study in the hope that it may help others undertaking fieldwork researching ageing or using a phenomenological lens in empirical work. As discussed in Chapter 3, the practical experience of undertaking longitudinal research is rarely discussed in studies of work. Part of the reason for this may be that qualitative longitudinal accounts are relatively rare in management and organization studies. Similarly, while it is more common for studies across the humanities and social sciences to draw on a phenomenological lens to understand a given research phenomenon, relatively few discuss how a commitment to phenomenology informs the way in which researchers themselves experience the empirical research process as related to negotiating fieldwork.

For me, a qualitative longitudinal approach sits comfortably with exploring ageing. Given that ageing is an experience that we often get to know in and through time, exploring it through a methodological mode that recognizes the richness of temporality feels like a good place to start. Longitudinal research is broadly concerned with 'how time interacts and interplays with the collection and analysis of qualitative data' (Saldana, 2003: 5) and is often chosen due to a concern with understanding and tracking patterns and changes over time. Such an approach is assumed to provide us with either a better consideration of future trajectories, or how past biographical aspects shape actions and behaviours, gaining insights or predications that would otherwise be difficult to explore within cross-sectional encounters.

In general, any extended engagement with the field or with research participants takes extensive planning as well as a commitment of resources and the continued goodwill of gatekeepers. While the parameters of longitudinal research focus on engagement for a 'prolonged duration', what constitutes 'prolonged' and how measurement or analysis occurs within these parameters is subject to disciplinary or paradigmatic expectations. Some research may be continuous in the sense of a set period, and will engage with participants at formative points in their lives. Other research differentiates between a prospective view (in terms of being based on an event, and the collation of new data) or retrospective view (through analysing data such as medical records or diaries and memoirs) as a way of tracking the journey of particular ideas (Neale and Bishop, 2012). Alternatively, research may be considered longitudinal through 're-studies' where scholars revisit sites that were the focus of previous accounts undertaken by themselves or other teams or authors). For example, Johnson et al (2007) revisited 20 surviving residential care homes that constituted part of Peter Townsend's study of 173 homes in the 1950s. Such studies are all mindful of the broader challenge of longitudinal analysis in the social sciences more broadly, such as 'drowning' in data or losing focus in the phenomenon under investigation.

Longitudinal studies of ageing are also influenced by certain disciplinary heritages. For example, 'Inventing adulthoods' explored transitions of 100 adults over ten years that included a concern with work as both an actualized and imagined part of their future as central to a sense of belonging (Henderson and Thompson, 2014). As rich as they are, following traditions of youth studies places an emphasis on transitions in and around emerging adulthood, exploring different phenomenon (such as work) through this lens rather than considering a broader landscape of the ageing experience. Within studies of work and organizations, longitudinal elements are mainly found in case study approaches, where the level of analysis is often at a department or firm level rather than focusing on the working lives of those located there. As a result, there is less concern with how specific occupational logics or situated acts or practices are constituted in and through a phenomenon such as ageing, and how they are enacted through, or enacting with, normative organizational expectations of capability and performance, even though these elements intimately inform organizational interdependencies and subjectivities.

The value of qualitative longitudinal studies in ageing has been noted in the ability to provide 'a rich and nuanced understanding of human experience across the life course and the aging process' (Nevedal et al, 2019: e796–e797). The inherent interest in tracking people's lives has been transplanted into popular culture formats, such as the documentary *7-Up* in the UK, which followed 14 individuals, revisiting them every seven years, with the last instalment (*63 Up*) being broadcast in 2019. At the same time, research that is longitudinal, such as the English Longitudinal Study of Ageing (ELSA) and the Longitudinal Studies of Aging (LSOA) in the US, is incredibly costly and increasingly difficult to attract funding, since the payouts are so often in a future that cannot garner a value in the present – a feature that challenges increasingly scruitinised research budgets in policy and academia through relatively short cycles of evaluation and impact. There are also criticisms that age-related surveys tend to focus on health rather than a more holistic landscape of ageing and this may also result in inadvertently diminishing the fecundity of the ageing experience.

In thinking through what a phenomenological approach to longitudinal research work might involve, it is worth briefly noting that empirical studies taking a phenomenological approach often follow one of three paths. The first approach uses phenomenology as a theoretical inspiration through which to explore a given phenomenon, but has limited influence in terms of method or analysis. While it may consider how to 'access' or invoke data that can be subject to phenomenological interpretation, it often does not carry through to a consideration of, for example, research questions in an interview where they often use standardized qualitative approaches to research design and analysis. However, in their (re)presentation, they would seek to embody a phenomenological attitude – what van Manen (2016: 19), following Spiegelberg (1975), terms a 'agogical approach' that 'aims to guide the person to the project and pathos of phenomenological inquiry and to help stimulate personal insights, sensibilities, and sensitivities for a phenomenology of practice'.

The second approach is often concerned with how phenomenological research is used as a broader methodological mode of inquiry. This approach has been particularly important in studies of health and nursing, perhaps in part because it serves as a contrast with dominant paradigms in medical fields that privilege objectivity (cf. Flood, 2010). However, this can also include reference to normative modes of presenting data, such as through 'structural descriptions' (for example, Moustakas, 1994) that may be in tension with the way in which phenomenology has been interpreted across the social sciences.

This tension can also be found in the final approach where a broader phenomenological commitment informs established research traditions, such as ethnomethodology. That said, within life course studies, we may find that cross-sectional studies are often driven through a concern with being and doing in and over time that feels phenomenologically charged. This might include the retrospective methods are employed in, for example, biographical interviews (Rosenthal, 1993) or life course accounts (Bernardi et al, 2019), or how research designs focus on participants making sense of the present and possible future trajectories through placing an emphasis on the past or playing with temporal dynamics. Here phenomenological theory provides inspiration for the variegated ways in which to consider and generate eidetic modes of representation, although attention to translating the phenomenological method into a research practice is more implicit.

Within this landscape, few studies have considered how phenomenological inquiry might be embedded within a longitudinal research programme. For those longitudinal research teams that do engage with phenomenological concerns, preference is given to engaging either with the general ethos of phenomenology or using specific phenomenological concepts to inform or guide their research design. For example, Snelgrove's (2014) three-wave study suggests that the phenomenological term 'bracketing' provides a means through which to articulate and better understand the dynamics at play within longitudinal research, while Woll (2013: 7) suggests that diary methods, when considered phenomenologically, enable an articulation of how participants can themselves reflect 'on difficulties and inner feelings … an example of a democratization process in phenomenological research'.

Within psychology, where an interpretative phenomenological analysis (IPA) framework is popular, longitudinal studies have emphasized its value in terms of being able to 'reveal the changing meaning of an experience as it is lived through that person's trajectory' (Farr and Nizza, 2019: 200). Many studies following this approach, termed longitudinal interpretive phenomenological analysis (LIPA), and focus on a particular event (such as a transition into care, or a health episode), change, or progression. In doing so, they seek to identify the ideographic trajectories relating to a given phenomenon. This of course challenges a disciplinary pull towards generalizability and in many studies employing LIPA, the researcher appears to be faced with a compromise between a rich description of one's world as it unfolds and undertaking an inevitably reductive process that may speak across people's experiences at the possible cost of richness. However, the phenomenological method can also provide longitudinal researchers with not only a source of theoretical inspiration, but also a means of orientating themselves to a particular ethos and practice of research. In other words, it can inform the 'being' in empirical research, in terms of researcher positioning, reflexivity and means of articulating dynamics underpinning the study, and the 'doing' or empirical research, in terms of the practicalities of research design, method and analytical choices. This not only requires particular attention to the substantive research phenomenon under study, but also how methodological choices are central to informing the calibration of self-other-setting– relations that de Beauvoir, Merleau-Ponty and others discuss.

Longitudinal research should of course consider both the context in which accounts take place, and the people upon which the production of these accounts relies. A phenomenological pursuit recognizes that the study of ageing cannot be extrapolated from the web of relations through which the research is experienced. Longitudinal research evolves in ways which mean that the researcher is thrown into situations, places, locations and relations through which the data emerges that happen as the researcher moves across their own biographically situated position. This situated knowledge points to how representation is always multilayered and incomplete, like a rich but partial description of a work of art where 'in this sustained engagement, invisibility, partial vision and blindness play an important role' (Horstkotte, 2017: 149).

Such a pursuit requires us to think about trying to detangle the variegated ideas, people and activities we encounter in the field as part of an attempt to glimpse into how a given phenomenon is revealed, constituted and circulated in and through the bodies in a given setting. 'Getting a grip', as discussed in Chapter 3, refers to a generative pursuit enacted in situ – of a research interview or observation, for example – that might tell us something about the way in which such processes play out in other contexts. To consider the grip, as Merleau-Ponty explains, is to recognize the mutual experience of the world taking 'hold' on the individuals in terms of their actions or socialized dispositions. Yet it simultaneously refers to the experience of how we get to know the world and the capacities it affords us; how we all 'grasp'. This is central to how we methodological pursue research in an inherently embodied way, where 'the body is not a thing, it is a situation: it is our grasp on the world and our sketch of our project' (de Beauvoir, 2015 [1949]: 103). Within longitudinal research, we recognize that this carries a temporal element: through experience, we come to anticipate how we engage with the world as well as how we receive it, and it receives us. For example, a researcher's previous biographical experience of research may mean that they are drawn to settings or phenomenon, while our respondent's experiences of being interviewed in other settings, from job interviews to watching parodic representations of work on the television, all shape how they perceive the research space.

For me, the most important aspect that a phenomenological commitment in longitudinal research brings is taking the temporal politics of longitudinal research seriously – and critically engaging with we might understand as the chronopolitical dynamics of longitudinal research. By 'chronopolitical', I am not necessarily referring to the relationship between time and political activities at a meso- or macro-level (cf. Wallis, 1970), but rather the embodied enmeshment of a power nexi, political settings, and the potential to enable or constrain participants' shape, rhythmic relations and practices in and over time.

In practice, this related to my own stack of privilege and gathering of social and professional capital that enabled and shaped engagement and a continued commitment to undertaking longitudinal research. Throughout the research, I continued to benefit from the affordances of a situated set of circumstances I had as a researcher at the start of the research that has subsequently been leveraged over time. At the time the study commenced in 2010, I had a permanent faculty position having completed my PhD in 2007 – a situation that contrasts with the growing landscape of postdoctoral precarity that is now the case in the UK. I had gained the early accoutrements of a permanent position and promotion to senior lecturer that enabled me to be a bit more meandering about my research on ageing. At the time, I was 30, had no children and lived with a partner who also worked full-time, and our two salaries meant we could live in central London in the UK – the equivalent of a sweet shop for organizational researchers interested in a variety of different types of work. My own worktime was pliable: I could work late or at weekends should I wish and had the corporeal capacity to do this while maintaining a social life with people who were equally untied and untired. I write this not to produce some romanticized hagiography, but to highlight that these were the age-situated conditions from which the study emerged. In other words, the longitudinal research was enacted through an elasticity that came from my own 'time of life' to engage in research in this way that I doubt I could replicate now.

This reverberates with Beauvoir's own reflections on who has the time to study, reflect and write about life, saying 'The main source of my example is the writing of the privileged few who, as we have seen, were almost the only people to have the means and the leisure to record their evidence' (de Beauvoir, 1986 [1970]): 313). Yet it also points to the chronopolitical dynamics of the focus on a longitudinal phenomenological concern and how we extrapolate from certain people's experiences. A key feature of longitudinally researching ageing is the ongoing intellectual ambition to make broader theoretical claims about ageing which, as a phenomenon, continues to be so ontologically elusive. But it also requires us to consider the unevenness or selectivity of the practical acts and accomplishments that are involved in this. In doing so, we must consider how the experiences of the few, who may be privileged in terms of their socioeconomic, gendered or other social position, are not representing the experiences of the many, while also considering how the experiences that are gradually revealed in and over time may point to something that also relates to the perceptual experience of others. In other words, a phenomenological commitment in longitudinal research creates theoretical insights not simply from participant replication or patterns in and over time, but from the experiential flow of their testimony. To this extent, phenomenological longitudinal work follows Burke et al's (2023: 275) suggestion that 'phenomenologically, a testimony, experience, or event is not significant insofar as it is statistically generalizable but insofar as it discloses meaning that is deeply, collectively important.'

Three points of orientation in figuring-in longitudinal qualitative research

My discussion in Chapter 3 introduced figuring-in ageing as a methodological intervention that seeks to contribute to debates on how we undertake longitudinal research that opens, rather than measures, lived experience. Central to this is considering the embodied experience of longitudinal research. By way of an example, in what follows, I suggest three ways that corporeality marks the researchers' experience of figuring-in longitudinal research.

Capsuling

Longitudinal research spaces are not simply *about* time, but are part of a temporal experience where interactions themselves set up lines of flight, encountering a person in the moment and calling them into account in their situated positionality in time. When deciding to go back to HFUK in 2012 for a second time, I considered of how a lingering cult of the present that delineated financial capitalism might thwart encouraging accounts of ageing as beyond the spatial and temporal parameters usually encountered in people's organizational lives. This led to developing a personalized one-page sheet of memorable or verbatim quotations for each person I had interviewed. While initially a personal aide-mémoire to myself to help me, during my second interview with Nathan, he peered over to look at them and began a dialogue between himself 'in person' and 'on paper': 'This is strange, I know that is me saying that one, but I completely disagree with this, I have no idea what I was thinking then [pause], yes, that's me [pause] are you sure that's right? Ah that would have been when I'd just had a fight with a colleague' (Nathan, 2012, Y2).

I subsequently repeated this for all interviews across each the wave, gradually building up several one-page 'time capsules' for each person that were revisited during each of their interviews. The engagement with their personalized 'time capsules' ranged from a keenness to hear themselves to feeling they were calling themselves to account in some way 'like the ghost of Christmas Past', as Jack (2018, Y8) suggested. Some asked to keep them to show their partners or friends, while others were very keen to make sure they were destroyed securely immediately after the interview. In general, they were surprised at how much they had disclosed and described the 'bite' of recounting their past emotions:

Oh God. Reading that made me feel like one of Alan's employees all of a sudden, and then the fear of him reading that. But now, obviously, I remember that it's all over and that he's not my boss anymore and it doesn't matter, although we're still friends. But that's just funny. I didn't realize I would have been so scathing. I just sort of sat there and said exactly how I felt. (Finn, 2014, Y4)

On a practical level, the time capsule became one way to encourage people to stay with the process. Few of those in the study kept a detailed journal or diary and many suggested that the time capsule provided them with an insight into their own feelings and ideas at a particular moment that was rarely captured anywhere else in their lives, placing them into a different time and space through their own testimonies. That is not to say that engaging with their capsules was always a comforting or affirming experience. They could, for example, confront people with a realization of unfulfilled ambitions, or echo an accumulative ambivalence around their work or lives in ways that was profoundly uncomfortable. Liam (2018, Y8) summed this up during a later interview when, despite enjoying taking part in the study, he proclaimed: 'Oh, God, I hate it when you do this. This is the worst bit because basically it's just a catalogue of my life getting progressively worse.' Such comments were often made in jest, such as Ollie (2016, Y6) playfully referring to them as 'destructor of dreams', but his response made me carefully consider when and how they were framed during our encounters.

I subsequently became more aware of how the personalized time capsules were introduced, while also recognizing their potential to productively agitate the structure of the interview experience. Their time capsules operated not as factual accounts, but rather an analytical manoeuvre, bringing to bear the subject–object paradox that lies at the very heart of phenomenological inquiry. In many ways, engaging with capsuling as a conscious practical activity during the interview was analogous to the ontological quandry of 'being of a subject for the world and at the same time being of an object in the world' (Husserl, 1970: 178). Pulling towards a recognition of the subject appearing as an 'object' in relation to their own words on paper demanded a consideration of the self beyond the temporally present 'I' of the interview. In many instances, this invited an openness to the fabric of their ageing experiences, encouraging them to explore, articulate and connect with some of the more paradoxical and ambiguous elements.

Wasting

When people talk about growing older, wasting – particularly in relation to time – is often positioned as contrary to what ageing productively should be. Accounts of procrastination, distractions, musings and other activities all contribute to a broader moral economy that encourages us to make each moment accountable in terms of a quantified value. Here, time is conceptualized as something that can be 'wasted' through being frittered away or squandered, but also does so in age-coded ways – for example, a misspent youth may be more socially forgivable than an idle old age. This informed the backdrop of participants talking to me about ageing as perhaps a rather wasteful activity in itself – something that is viewed as both incidental and pointless due to its inevitability, 'given you are going to grow older anyway, whether you like it or not' (Russell, 2010, Y0). People's lives are busy; often the last thing they need is a researcher adding to the burden and impinging pressures, and in longitudinal research you ask not only for their insights but also for their time, repeatedly. This is exacerbated when undertaking research in a setting where cultures and ways of interacting are often inscribed into the very logic of financial capitalism as a mode of organizing. What you are inviting people to do is allocate their resources in a way that is difficult to justify as part of an economic or transactional exchange.

However, it emerged that in the refusal of the research to be consigned to such as transactional relationship, wasting becomes a fruitful way of considering the ethos of longitudinal research. On the one hand, it speaks to a more holistic feeling of reciprocity in the research where longitudinal research has broader possibilities in what it 'gives' to those participating with the researcher. Many of those being interviewed enjoyed the confidential space to say what they wanted compared to the tightly regulated and panoptic spaces of work. Others discussed the 'opportunity to reflect' (Kieran, 2018, Y8) as an unusual experience, with one suggesting that 'I find it very therapeutic seeing you every couple of years' (Liam, 2016, Y6). This is not to confuse the interviews with a medical or health-based intervention, but rather that interviews absorbed their feelings and thoughts in a way that sat outside the normative confines of 'use' in their daily working lives. In other words, in refusing to be seen as 'useful' in the utilitarian sense, research relations move away from ideas of extraction or transaction towards a more embodied feeling of connection and interaction. This is particularly the case in financial capitalism, where work encourages a sequestering or deferral of more existential aspects of life, or even away from reflecting on what we are doing, as Finn suggests:

> When you're just like in something every day, like I find it quite hard to see my job objectively when I'm in it every day cos I don't get a moment's peace. But sometimes, just occasionally I get a little glimpse and I see it with clarity, usually when I'm on holiday and I'm switched off, or in these interviews, and I'm like actually, it's shit, isn't it. Why do I take that every day? Or actually I thought I wasn't very good at that but actually I'm pretty good at that. (Finn, 2016, Y6)

Wasting also speaks to the processes involved in longitudinal research. Wasting can be about recognizing that we create something from the rubble of organizational experiences in which we rummage during extended fieldwork. Researchers become master scavengers in and over time, and the iterative development and practical act of longitudinal research has a necessary element of waste. This is not just about disposal. Insights are generated from asides or throwaway comments that are then pursued somewhat intuitively. Interactions are populated with meaning which we follow. During the process of analysis, some ideas begin to decay, others start to feel a bit 'off' or are left to rot in legacy files or scribbles. Unexpected emails, online messages or texts from participants pop up intermittently, alongside various artefacts or 'debris' that come to our attention, including newspaper articles on ageing, conversations with colleagues, friends and strangers or other pieces of research being undertaken at the same time. Different fragments of ideas, information or incidental details about different lives come together in ways that would otherwise not have been encountered. Figuring-in involves stitching these fragments together into a kind of imperfect and incomplete patchwork of resonances and recollections. Wasting thus moves from being an inconvenience or moral failure to a generative activity that recognizes the irreducibility of the research process for all of those involved and an experience that cannot be fully accounted for through standardization.

Weighting

As I mentioned at the beginning of Chapter 3, when I began the study, it was never intended to be longitudinal. Longitudinal studies involve a particular type of labour that requires persistence, but also recognition of bearing the load in an embodied sense of endurance. Over the course of the research, I moved across three different employers, each time bargaining my value in the labour market based on a piece of research with few immediate short-term outputs. This is difficult in the shorter cyclic rounds of National assessment exercises that are increasingly dominating higher education, such as the UK REF.

At the same time, there is a creeping feeling of weight, both in the sense that I 'should be done' by now, secret fears that I was losing patience, and losing faith over whether I was doing the right thing. On the one hand, exploring these affective expressions is tending towards a phenomenological concern, seeking to understand an emotive intentionality that is part of what Steinbock (2014: 21) calls 'the mystery in the ordinary'. This manifested throughout the time spent on the project, expanding over the years, with intermittent bursts of activity and a manifold escalation of commitment entwined into a sibling relation of a creeping boredom. I also faced the encumbrance of increasing responsibilities for and to others at work in terms of larger and more significant administrative and managerial roles. This made more of my time belong to others and resulted in much less flexibility to fit around the busy schedules of participants, whose own lives were becoming more demanding as the study progressed. Preparing and undertaking interviews was incidental, but required a responsiveness over different time zones and staying up late to have online chats and arrange interviews for the short time when I flew from Australia to the UK during the middle of the study, all happening while I was physically ground down by pregnancies. If this sounds like I moaning, I was, but with that there was also a weight of guilt that I was aware I had the privilege of being able to undertake the research thanks to having a permanent faculty position and to some very patient participants, not to mention having a partner who took the load of family and domestic life in order to allow me to travel for fieldwork.

For participants, although their engagement with research was more ad hoc, it also could have consequences beyond the burden of being repeatedly contacted. While following-the-people involved directly negotiating with individuals, moving across different workplaces and employers meant a contingency relating to the possible costs of staying involved. For example, during 2014, one told me that he was participating while being employed for a firm with 'a proper scary in-house law team' that continually monitored employees to ensure they did not bring the company into disrepute. Year 4 was marked more broadly by some of the larger group of people I had interviewed not replying to emails, and one saying they were actively choosing to drop out. At the same time, by 2016, the cumulative relations built up with people made research exchanges far easier and an increasing lightness came from a depth of my relationships with participants. By the halfway point of the project, those still agreeing to take part were clearly in it for the long haul: they still might not fully understand what I was trying to do, but there was a familiarity that bred a sense of mutual commitment. Interactions became easier and often took place beyond formal workspaces, such as restaurants, cafes or people's homes. Interviews were often scheduled for a less bounded hour and participants were keen to quickly get through the standard forms and ethical protocols and start talking. In this sense longitudinal research became less about the need to complete an interview and more about 'picking up from where we left off' (Ollie, 2018, Y8).

References

Ahmed, S. (2006). *Queer Phenomenology: Orientations, Objects, Others*. Durham, NC: Duke University Press.

Ahmed, S. (2007). A phenomenology of whiteness. *Feminist Theory*, 8(2), 149–168.

Ainsworth, S. (2002). The 'feminine advantage': A discursive analysis of the invisibility of older women workers. *Gender, Work & Organization*, 9(5), 579–601.

Ainsworth, S. and Hardy, C. (2008). The enterprising self: An unsuitable job for an older worker. *Organization*, 15(3), 389–405.

Alford, C.F. (1989). *Melanie Klein and Critical Social Theory: An Account of Politics, Art, and Reason Based on Her Psychoanalytic Theory*. New Haven: Yale University Press.

Amin, G.S. and Kat, H.M. (2003). Hedge fund performance 1990–2000: Do the "money machines" really add value? *Journal of Financial and Quantitative Analysis*, 38(2), 251–274.

Arber, S., Andersson, L. and Hoff, A. (2007). Changing approaches to gender and ageing: Introduction. *Current Sociology*, 55(2), 147–153.

Arnett, J.J. (2000). Emerging adulthood: A theory of development from the late teens through the twenties. *American Psychologist*, 55(5), 469–480.

Arp, K. (2001). *The Bonds of Freedom: Simone de Beauvoir's Existentialist Ethics*. Chicago: Open Court Publishing.

Arp, K. (2005). The joys of disclosure: Simone de Beauvoir and the phenomenological tradition. *Analecta Husserliana*, 88, 393–406.

Arp, K. (2016). Old age in existentialist perspective. In G. Scarre (ed). *The Palgrave Handbook of the Philosophy of Aging* (pp 135–148). London: Palgrave MacMillan.

Augé, M. (1996). Paris and the ethnography of the contemporary world. In M. Sheringham (ed), *Parisian Fields*, 1(1), 175–181. London: Reaktion.

Australian Government (2025). National Mental Health Lived Experience Peak Bodies Project. https://www.health.gov.au/contacts/lived-experience-section

Ayalon, L. (2022). Ageism towards oneself vs. ageism towards others in the context of views of aging. In Y. Palgi, A. Shrira and M. Diehl (eds), *Subjective Views of Aging: Theory, Research, and Practice* (pp 41–58). Cham: Springer International Publishing.

Baars, J. (2012). *Aging and the Art of Living.* Baltimore: JHU Press.

Bahnisch, M. (2000). Embodied work, divided labour: Subjectivity and the scientific management of the body in Frederick W. Taylor's 1907 'Lecture on Management'. *Body & Society*, 6(1), 51–68.

Bakhtin M. (1981). *The Dialogic Imagination: Four Essays by MM Bakhtin.* Austin: University of Texas Press.

Banks J and Casanova M. (2003). Work and retirement. In M. Marmot, J. Banks, R. Blundell, C. Lessof and J. Nazroo (eds), *Health, Wealth and Lifestyles of the Older Population in England: The 2002 English Longitudinal Study of Ageing* (pp 127–142). London: Institute of Fiscal Studies.

Bartky, S.L. (1990). *Femininity and Domination: Studies in the Phenomenology of Oppression.* London: Routledge.

Beck, V. (2014). Employers' views of learning and training for an ageing workforce. *Management Learning*, 45(2), 200–215.

Beck, V. and Williams, G. (2015). The (performance) management of retirement and the limits of individual choice. *Work, Employment and Society*, 29(2), 267–277.

Berger, E. (2021). *Ageism at Work: Deconstructing Age and Gender in the Discriminating Labour Market.* Toronto: University of Toronto Press.

Bergoffen, D. (1997). *The Philosophy of Simone de Beauvoir: Gendered Phenomenologies, Erotic Generosities.* New York: SUNY Press.

Bernardi, L., Huinink, J. and Settersten Jr., R.A. (2019). The life course cube: A tool for studying lives. *Advances in Life Course Research*, 41, 1–13.

Beunza, D. (2019). *Taking the Floor: Models, Morals, and Management in a Wall Street Trading Room.* Princeton: Princeton University Press.

Biggart, A., Stauber, B. and Walther, A. (2001). Avoiding misleading trajectories: Transition dilemmas of young adults in Europe. *Journal of Youth Studies*, 4(1), 101–118.

Biggs, S. and Powell, J.L. (2001). A Foucauldian analysis of old age and the power of social welfare. *Journal of Aging & Social Policy*, 12(2), 93–112.

Blöndal, S. and Scarpetta, S. (1999). *The Retirement Decision in OECD Countries.* OECD Economics Department Working Papers, No. 202, Paris: OECD Publishing,

Bourdieu, P. (1977). *Outline of a Theory of Practice*, R. Nice (trans.). Cambridge: Cambridge University Press.

Bowman, D., McGann, M., Kimberley, H. and Biggs, S. (2017). 'Rusty, invisible and threatening': Ageing, capital and employability. *Work, Employment and Society*, 31(3), 465–482.

Bratt, C., Abrams, D., Swift, H.J., Vauclair, C.M. and Marques, S. (2018). Perceived age discrimination across age in Europe: From an ageing society to a society for all ages. *Developmental Psychology*, 54(1), 167–180.

Brown, A.D. (2015). Identities and identity work in organizations. *International Journal of Management Reviews*, 17(1), 20–40.

Brown, S.D., Kanyeredzi, A., McGrath, L., Reavey, P. and Tucker, I. (2020). Organizing the sensory: Ear-work, panauralism and sonic agency on a forensic psychiatric unit. *Human Relations*, 73(11), 1537–1562.

Brown-Séquard, C.E (1889). Note on the effects produced on man by subcutaneous injections of a liquid obtained from the testicles of animals. *The Lancet*, 20 July, 105–107.

Burgelman, R.A. (2010). Strategic consequences of coevolutionary lock-in: Insights from a longitudinal process study. In G. Schreyoegg and J. Sydow (eds), *The Hidden Dynamics of Path Dependence: Institutions and Organizations* (pp 233–248). Basingstoke: Palgrave Macmillan.

Burke, M., Ferrari, M. and Mann, B. (2023). Toward a feminist phenomenology of temporal harm. *Signs: Journal of Women in Culture and Society*, 48(2), 269–290.

Butler, C. (2020). Managing the menopause through 'abjection work': When boobs can become embarrassingly useful, again. *Work, Employment and Society*, 34(4), 696–712.

Butler, J. (1986). Sex and gender in Simone de Beauvoir's *Second Sex*. *Yale French Studies*, 72, 35–49.

Butler, J. (1993). *Bodies That Matter: On the Discursive Limits of Sex*. London: Routledge.

Butler, J (1990). *Gender Trouble*. London: Routledge.

Butler, J. (2021). The surface is rippled: Interview with Judith Butler. *Psychoanaliterature Podcast: Psychoanalysis, Literature, and All That Lie in Between*. https://podcasters.spotify.com/pod/show/psychoanaliterature/episodes/The-Surface-is-Rippled-Interview-with-Judith-Butler-part-II-e1c5rq8

Bytheway, B. (1994). *Ageism*. Basingstoke: McGraw-Hill Education.

Cairns, D., de Almeida Alves, N., Alexandre, A. and Correia, A. (2020). *Youth Unemployment and Job Precariousness: Political Participation in a Neoliberal Era*. London: Palgrave Macmillan.

Calasanti, T. and King, N. (2005). Firming the floppy penis: Age, class, and gender relations in the lives of old men. *Men and Masculinities*, 8(1), 3–23.

Calasanti, T.M. and Slevin, K.F. (2013). *Age Matters: Re-aligning Feminist Thinking*. London: Routledge.

Canduela, J., Dutton, M., Johnson, S., Lindsay, C., McQuaid, R.W. and Raeside, R. (2012). Ageing, skills and participation in work-related training in Britain: Assessing the position of older workers. *Work, Employment and Society*, 26(1), 42–60.

Chia, R. and Holt, R. (2006). Strategy as practical coping: A Heideggerian perspective. *Organization Studies*, 27(5), 635–655.

Cho, S., Crenshaw, K.W. and McCall, L. (2013). Toward a field of intersectionality studies: Theory, applications, and praxis. *Signs: Journal of Women in Culture and Society*, 38(4), 785–810.

Chonody, J.M. and Wang, D. (2014). Ageism among social work faculty: Impact of personal factors and other 'isms'. *Gerontology & Geriatrics Education*, 35(3), 248–263.

Choudhry, M.T., Marelli, E. and Signorelli, M. (2012). Youth unemployment rate and impact of financial crises. *International Journal of Manpower*, 33(1), 76–95.

Čič, Ž.V. and Žižek, S.Š. (2017). Intergenerational cooperation at the workplace from the management perspective. *Naše Gospodarstvo/Our Economy*, 63(3), 47–59.

Cicero, M.T. (2016 [44 BC]). *How to Grow Old: Ancient Wisdom for the Second Half of Life*, P. Freeman (trans.). Princeton: Princeton University Press.

Cole, T.R. (2016). Rereading Simone de Beauvoir's The Coming of Age from a distance of some forty years. *Age, Culture, Humanities: An Interdisciplinary Journal*, 3, 207–216.

Conen, W.S., van Dalen, H.P. and Henkens, K. (2012). Ageing and employers' perceptions of labour costs and productivity: A survey among European employers. *International Journal of Manpower*, 33(6), 629–647.

Crawford, R., Cribb, J., Emmerson, C. and Simpson, P. (2020). Retirement expectations, attitudes and saving behaviour: How have these changed during a decade of pension reforms? *Institute for Fiscal Studies*. https://www. nber.org/sites/default/files/2020-05/NB19-13%20Crawford%2C%20Cribb%2C%20Emmerson%2C%20Simpson%20FINAL.pdf

Crisp, R. and Powell, R. (2017). Young people and UK labour market policy: A critique of 'employability' as a tool for understanding youth unemployment. *Urban Studies*, 54(8), 1784–1807.

Cruikshank, M. (2009). *Learning to Be Old: Gender, Culture, and Aging*. Plymouth: Rowman & Littlefield.

Cutcher, L. (2021). Mothering managers: (Re)interpreting older women's organizational subjectivity. *Gender, Work & Organization*, 28(4), 1447–1460.

Cutcher, L., Riach, K. and Tyler, M. (2022). Splintering organizational subjectivities: Older workers and the dynamics of recognition, vulnerability and resistance. *Organization Studies*, 43(6), 973–992.

Dale, K. (2005). Building a social materiality: Spatial and embodied politics in organizational control. *Organization*, 12(5), 649–678.

De Beauvoir, S. (1965 [1960]). *The Prime of Life*, P. Green (trans.). Harmondsworth: Penguin.

De Beauvoir, S. (1976 [1958]). *Memoires of a Dutiful Daughter*, J. Kirkup (trans.). Harmondsworth: Penguin.

De Beauvoir, S. (1985 [1963]) *Force of Circumstance*, R. Howard (trans.). Harmondsworth: Penguin.

De Beauvoir, S. (1986 [1970]). *Old Age*, P. O'Brian (trans.). Harmondsworth: Penguin.

De Beauvoir, S. (1988 [1972]). *All Said and Done*. P. O'Brian (trans.). London: Penguin.

De Beauvoir, S. (2004 [1944]). Pyrrhus and Cineas. In M.A. Simons, M. Timmerman and M. Mader (eds), *Simone de Beauvoir: Philosophical Writings* (pp 77–150). Urbana: University of Illinois Press.

De Beauvoir, S. (2004 [1945]). A review of *The Phenomenology of Perception* by Maurice Merleau-Ponty (1945). In M.A. Simons, M. Timmerman and M. Mader (eds), *Simone de Beauvoir: Philosophical Writings* (pp 151–154). Urbana: University of Illinois Press.

De Beauvoir, S. (2004 [1947]). An existentialist looks at Americans. In M.A. Simons, M. Timmerman and M. Mader (eds), *Simone de Beauvoir: Philosophical Writings* (pp 299–317). Urbana: University of Illinois Press.

De Beauvoir, S. (2005 [1945]). Moral idealism and political realism. In M.A. Simons, M. Timmerman and M. Mader (eds), *Simone de Beauvoir: Philosophical Writings* (pp 165–194). Urbana: University of Illinois Press.

De Beauvoir, S. 2006 [1965]. The art of fiction. *The Paris Review* No. 35, 3–21.

De Beauvoir, S. (2012 [1946]). *An Eye for an Eye,* L. Lieberman (trans.). Now and Then. https://www.goodreads.com/book/show/13631 780-an-eye-for-an-eye

De Beauvoir, S. (2015 [1949]). *The Second Sex*, C. Borde (trans.), S. Malovany-Chevallier (trans.), S. Rowbotham (other). London: Vintage.

De Beauvoir, S. (2018 [1947]). *The Ethics of Ambiguity*, B. Frechtman (trans.). New York: Open Road.

De Beauvoir, S. (2021 [1954]). *The Inseparables*, L. Elkin (trans.). Dublin: Penguin Random House.

De Gregoriou, G.N. (2002). Hedge fund survival lifetimes. *Journal of Asset Management*, 3(3), 237–252.

De Meulenaere, K., Boone, C. and Buyl, T. (2016). Unravelling the impact of workforce age diversity on labor productivity: The moderating role of firm size and job security. *Journal of Organizational Behavior*, 37(2), 193–212.

De Saint Aubert, E. (2006). La 'promiscuité': Merleau-Ponty à la recherche d'une psychanalyse ontologique. *Archives de Philosophie*, 69(1), 11–35.

De Saint Aubert, E. (2019). The blood of others: Maurice Merleau-Ponty and Simone de Beauvoir, J. McWeeny (trans.). *Simone de Beauvoir Studies*, 30(1), 33–65.

De Saint Aubert, E. (2020). A poetics of co-naissance via André Breton, Paul Claudel, and Claude Simon. In G.A. Johnson, M. Carbone and E. de Saint Aubert (eds), *Merleau-Ponty's Poetic of the World: Philosophy and Literature* (pp 31–67). New York: Fordham University Press.

De Saint Aubert, E. (2020). Metaphoricity: Carnal infrastructures and ontological horizons. In G.A. Johnson, M. Carbone and E. de Saint Aubert (eds), *Merleau-Ponty's Poetic of the World: Philosophy and Literature* (pp 121–158). New York: Fordham University Press.

Duffy, K., Hancock, P. and Tyler, M. (2017). Still red hot? Postfeminism and gender subjectivity in the airline industry. *Gender, Work & Organization*, 24(3), 260–273.

Dumas, G. et al (2019). Mottling score is a strong predictor of 14-day mortality in septic patients whatever vasopressor doses and other tissue perfusion parameters. *Critical Care*, 23, 1–9.

Duncan, C. (2003). Assessing anti-ageism routes to older worker re-engagement. *Work, Employment and Society*, 17(1), 101–120.

Duncan, C. and Loretto, W. (2004). Never the right age? Gender and age-based discrimination in employment. *Gender, Work & Organization*, 11(1), 95–115.

DWP (Department for Work and Pensions) (2017). *Fuller Working Lives: Evidence Base*. London: Department for Work and Pensions. https://assets.publishing.service.gov.uk/media/5a81c52ded915d74e623405f/fuller-working-lives-evidence-base-2017.pdf

Egdell, V., Hussein, R., Harrison, D., Bader, A.K. and Wilson, R. (2023). 'I find it daunting ... that I'm gonna have to deal with this until 60': Extended working lives and the sustainable employability of operational firefighters. *Work, Employment and Society*, 37(3), 721–739.

Elder Jr, G.H. (1994). Time, human agency, and social change: Perspectives on the life course. *Social Psychology Quarterly*, 57(1), 4–15.

Erikson, E.H. (1980). On the generational cycle: An address. *International Journal of Psychoanalysis*, 61, 213–223.

Erikson E.H. (1982). *The Life Cycle Completed: A Review*. New York: W.W. Norton.

Erikson, E.H. (1994). *Identity and the Life Cycle*. New York: W.W. Norton.

Farr, J. and Nizza, I.E. (2019). Longitudinal interpretative phenomenological analysis (LIPA): A review of studies and methodological considerations. *Qualitative Research in Psychology*, 16(2), 199–217.

Farrugia, D. (2018). *Spaces of Youth: Work, Citizenship and Culture in a Global Context*. Abingdon: Routledge.

Fanon, F. (2008 [1952]). *Black Skin, White Masks*, R. Philcox (trans.). Dublin: Penguin

Fasang, A.E. (2012). Retirement patterns and income inequality. *Social Forces*, 90(3), 685–711.

Featherstone, M. and Wernick, A. (eds). (1995). *Images of Ageing: Cultural Representations of Later Life*. London: Routledge.

Fisher, L. (2014). The Other without and the Other within. In S Stoller, ed. *Simone de Beauvoir's Philosophy of Age: Gender Ethics and Time* (pp 107–121). Berlin: Walter de Gruyter.

Fisher, M.S. (2012). *Wall Street Women*. Durham, NC: Duke University Press.

Fiske, S.T. (2017). Prejudices in cultural contexts: Shared stereotypes (gender, age) versus variable stereotypes (race, ethnicity, religion). *Perspectives on Psychological Science*, 12(5), 791–799.

Flood, A. (2010). Understanding phenomenology. *Nurse Researcher*, 17(2), 7–15.

Foster, C. and Resnick, S. (2013). Service worker appearance and the retail service encounter: The influence of gender and age. *Service Industries Journal*, 33(2), 236–247.

Freeman, E. (2010). *Time Binds: Queer Temporalities, Queer Histories*. Durham, NC: Duke University Press.

Freiman, M. (2017). Exphrasis as Enactment. *Axon*, 7(2). https://www.axon journal.com.au/issues/7-2/ekphrasis-enactmen

Furlong, A. (2012). *Youth Studies. An Introduction*. London: Routledge.

Furlong, A. and Cartmel, F. (2006). *Young People and Social Change*. New York: McGraw-Hill.

Gabriel, Y., Gray, D.E. and Goregaokar, H. (2010). Temporary derailment or the end of the line? Managers coping with unemployment at 50. *Organization Studies*, 31(12), 1687–1712.

Garsten, C. and Jacobsson, K. (2011). Transparency and legibility in international institutions: The UN Global Compact and post-political global ethics. *Social Anthropology/Anthropologie Sociale*, 19(4), 378–393.

Gatrell, C. (2019). Boundary creatures? Employed, breastfeeding mothers and 'abjection as practice'. *Organization Studies*, 40(3), 421–442.

Gendron, T.L., Inker, J. and Welleford, A. (2018). 'How old do you feel?' The difficulties and ethics of operationalizing subjective age. *The Gerontologist*, 58(4), 618–624.

Genovese, E.D. (2012). *The Political Economy of Slavery: Studies in the Economy and Society of the Slave South*. Middletown, CT: Wesleyan University Press.

Gioia, D.A., Corley, K.G. and Hamilton, A.L. (2013). Seeking qualitative rigor in inductive research: Notes on the Gioia methodology. *Organizational Research Methods*, 16(1), 15–31.

Grant-Smith, D. and McDonald, P. (2018). Ubiquitous yet ambiguous: An integrative review of unpaid work. *International Journal of Management Reviews*, 20(2), 559–578.

Guenther, L. (2019). Critical phenomenology. In G. Weiss, A.V. Murphy and G. Salamon (eds), *50 Concepts for a Critical Phenomenology* (pp 11–16). Evanston, IL: Northwestern University Press.

Hagestad, G.O. and Settersten Jr, R.A. (2015). Subjective aging and new complexities of the life course. *Annual Review of Gerontology and Geriatrics*, 35(1), 29–53.

Harding, N. (2013). *On Being at Work: The Social Construction of the Employee*. London: Routledge.

Havighurst. R.J. and Albrecht, R. (1953). *Older People*. New York: Longmans.

Heffernan, J. (1993). *Museum of Words: The Poetics of Ekphrasis from Homer to Ashbery*. Chicago: University of Chicago Press.

Heidegger, M. (1951). Building dwelling thinking. In J. Morra and M. Smith (eds) *Visual culture: Critical Concepts in Media and Cultural Studies* (pp 66–76). London: Routledge.

Heidegger, M. (1988 [1807]). *Hegel's phenomenology of spirit*. P. Emad and K. Maly (trans.). Bloomington: Indiana University Press.

Henderson, S. and Thomson, R. (2014). Inventing adulthoods: A qualitative longitudinal study of growing up. In A. Clark, R. Flewitt, M. Hammersley and M. Robb (eds), *Understanding Research with Children and Young People* (pp 210–222). London: Sage.

Hengehold, L. and Bauer, N. (eds). (2017). *A Companion to Simone de Beauvoir*. Hoboken: Wiley Blackwell.

Ho, K. (2009). *Liquidated: An Ethnography of Wall Street*. Durham, NC: Duke University Press.

Hockey, J. and James, A. (2002). *Social Identities across the Life Course*. Basingstoke: Palgrave Macmillan.

Horstkotte, S. (2017). Ekphrasis as genre, ekphrasis as metaphenomenology. In R. Bodola and G. Isekenmeier (eds), *Literary Visualities: Visual Descriptions, Readerly Visualisations, Textual Visibilities* (pp 127–164). Berlin: De Gruyter.

Husserl, E. (1970 [1954]). *The Crisis of European Sciences and Transcendental Phenomenology: An Introduction to Phenomenological Philosophy*, D. Carr (trans.). Evanston, IL: Northwestern University Press.

Irni, S. (2009). Cranky old women? Irritation, resistance and gendering practices in work organizations. *Gender, Work & Organization*, 16(6), 667–683.

Istenič, T., Redek, T. and Farčnik, D. (2024). Gender and age wage–productivity gaps in intangible and non-intangible work occupations. *Economic and Business Review*, 26(1), 1–12.

Itzen, C. and Newman, J. (eds). (2003). *Gender, Culture and Organizational Change: Putting Theory into Practice*. London: Routledge.

Jack, G., Riach, K. and Bariola, E. (2019). Temporality and gendered agency: Menopausal subjectivities in women's work. *Human Relations*, 72(1), 122–143.

Jameson, F. (1991) *Postmodernism, or The Cultural Logic of Late Capitalism*. Durham, NC: Duke University Press.

Jenkins, A. and Poulston, J. (2014). Managers' perceptions of older workers in British hotels. *Equality, Diversity and Inclusion: An International Journal*, 33(1), 54–72.

Johnson, J., Rolph, S., Smith, S., Bernard, B. and Scharf, T. (eds). (2007). *Critical Perspectives on Ageing Societies*. Bristol: Policy Press.

Johnson-Hillery, J., Kang, J. and Tuan, W.J. (1997). The difference between elderly consumers' satisfaction levels and retail sales personnel's perceptions. *International Journal of Retail & Distribution Management*, 25(4), 126–137.

Junkers, G. (2019) Editor's preface. In G. Junker (ed), *Is It Too Late? Key Papers on Psychoanalysis and Ageing* (pp xi–xxii). Abingdon: Routledge.

Jyrkinen, M. and McKie, L. (2012). Gender, age and ageism: Experiences of women managers in Finland and Scotland. *Work, Employment and Society*, 26(1), 61–77.

Keats, J. (2000 [1819]). Ode on a Grecian urn. *Journal of Museum Education*, 25(1–2), 20.

Kenny, K. (2019). *Whistleblowing: Toward a New Theory*. Cambridge, MA: Harvard University Press.

Kindelan, A. (1998). Older workers can alleviate labor shortages. *HR Management*, 43(10), 200–200.

King, P. (2020). *Time Present and Time Past: Selected Papers of Pearl King*. Abingdon: Routledge.

Klein, M. (n.d.) Unpublished notes from Melanie Klein's archive. *Wellcome Collection*. https://wellcomecollection.org/works/kzj85gmv/items?canvas=11

Klein, M. (1948 [1940]). Mourning and its relation to manic-depressive states. In *Contributions to Psycho-analysis 1921–1945, No. 34* (pp 311–338). London: Hogarth Press and the Institute for Psychoanalysis.

Klein, M. (1997 [1932]). *The Psychoanalysis of Children*. London: Vintage.

Kleissner, V. and Jahn, G. (2020). Dimensions of work-related age stereotypes and in-group favoritism. *Research on Aging*, 42(3–4), 126–136.

Köttl, H., Gallistl, V., Rohner, R. and Ayalon, L. (2021). 'But at the age of 85? Forget it!': Internalized ageism, a barrier to technology use. *Journal of Aging Studies*, 59, 100971.

Krekula, C. (2009). Age coding: On age-based practices of distinction. *International Journal of Ageing and Later Life*, 4(2), 7–31.

Kruks, S. (2012). *Simone de Beauvoir and the Politics of Ambiguity*. Oxford: Oxford University Press.

Lain, D. (2018). *Reconstructing Retirement*. Bristol: Policy Press.

Lain, D., Airey, L., Loretto, W. and Vickerstaff, S. (2020). Older workers and ontological precarity: Between precarious employment, precarious welfare and precarious households. In A. Grenier, C. Phillipson and R.A Settersten Jr. (eds), *Precarity and Ageing* (pp 91–114). Bristol: Policy Press.

Lamont, R.A., Swift, H.J. and Abrams, D. (2015). A review and meta-analysis of age-based stereotype threat: Negative stereotypes, not facts, do the damage. *Psychology and Aging*, 30(1), 180–193.

Landes, D. (2014). Translator's introduction. In M. Merleau-Ponty, *Phenomenology of Perception* (pp xxx–li). New York: Routledge.

Leder, D. (1990). *The Absent Body*. Chicago: University of Chicago Press.

Li, Q., Lourie, B., Nekrasov, A. and Shevlin, T. (2022). Employee turnover and firm performance: Large-sample archival evidence. *Management Science*, 68(8), 5667–5683.

MacKenzie, D. (2008). *Material Markets: How Economic Agents Are Constructed.* Oxford: Oxford University Press.

Maltby, T. (2007). The employability of older workers: what works? In W. Loretto, S. Vickerstaff and P. White (eds), *The Future for Older Workers* (pp 161–184). Bristol: Policy Press.

Mann, B. (2012). Gender as justification in Simone de Beauvoir's *Le Deuxième Sexe. Sapere Aude*, 3(6), 200–213.

Marshall, B.L. (2002). Hard science: Gendered constructions of sexual dysfunction in the Viagra age. *Sexualities*, 5(2), 131–158.

Martin, G., Dymock, D., Billett, S. and Johnson, G. (2014). In the name of meritocracy: Managers' perceptions of policies and practices for training older workers. *Ageing & Society*, 34(6), 992–1018.

McDowell, L. (1997). *Capital Culture: Gender at Work in the City.* Oxford: Blackwell.

McDowell, L. (2009). New masculinities and femininities. In A. Furlong (ed), *Handbook of Youth and Young Adulthood: New Perspectives and Agendas* (pp 58–65). New York: Routledge.

McDowell, L. (2010). Capital culture revisited: Sex, testosterone and the city. *International Journal of Urban and Regional Research*, 34(3), 652–658.

McLaughlin, J.S. and Neumark, D. (2024). Gendered ageism and disablism and employment of older workers. In S. Westwood and N.J. Knauer (eds), *Research Handbook on Law, Society and Ageing* (pp 247–264). Cheltenham: Edward Elgar.

McQuaid, R.W. and Lindsay, C. (2005). The concept of employability. *Urban Studies*, 42(2), 197–219.

McVittie, C., McKinlay, A. and Widdicombe, S. (2003). Committed to (un) equal opportunities? 'New ageism' and the older worker. *British Journal of Social Psychology*, 42(4), 595–612.

McWeeny, J. (2016). Flesh possessed: On the promiscuity of subjectivity in Merleau-Ponty's ontology. *Chiasmi International*, 18, 235–249.

McWeeny, J. (2021). How does your mind grasp your body? Recovering phenomenological figures in 'The Second Sex'. Keynote presentation delivered at *Simone de Beauvoir: New Perspectives for the Twenty-First Century.* Institute of Philosophy, Leuven, Belgium, 2 June.

Merleau-Ponty, M. (2014 [1945]). *Phenomenology of Perception*, D. Landes (trans.). Abingdon: Routledge.

Merleau-Ponty, M. (1968 [1964a]). *The Visible and the Invisible*, A. Linguis (trans.). Evanston, IL: Northwestern University Press.

Merleau-Ponty, M. (1964b). *Sense and Non-sense.* Evanston, IL: Northwestern University Press.

Merleau-Ponty, M. (1964c). Eye and mind. In M. Merleau-Ponty, C. Dallery (trans.), *Primacy of Perception* (pp 159–190). Evanston, IL: Northwestern University Press.

Maslakovic, M. (2010). *IFSL Hedge Funds 2010.* https://thehedgefundjour nal.com/ifsl-hedge-funds-2010/

McRobbie, A. (2009). Top girls? Young women and the post-feminist sexual contract. In A. Elliott and P. du Gay (eds), *Identity in Question* (pp 79–97). London: Sage.

Merleau-Ponty, M. (2012). *Phenomenology of Perception*, D.A. Landes (trans.). New York: Routledge.

MIND (2023). *The Influence and Participation Toolkit.* https://www.mind. org.uk/workplace/influence-and-participation-toolkit/

Moi, T. (2008). *Simone de Beauvoir: The Making of an Intellectual Woman.* New York: Oxford University Press.

Moulaert, T. and Biggs, S. (2013). International and European policy on work and retirement: Reinventing critical perspectives on active ageing and mature subjectivity. *Human Relations*, 66(1), 23–43.

Moustakas, C. (1994). *Phenomenological Research Methods.* London: Sage.

National Survivor User Network (2023). Meaningful engagement of people with lived experience: A framework and assessment for measuring and increasing lived experience leadership across the spectrum of engagement. Available at https://nationalsurvivornetwork.org/wp-content/uploads/ 2023/01/2023-Meaningful-Engagement-of-People-With-Lived-Experie nce-Toolkit.pdf

Neale, B. and Bishop, L. (2012). The Timescapes archive: A stakeholder approach to archiving qualitative longitudinal data. *Qualitative Research*, 12(1), 53–65.

Neely, M.T. (2022). *Hedged Out: Inequality and Insecurity on Wall Street.* Oakland: University of California Press.

Nevedal, A.L., Ayalon, L. and Briller, S.H. (2019). A qualitative evidence synthesis review of longitudinal qualitative research in gerontology. *The Gerontologist*, 59(6), e791–e801.

Nickson, D. and Baum, T. (2017). Young at heart, but what about my body? Age and aesthetic labour in the hospitality and retail industries. In E. Parry and J. McCarthy (eds), *The Palgrave Handbook of Age Diversity and Work* (pp 539–559). London: Palgrave Macmillan.

Nielsen, G.P. (1982). *Sky Girl to Flight Attendant: Women and the Making of a Union.* Ithaca, NY: ILR Press.

North, M.S. and Fiske, S.T. (2015). Modern attitudes toward older adults in the aging world: A cross-cultural meta-analysis. *Psychological Bulletin*, 141(5), 993–1021.

Nussbaum, M.C. and Levmore, S. (2017). *Aging Thoughtfully: Conversations about Retirement, Romance, Wrinkles, and Regret.* New York: Oxford University Press.

OECD (Organisation for Economic Co-operation and Development) (2006) *Live Longer, Work Longer.* Paris: OECD Publishing. https://www.oecd. org/en/publications/2006/02/live-longer-work-longer_g1gh607a.html

Pain, R. (2003). Youth, age and the representation of fear. *Capital & Class*, 27(2), 151–171.

Petery, G.A., Wee, S., Dunlop, P.D. and Parker, S.K. (2020). Older workers and poor performance: Examining the association of age stereotypes with expected work performance quality. *International Journal of Selection and Assessment*, 28(4), 510–521.

Phillipson, C. (2019). 'Fuller' or 'extended' working lives? Critical perspectives on changing transitions from work to retirement. *Ageing & Society*, 39(3), 629–650.

Plato (2010 [360BC]). *Meno and Phaedo*, D. Snedly (ed). Cambridge: Cambridge University Press.

Pitt-Catsouphes, M., Matz-Costa, C. and Besen, E. (2013). Linking age to the quality of employees' work experiences. In P. Taylor (ed), *Older Workers in an Ageing Society* (pp 202–222). Cheltenham: Edward Elgar,

Porter, R. (1998). *London: A Social History*. Cambridge, MA: Harvard University Press.

Previtali, F. and Spedale, S. (2021). Doing age in the workplace: Exploring age categorisation in performance appraisal. *Journal of Aging Studies*, 59, 100981.

Pritchard, K. and Whiting, R. (2014). Baby boomers and the lost generation: On the discursive construction of generations at work. *Organization Studies*, 35(11), 1605–1626.

Rawlings, A. V. (2006). Ethnic skin types: Are there differences in skin structure and function? 1. *International Journal of Cosmetic Science*, 28(2), 79–93.

Ray, R.E. (1996). A postmodern perspective on feminist gerontology. *The Gerontologist*, 36(5), 674–680.

Riach, K. (2007). 'Othering' older worker identity in recruitment. *Human Relations*, 60(11), 1701–1726.

Riach, K. (2009). Managing 'difference': Understanding age diversity in practice. *Human Resource Management Journal*, 19(3), 319–335.

Riach, K. and Cutcher, L. (2014). Built to last: Ageing, class and the masculine body in a UK hedge fund. *Work, Employment and Society*, 28(5), 771–787.

Riach, K. and Kelly, S. (2015). The need for fresh blood: Understanding organizational age inequality through a vampiric lens. *Organization*, 22(3), 287–305.

Riach, K. and Loretto, W. (2009). Identity work and the 'unemployed' worker: Age, disability and the lived experience of the older unemployed. *Work, Employment and Society*, 23(1), 102–119.

Riach, K. and Wilson, F. (2014). Bodyspace at the pub: Sexual orientations and organizational space. *Organization*, 21(3), 329–345.

Roberts, I. (2006). Taking age out of the workplace: Putting older workers back in? *Work, Employment and Society*, 20(1), 67–86.

Rogers, J. and Terriquez, V. (2016). 'It shaped who I am as a person': Youth organizing and the educational and civic trajectories of low-income youth. In J. Conner and S. Rosen (eds), *Contemporary Youth Activism: Advancing Social Justice in the United States: Advancing Social Justice in the United States* (pp 141–162). Santa Barbara: Praeger.

Rosenthal, G. (1993). Reconstruction of life stories: Principles of selection in generating stories for narrative biographical interviews. *The Narrative Study of Lives*, 1(1), 59–91.

Rudman, D.L. (2006). Shaping the active, autonomous and responsible modern retiree: An analysis of discursive technologies and their links with neo-liberal political rationality. *Ageing & Society*, 26(2), 181–201.

Rudman, D.L. and Molke, D. (2009). Forever productive: The discursive shaping of later life workers in contemporary Canadian newspapers. *Work*, 32(4), 377–389.

Sabelis, I. and Schilling, E. (2013). Frayed careers: Exploring rhythms of working lives. *Gender, Work & Organization*, 20(2), 127–132.

Saldaña, J. (2003). *Longitudinal Qualitative Research: Analyzing Change through Time*. Oxford: AltaMira.

Schwarzer, A. and de Beauvoir, S. (1984). *After The Second Sex: Conversations with Simone de Beauvoir*, M. Havarth (trans.). New York: Pantheon.

Seamon, D. (2015). *A Geography of the Lifeworld: Movement, Rest and Encounter*. London: Routledge Revivals.

Segal. L. (2014). *Out of Time: The Pleasures and Perils of Ageing*. London: Verso.

Segal. L. (2023). *Lean on Me: A Politics of Radical Care*. London: Verso.

Settersten Jr., R.A. (2003). Invitation to the life course: The promise. In R.A. Settersten, Jr. (ed), *Invitation to the Life Course: Towards New Understandings of Later Life* (pp 1–11). London: Routledge.

Sharps, M.J., Price-Sharps, J.L. and Hanson, J. (1998). Attitudes of young adults toward older adults: Evidence from the United States and Thailand. *Educational Gerontology: An International Quarterly*, 24(7), 655–660.

Shaxson, N, (2013). The zombies of Mayfair. *New Statesman*, 142(5164), 30–33.

Shore, C., Wright, S. and Però, D. (eds) (2011). *Policy Worlds: Anthropology and the Analysis of Contemporary Power*. Oxford: Berghahn Books.

Simons, M.A. (ed). (2006). *The Philosophy of Simone de Beauvoir: Critical Essays*. Bloomington: Indiana University Press.

Skeggs, B. (1997). *Formations of Class & Gender: Becoming Respectable*. Thousand Oaks: Sage.

Snelgrove, S.R. (2014). Conducting qualitative longitudinal research using interpretative phenomenological analysis. *Nurse Researcher*, 22(1), 20–25.

Sontag, S. (1979). The double standard of aging. In J. Williams (ed), *Psychology of Women* (pp 462–478). San Diego: Academic Press.

Spedale, S. (2019). Deconstructing the 'older worker': Exploring the complexities of subject positioning at the intersection of multiple discourses. *Organization*, 26(1), 38–54.

Spiegelberg, H. (1975). *Doing Phenomenology: Essays on and in Phenomenology.* The Hague: Springer Dordecht.

Stanier, J., Miglio, N. and Dolezal, L. (2022). Pandemic politics and phenomenology: Editors' introduction. *Puncta: Journal of Critical Phenomenology*, 5. https://doi.org/10.5399/pjcp.v5i1.1

Statista (2024). Value of assets managed by hedge funds worldwide from 1997 to the second quarter of 2024. https://www.statista.com/statistics/271771/assets-of-the-hedge-funds-worldwide/

Steinbock, A. (2014). *Moral Emotions: Reclaiming the Evidence of the Heart.* Evanston, IL: Northwestern University Press.

Stoller, S. (2013). The indeterminable gender: Ethics in feminist phenomenology and poststructuralist feminism. *Janus Head*, 13(1), 17–34.

Stoller, S. (2014). We in the other, and the child in us. In S. Stoller (ed), *Simone de Beauvoir's Philosophy of Age: Gender Ethics and Time* (pp 195–210). Berlin: Walter de Gruyter.

Taskin, L., Courpasson, D. and Donis, C. (2023). Objectal resistance: The political role of personal objects in workers' resistance to spatial change. *Human Relations*, 76(5), 715–745.

Tidd, U. (1999). *Simone de Beauvoir, Gender and Testimony.* Cambridge: Cambridge University Press.

Tidd, U. (2004). *Simone de Beauvoir.* London: Routledge.

Tornstam, L. (2006). The complexity of ageism: A proposed typology. *International Journal of Ageing and Later Life*, 1(1), 43–68.

Trethewey, A. (1999). Disciplined bodies: Women's embodied identities at work. *Organization Studies*, 20(3), 423–450.

Tuan, Y.F. (1986). Strangers and strangeness. *Geographical Review*, 76(1), 10–19.

Tulle, E. (2008). The ageing body and the ontology of ageing: Athletic competence in later life. *Body & Society*, 14(3), 1–19.

Tyler, M. (2019). *Judith Butler and Organization Theory.* London: Routledge.

Ugargol, A.P. and Parvathy, L. (2023). Precarity of informal work, absence of social security, and ageism: The persistence of social inequalities and challenges for older adults' labor force participation in India. In S. Irudaya Rajan (ed), *Handbook of Aging, Health and Public Policy: Perspectives from Asia* (pp 1–29). Singapore: Springer Nature.

UK Government (2023). *Employment Tribunal and Employment Appeal Tribunal Accessible Tables 2022 to 2023.* https://www.gov.uk/government/statistics/tribunal-statistics-quarterly-april-to-june-2023

Van Dyk S. (2016). The othering of old age: Insights from postcolonial studies. *Journal of Aging Studies*, 39(2), 109–120.

Van Manen, M. (2016). *Phenomenology of Practice: Meaning-Giving Methods in Phenomenological Research and Writing*. Abingdon: Routledge.

Vickerstaff, S. (2006). 'I'd rather keep running to the end and then jump off the cliff'. Retirement decisions: Who decides? *Journal of Social Policy*, 35(3), 455–472.

Vickerstaff, S. and Loretto, W. (2017). The United Kingdom – a new moral imperative: Live longer, work longer. In Á. Ní Léime, D. Street, S. Vickerstaff, C. Krekula and W. Loretto (eds), *Gender, Ageing and Extended Working Life* (pp 175–192). Bristol: Bristol University Press.

Vickerstaff, S. and van der Horst, M. (2021). The impact of age stereotypes and age norms on employees' retirement choices: A neglected aspect of research on extended working lives. *Frontiers in Sociology*, 6, 686645.

Vickerstaff, S., Phillipson, C. and Loretto, W. (2015). Training and development: The missing part of the extending working life agenda? *Public Policy & Aging Report*, 25(4), 139–142.

Walker, A. (2002). A strategy for active ageing. *International Social Security Review*, 55(1), 121–139.

Wallis G. (1970). Chronopolitics: The impact of time perspectives on the dynamics of change. *Social Forces* 49(1), 102–108.

Wanka, A. (2020). No time to waste. How the social practices of temporal organisation change in the transition from work to retirement. *Time & Society*, 29(2), 494–517.

Walter, C. (2020). *Immortality, Inc: Renegade Science, Silicon Valley Billions, and the Quest to Live Forever*. Washington, DC: National Geographic Society.

Waring, A. and Waring, J. (2009). Looking the part: Embodying the discourse of organizational professionalism in the City. *Current Sociology*, 57(3), 344–364.

Webb, R. (2009). *Ekphrasis, Imagination and Persuasion in Ancient Rhetorical Theory and Practice*. Farnham: Ashgate.

Weick, K.E. (1995). *Sensemaking in Organizations*. London: Sage.

Willis, P. (2017 [1978]). *Learning to Labour: How Working Class Kids Get Working Class Jobs*. Abingdon: Routledge.

Willson, A.E., Shuey, K.M. and Elder, Jr., G.H. (2007). Cumulative advantage processes as mechanisms of inequality in life course health. *American Journal of Sociology*, 112(6), 1886–1924.

Wittgenstein, L. (2001 [1953]). *Philosophical Investigations*. Malden, MA: Blackwell.

Woll, H. (2013). Process diary as methodological approach in longitudinal phenomenological research. *Indo-Pacific Journal of Phenomenology*, 13(2), 1–11.

Woodward K. (1995). Simone de Beauvoir: Aging and its discontents. In S. Benstock (ed), *The Private Self: Theory and Practice of Women's Autobiographical Writings* (pp 90–113). Chapel Hill: University of North Carolina.

World Health Organization (2002). *Active Ageing: A Policy Framework.* Geneva: World Health Organization.

World Health Organization (2021). *Global Report on Ageism.* Geneva: World Health Organization.

Yeo, M. (1992). Perceiving/reading the other: Ethical dimensions. In T.W. Busch and S. Gallagher (eds), *Merleau-Ponty, Hermeneutics, and Postmodernism* (pp 37–52). Albany: State University of New York Press.

Zaloom, C. (2006). *Out of the Pits: Traders and Technology from Chicago to London.* Chicago: University of Chicago Press.

Index

References to notes show both the page number and the note number (143n1).
Comments from research subjects can be found under *interviewees*.